# Allies as Rivals

# ALLIES AS RIVALS
## The U.S., Europe, and Japan in a Changing World-System

*edited by*
*Faruk Tabak*

Political Economy of the World-System Annuals, Volume XXVII
*Immanuel Wallerstein, Series Editor*

*Paradigm Publishers*
Boulder • London

Copyright © 2005 by Paradigm Publishers

Published in the United States by Paradigm Publishers, 3360 Mitchell Lane, Suite E, Boulder, Colorado 80301 USA.

Paradigm Publishers is the trade name of Birkenkamp & Company, LLC, Dean Birkenkamp, President and Publisher.

)

**Library of Congress Cataloging-in-Publication Data**

Allies as rivals : the U.S., Europe, and Japan in a changing world-system / edited by Faruk Tabak.
p. cm. — (Political economy of the world-system annuals ; v. 27)
"Product of the Twenty-seventh Annual Conference of the Political Economy of the World-System held at Georgetown University in April 24-25, 2003" — Acknowledgements.
Includes bibliographical references and index.
ISBN 1-59451-121-7 (hc : alk. paper)
1. World politics—1945-1989. 2. World politics—1989– 3. Economic history—1945– 4. Hegemony. 5. Peace. I. Tabak, Faruk. II. Political Economy of the World-System Conference (27th : 2003 : Georgetown University) III. Series.
D455.A44 2005
327'.09172'2090511—dc22

2005004919

Printed and bound in the United States of America on acid-free paper that meets the standards of the American National Standard for Permanence of Paper for Printed Library Materials.

Designed and Typeset by Straight Creek Bookmakers.

09  08  07  06  05
1  2  3  4  5

# CONTENTS

# ACKNOWLEDGMENTS

This volume is the product of the Twenty-Seventh Annual Conference of the Political Economy of the World-System held at Georgetown University April 24–25, 2003. The conference would not have been possible without the sponsorship of the Honorable Robert Galucci, Dean of Walsh School of Foreign Service. It is with utmost pleasure that the editor wants to thank James Reardon-Anderson, director of the Master of Science in Foreign Service for his unfailing support in the organization of the conference, and Samuel Barnes of the BMW Center for German Studies for providing additional financial support and guidance. Thanks are also due to the conference participants.

*Faruk Tabak*

# 1

# INTRODUCTION: HEGEMONY, RIVALRY, AND THE TRAJECTORY OF THE WORLD-SYSTEM

*Faruk Tabak*

## I.

There has been a striking resurgence lately in the volume of writings on the nature, structure, and destiny of empires. This, of course, is hardly surprising in light of current developments on the world political stage. The revival of interest in empires is more than likely a byproduct of the desire to chart, in a historically grounded fashion, probable destinies awaiting *pax Americana* in the coming decades. It is thus the advent of hegemonic decline and the concomitant rise of rivalry that informs the growing literature on empires. Whether or not Washington's dominion over the world-system, relatively weightless in nature due to its nonterritorial character (especially when compared with that of London), will eventually turn into one of flesh and bone—into an empire—has been the subject matter of many an analysis (Balakrishnan 2003; Howe 2002; Johnson 2004; Mann 2003; Todd 2002). To be fair, the specter of empire does not necessarily forebode a reincarnation of empires past—recent or distant. However unclear the general contours of this emergent empire may be, some scholars anticipate that if an imperial polity were to gradually emerge from the

1

debris left behind by the "withering away" of nation-states, it would be unlike any other—without an emperor and central command, for one—due in large part to the transnational character of the structures that have come to envelop the world-system since the 1970s (Hardt and Negri 2000).

The specter of empire therefore evokes mixed sentiments, ranging from aversion to enthusiasm, depending on whether one anticipates that the passing of *pax Americana* would unleash a depressingly all too familiar tale of imperial rivalry or that the transformations ushered in by the passing of the *pax* would open up a world endowed with a rich inventory of possibilities. However well represented these diametrically opposed scenarios may be in the recent crop of writings on the future of *pax Americana,* they hardly exhaust, but merely bracket, the possibilities raised in discussions surrounding empires and rivalry.

In determining which of the trajectories highlighted in the literature is more likely to be followed than not, the crucial task has been to excavate the historiography on empires with the express purpose of constructing a comparative frame of reference within which the destiny of U.S. hegemony can meaningfully be plotted. The popularity of this approach emanates from the fact that, even in failure, it is anything but an exercise in futility. Precisely because even when the task of finding historical lineages of or affinities for *pax Americana* proves futile, the exercise designates and enshrines it as incomparable, if not unique, in its resilience against forces precipitating decline (cf. O'Brien 2003). In either case, though, historical surveys that chart divergences or convergences among instances of imperial grandeur and decline have come to lay the historical and theoretical foundations of differing scenarios on if and how U.S. hegemony will unfold in the immediate and not so immediate future.

Tracing the historical pedigree of empires to determine which, among the eligible few, would form the basis of comparison almost invariably extends the temporal compass of these analyses back to no less than the decline of the Roman empire (Amin 1980; Debray 2002; Hardt and Negri 2000). Despite the temporal distance, the challenges posed by Christians of the later Roman empire to the territorial order of the day seem more relevant to the current situation than the dissolution of the later reincarnations of empire, colonial or dynastic. So does Emperor Caracalla's declaration, in the face of the impending disintegration of his empire, which endowed every free man, "barbarian" foremost, a citizen of Rome. Given the drastic nature of the transformations that accompanied the decline of the Roman empire, it goes without saying that those who establish an affinity between the ends of *pax Americana* and *pax Romana* anticipate nothing short of the dawn of a new world order.

If the search for comparable genealogies of decline has led some to narrate the current conjuncture in a tense of the deepest past, others, by contrast, have taken a much shorter view. In this approach, the erosion of U.S. hegemony from the late 1970s is compared to the gradual weakening, from the late 1870s, of the command London exercised over the world-economy. This set of writings finds telling parallels (or by the same token, differences) between these two world orders. In the case of *pax Britannica,* the enfeeblement of the empire and the erosion of the centrality of London in world economic flows were accompanied and caused by growing hegemonic rivalry. The period of rivalry that triggered a proliferation in the number of colonial empires around the globe eventually culminated in the explosion of the Thirty Years War, from 1914 to 1944. In the case of *pax Americana,* the events of the last few decades have heralded, much to the dismay and disbelief of those manning the commanding heights of its political apparatus, a growing challenge to its previously uncontested rule. The transformation over a span of two decades of the erstwhile timid German insouciance toward U.S. pressure in the 1980s in matters relating to the importation of natural gas from the Soviet Union, into outright defiance during the Second Gulf War, leaves no doubt as to the directionality of this change.

The resurfacing of rivalry, however timorous and embryonic, has invited comparisons between the end of *pax Britannica* and the present state of *pax Americana.* Having the luxury to diagnose, in historical hindsight and with closer scrutiny, the afflictions of British rule at its twilight is seen by some as providential. For analyses of this demise are expected to provide precious clues for detecting early signs of hegemonic rivalry, which, if left unshepherded, could turn into full-fledged warfare. It is hoped that if necessary precautions and measures were to be taken in a timely fashion, then a conflagration like the Thirty Years War could be avoided in some fashion, however unpalatable this option may turn out to be for the would-be rivals (Calleo 2003; Kagan 2003; Pfaff 2003).

The delusion of curbing hegemonic rivalry is not the only prescription that a historical reevaluation of the turn of the twentieth century has to offer, though. Also of concern is the impact this rivalry had, during the interwar period, on the welfare of the world's populations and on the free market "utopia" dear to *pax Britannica.* When seen from this vantage point, core/corporate capital, which has managed since the 1970s to establish its demands on the world-system's states with ease due to its regained mobility, is expected to unleash once again the kind of destruction the previous phase of rivalry had on peoples' livelihood. As some argue happened during the interwar period, deepening rivalry would once again annihilate, in Polanyi's lexicon, social mechanisms of self-protection as well as fracture the unity of the world market (James 2001; Stiglitz 2002).

In contrast to these comparative analyses, which advance the notion that there exists a systemic affinity between these two periods—or episodes—of decline, others, while still utilizing British hegemony as their frame of reference, stress the contrasting features of the two periods to underline how the structure of *pax Americana* has essentially been different from that of *pax Britannica.* The awesome military power the United States commands in comparison not only to that of its individual main rivals but to the rest of the core states' collective capacity, and the encompassing transborder links U.S.- and core-based capital has woven among distant corners of the globe, are enumerated to assert that the age-old dynamic of rivalry has become merely a thing of the past and that the landscape within which the world-system operates today is fashioned anew as a result of U.S. hegemony. In this view, the structural traits, or the unintended consequences, of U.S. hegemony set it apart from its predecessor, *pax Britannica,* and a comparative exercise between the two is consequently found to be lacking in historical merit (Kennedy 1999; O'Brien 2003).

A similar line of inquiry sets out to contrast *pax Britannica* with *pax Americana* in order to highlight the differences between the two and stresses the significance of viewing the latter through the prisms of the former—that is, through the mirror of formal empire. This approach designates the informal nature of *pax Americana,* its quintessential property, as its biggest failing. It underlines the fact that the two hegemonies do not share a common lineage, but it does this by underplaying the nature and structure of American rule. It portrays the "weightless" character of *pax Americana* as its principle weakness, for the inability of this behemoth to lay anchor in distant corners of the globe in a colonial fashion, as Britain did as the disseminator of "democracy and industrialization," denies it the tools available to proper, or territorial, empires (Ferguson 2003).

Not all analyses subscribe to the idea that the differences or similarities between the structural traits of *pax Americana* and *pax Britannica* can be of use in determining the coordinates of the structures that are likely to emerge in the near future. Instead, they argue that, given the interconnectedness and holism of the processes at work, the dynamics of the present situation cannot be fully grasped and conceptualized through the lens of a nation state–based approach. In this light, the speed with which trans- and cross-border operations have been interweaving distant quarters of the globe renders the concept of hegemony obsolete and devoid of function. In fact, the transnational space built by expanding structures of corporate accumulation and the emergence since the late nineteenth century of political bodies with sweeping, cross-border jurisdictions are seen as harbingers of an incipient world community and of a world where existing lines of division, social as well as political, are becoming blurred, laying the basis of a world of possibilities (Hardt and Negri 2000; Iriye 2002).

However historically informed these approaches may seem at first sight, the temporal span of their analyses falls seriously short of capturing the longevity of the capitalist world economy. For most of these studies start from the assumption that the foundations of the modern world-system have been put in place by the British empire from the late eighteenth century (cf. Frank 1998; Pomeranz 2000). Affixing the origins of the world-system in the late eighteenth century does not leave too much room for meaningful cross-historical comparison, save for the two hegemonies of the past two centuries. This is clearly evident in the literature on "globalization" and its "two waves": the onset of the first wave is dated to the end of the nineteenth century, and the second, the end of the twentieth (James 2001; O'Rourke and Williamson 2001). Such a short pedigree fails to capture not only the longevity of the world-system, but equally important, how each hegemonic rise and decline has shaped the system's long-term trajectory.

Naturally, the periodic rise and demise of the world-system's hegemonic powers inform a considerable part of this literature. Here, the three instances of hegemony that have come to characterize the capitalist world-system, those of *pax Neerlandica, pax Britannica,* and *pax Americana,* serve as the frame of reference for charting the likely course of hegemonic rivalry accompanying the waning of American rule. The periodic nature of hegemonic cycles does not point to a mere replication of a historically set scenario, however. Periods of hegemony are not merely a succession of repeated movements, albeit with variations and revivals. They are moments in the life-span of the world-system and have their distinctive characteristics, since they embody cumulative systemic change. They are not necessarily episodes with comparable qualities. Crucially, hegemonic moments constitute significant turning points in extending the system's territorial sweep, deepening its social reach, and in the process, laying the basis of its eventual dissolution (Hopkins 1993; Wallerstein 2003).

Current transformations, too, frequently portrayed as the epitome of "globalization," register a historical moment in the life-span of the world-system. As such, they are more than simple reincarnations of the processes associated with the passing of British hegemony. Rather, they have more to share with a relatively distant, and not recent, past. It was not by mere chance that the fatal cycle of worldly fortune, *circulus vicissitudinis rerum humanorum,* was staged in the mid-sixteenth century by the burgers of Antwerp—in the annual processions through the city during the Feast of the Circumcision. The cycle, as envisioned then, was composed of eight stages: it started with the "triumph" of the world and moved successively through riches, pride, envy, war, want, humility, and peace. The cycle was "ominously" resumed as peace started to mother riches in the final "triumph" (Schama 1987, 326–327).

## II.

If one way of analyzing periods of hegemony is to view them as "moments" in the long-term trajectory of the world-system rather than as recurrent stages in the fatal cycle of worldly fortune, then it follows that the end of the U.S. hegemonic moment has to be assessed in more than one register. After all, a moment can be invested with variegate meanings depending on the temporality in which it is placed. When viewed from the vantage point of the world-system's cycles of hegemony, for instance, it can be argued that U.S. hegemony was anything but a simple *bis repetita* of British hegemony. For it transformed the colonial order forged by *pax Britannica* into an informal empire. What is more, stateness, initially imposed on and broadcast in the newly incorporated regions of the world-economy by and through colonization, has come to reign as the systemic mold available for organizing body politics worldwide. It is telling that by the turn of the twentieth century, even attempts to undermine or subvert the system had taken the form of building new nation-states, not to mention of course the proliferation in the number of nation-states that resulted from decolonization. As U.S. hegemony was reaching its height, historical alternatives to stateness were forcefully eliminated.

More significantly, the transformation of the colonial order of the nine-teenth and twentieth centuries into a U.S.-centered informal empire has, by consolidating the global spread of stateness, brought the interstate order ini-tially enshrined by *pax Neerlandica* to a formal completion. So when seen from the vantage point of the world-economy's secular trends, it can be argued that the interstate system that was designed to govern relations in a relatively narrow geographical space of the world-system during the sixteenth and seventeenth centuries has come to constitute part and parcel of the world body politic. Put differently, the secular trend that had commenced in 1648 was brought to a close in 1968 (the year that symbolically represents the onset of the current crisis in 1967–1973). It is not surprising that the interstate system, as one of the central institutions of the world-system, has expanded in concert with the territorial spread of the world-economy. Now that the interstate system has come to traverse the whole globe, the closure of its territorial frontier is more than likely to mark a historical milestone. But this does not inevitably augur the end of the nation-states, much touted in the literature since the 1980s, due to the growing hold upon them under "globalization" of transnational institutions and enterprises. What the disappearance of the external arena signals is a pend-ing reconfiguration in the relationship between the interstate system and the interenterprise system, two systems that jointly constitute the basic networks of the world-economy.

Put differently, the end of U.S. hegemony, when seen from the vantage point of the world-system as a historical system, heralds the advent of structural change as well. The transformations underlying the demise of *pax Americana* may conceivably alter the basic premises of the world-system. This is partly because the synchronous and symbiotic expansion of the interstate and interenterprise systems, which has not necessarily been conflictive thus far ow-ing to the availability of new territories that could be incorporated in their fold, is not likely to be reproduced because of the closure of the world-economy's territorial frontier. For the transfer of a wide array of functions that early enter-prises had to perform (from warfare to welfare) and associated costs onto the states has hitherto allowed both systems to expand concomitantly and in har-mony, because territorial enlargement has offered new avenues of expansion for the interenterprise system.

Yet, this concordance has reached its limits. Since the closing of late of the world-economy's territorial frontier, the relationship between business en-terprises and states has been rendered more complex and problematic. An ex-pansion in the realm of the interenterprise system can now take place mostly at the expense of statal regimentation: hence the enthusiastic and forcible en-thronement of programs that set out to streamline states in part by extending the compass of "privatization" and "liberalization" worldwide. Collectively, these programs serve to extend the operational domain of business enterprises (from welfare to warfare) by trespassing into that of the states. In the final analysis, given the multiplicity of historical turning points *pax Americana* embodies, it is only fitting to evaluate the demise of American rule and the rise of triadic rivalry in multiple registers. In what follows, then, the three temporalities mentioned above—the world-system's hegemonic cycles, its secular trends, and its historical life-cycle—will receive brief but closer attention.

In the first register, that of the world-system's hegemonic cycles, the opening decades of the twenty-first century appear hardly to be a *bis repetita,* however loosely defined, of the opening decades of the twentieth. Quite the contrary, in fact. The consolidation of *pax Americana* after 1945 guaranteed a gradual transition from the territorial-colonial order of *pax Britannica* to a world order operated, as Braudel puts it, by "remote control" from Washington. Striking was the rapid pace of transition from the formal British empire to the informal American empire.

London's steady decline and relative loss of power, which ultimately culminated in the eventual dethronement of the city from the apex of the world-system, commenced roughly from the end of the Great Depression in the late 1890s to the end of the Thirty Years War in 1945. London found its much-coveted position taken over by New York rather precipitously—all in all, in less than half a century. Building on the massive colonization wave that picked up its pace in the 1880s and abetted the spread and consolidation of the interstate system, the new U.S. order, nonterritorial in nature, found a political environment supportive of its coming of age, as attested to by the lasting popularity of the Wilsonian doctrine of self-rule even in most distant quarters of the globe. By the time of the Land-Lease Act, the riches of the Edwardian *belle époque* had become a distant memory. Equally depressing for London, though not unexpected, was the loss of her empire in a remarkably brief span of time: the rise of U.S. power helped dismantle, albeit at times haltingly, the empires of the nineteenth century. What was at issue was not whether power was going to be devolved away from London and its imperial cadres, but whether the transfer would be gradual and orderly, without inflicting damage on the U.S. world order under construction.

Historically speaking, the swiftness of transition from British to American rule was in no way unique. Amsterdam's ascent to the pinnacle of the world-system was equally brisk. It, too, took place against a backdrop of an immense colonial enterprise, then undertaken by the Portuguese and Spanish empires from the latter half of the fifteenth century. Amsterdam overtook Antwerp with impressive speed and agility, from the late 1570s to 1625, in less than half a century. The shift in the center of gravity of the world-economy was so sudden that it was almost as if the "Spanish" Antwerp, a Portuguese and German creation, home to the Fuggers and Charles V, had "changed into Amsterdam." The city's climb to eminence, too, had repercussions reminiscent of the decolonization wave of the latter half of the twentieth century: as a result of Amsterdam's rise, "Portugal lost her empire in the Far East and very nearly lost Brazil as well" (Braudel 1984, 34, 187). Historically, the "modernity" and "weightlessness" at times were ascribed to the American and Dutch empires because of the systemic compliance successfully imposed by the former colonial empires in the regions newly incorporated into the world-system (Arrighi 1994).

The colonial world of the nineteenth and twentieth centuries provided the institutional scaffolding for the new hegemon to impose an ethereal control over the resources and economic flows of the world-economy. The British order paved the way by breaking down dynastic empires into scores of nation-states and by installing colonial states and instilling stateness in all quarters of its empire. The territorial gains of the period were deepened through the spread of stateness in the periphery—mostly in Asia and Africa—due, first, to the establishment by imperial powers of colonial states and, later during the postwar wave of decolonization, to the advent of the Cold War, which increased competition over newly independent states and absolved them momentarily from the strict logic of the world-market.

Import-substitution industrialization and the takeover and extension of the state apparatuses in most parts of the periphery took place during the 1945–1967/1973 period. It was this systemic expansion that set the stage and allowed for the relatively precipitous transition from the colonial order of *pax Britannica* to the imperial order of *pax Americana,* the defining transformation of the twentieth century. Ever since the completion of decolonization in the 1970s, which helped solidify the interstate system and the reconstruction of the unity of the world-market, the world-economy has started to follow a path distinctly different from the post-1945 period, as will be discussed later below.

In the second register, 1968 appears as the culmination of a secular trend that had started in 1648. After all, it was in that year and at the height of *pax Neerlandica* that the building of the interstate system engendered a set of arrangements in the wake of the expansionary period between 1450 and 1650. With Amsterdam's rise, not only the age of empire-building city-states came to an end. But also, imperial polities in Europe found themselves less dynastic and more territorial and subject, as codified by the Westphalia Treaty, to the rules of an institutionalized interstate system, tentative though it initially may have been. To be sure, tentative did not mean inefficacious. The new arrangements managed to survive even the tumultuous upheavals and the economic slowdown that set in during the 1650s and lasted till the 1750s.

The century-long slowdown was followed by the territorial expansion of the world-economy from 1750 to the turn of the twentieth century. The political reorganization of the newly incorporated regions, which followed the massive territorial expansion, brought the interstate system codified in 1648 to global dominion. The success registered in the consolidation of the interstate system worldwide was not without its drawbacks, however. The rise to global dominion of the interstate system unavoidably generated a new set of strains, as I will discuss below. This new wave of expansion and state-building was radically dissimilar from its two historical predecessors.

The territorial expansion of the first sixteenth century, which lasted from the mid-fifteenth century to the 1560s, stretched the boundaries of the global division of labor from the greater Mediterranean into and across the Atlantic. The reshaping of the economic arena was complemented later, in the second sixteenth century, from 1560 to 1650, with the expansion of stateness in the periphery of the system (in the Caribbean and New Spain) as the interstate system was being crafted and enthroned at home, thanks to the Westphalia Treaty. Similar in nature to the expansionary long sixteenth century, the expansionary period of the twelfth and thirteenth centuries too had allowed the empire-building city-states to firmly establish their hold over the Mediterranean. Its completion witnessed the emergence and strengthening of territorial states under the shadow of the towering city-states. That is, both long expansionary periods were eventually followed by political rearrangements that were codified and/or spread during periods of economic downswing; that is, during the fifteenth- and seventeenth-century crises.

The current turning point, 1968, too, represents the culmination point of the expansionary period that had started roughly in the mid-eighteenth century. It was during this period of massive territorial expansion under British command that the spatial stretch of the world-system came to cover, at the turn of the twentieth century, even the most far-flung corners of the globe. The post-1968 period hence shares similar characteristics with its historical predecessors c. 1350–1450 and 1650–1750. First, in all three periods of economic slow-down, the operational domain of the interenterprise system expanded at the expense of "public" domain. This tendency has taken the form of privatization through the sale of public offices, the sale of towns in the case of Spain, and the growing alienation of commons and eminent domain, just to name a few.

Secondly, all three periods have also witnessed a growing "securitization" of wealth through sophisticated, modern mechanisms of finance: the advent of private ownership of public debt (as in the case of *Casa di San Giorgio*), or by growing subscription by the accumulators to securitization of their wealth: witness the modernity of the Amsterdam stock market when compared with that of New York (Braudel 1982, 122; Neal 1990). The concentration and centralization of capital followed periods of impressive expansion of credit (and banking), centered first in Florence before and after 1300 (i.e., the high age of Champagne and Brie fairs); later in Genoa in the latter part of the sixteenth and the opening decades of the seventeenth century (i.e., the high age of Bisenzone and Lyons fairs); and finally in the latter part of the nineteenth and early half decades of the twentieth century (i.e., the high age of Rothschilds) (Arrighi 1994; Braudel 1982, 392, 522).

And thirdly, in all three cases, in consonance with capital's deepening rule, labor's force had accordingly been diminished due to the circumventing of organizations that defended and furthered its cause (guilds, trade unions) by ruralization of production or, in today's lexicon, by "outsourcing" or "flexible" accumulation. To wit, in the 1650–1750 period, political structuring from above was immediately accompanied by economic structuring from below because of the process then termed ruralization of manufacturing, which served two complementary purposes:

spreading the extent of market-mediated transactions into the countryside and using this avenue to tame and control urban-based labor.

In the fifteenth-century crisis, the migration of the textile industry out of north Italian cities and the transformation of the *arte della lana* into a rural activity contributed to the development of a rural industry in Ulm, Augsburg, and Nürnberg and in their vicinity. The spread and extent of this industry, based on *verlagssystem,* reached significant proportions. The second bout of dissemination of rural industries and the *verlagssystem* occurred during the seventeenth-century crisis. Although in the sixteenth century industrial activity had essentially been urban and concentrated along the axis running from the Netherlands to northern Italian city-states, in the following centuries it burgeoned on both sides of the axis as well and on a considerable scale. The eighteenth century is a period seen in the literature as the seedbed of "protoindustrialization," launching the careers of the great textile centers of later centuries (Tabak 2001).

When viewed in this light, the period that commenced in the 1970s can be placed alongside the seventeenth- and fourteenth-century secular downswings. Both periods and, judging by the performance it has shown so far, the twentieth century since the 1970s, have all been unforgiving, harsh, and, not paradoxically, rich, as Gentil de Silva (1984) appropriately termed them, in that they all have been immensely conducive to concentration of wealth in the hands of a few. Not unexpectedly, they also have been ridden with escalating strife (e.g., the Hundred Years War and the revolutions and rebellions of the "early modern" world). Unlike earlier periods where alternative forms of livelihood existed alongside wage employment, the post-1968 period, which has witnessed large portions of world populations turn into intermittent wage workers, will most likely experience similar social upheaval, especially in the face of the growing pace of urbanization and marginalization of agriculture in the peripheral regions of the world-economy (Davis 2004; Kasaba and Tabak 1995).

That the interstate system has come to cover the globe, however, in and of itself does not signal an end to the world-system. Yet, even though softened in the dim light of theories of globalization, the ferocity with which the streamlining of the states has been pursued and the speed with which most states were forced to vacate a wide array of the functions they have come to perform are meaningful indicators of the directionality of change. The functions that had devolved from private firms to the states during the life-span of the capitalist world-economy, stretching from underwriting wars to providing health care and entitlements, will seemingly revert back to their initial domicile, surely selectively and at the behest and convenience of the enterprises (Lane 1979; Minc 1993).

It is in this register of long-term and large-scale change that current developments find their proper place. In brief, historically, periods that followed major territorial expansion witnessed major systemic changes; the first, c. 1350–1450, the dissolution of feudal order; the second, c. 1650–1750, the end of empire-building city-states; and the third, 1968–?, no less than the end of the symbiotic relationship between the interstate and inter-enterprise systems.

# III.

The passing of America's hegemonic moment and the advent of rivalry, there-fore, should be assessed in more than one register. In the chapters that follow, the emphasis is placed primarily on the developments of the post-1945 period. Yet the analyses put forth here on the nature and future of the triadic rivalry are necessarily confined to the short term. They all bring into play changes of differing nature and duration. The ramifications of the end of *pax Americana* on the future transformation (and demise) of the world-system, the avenues opened up for contenders to the throne by the current easterly shift in the center of gravity of the world-economy, and the possibilities of either revamping imperial struc-tures or fashioning new political arrangements by hegemonic rivals to make better use of the disintegration of the existing order are all entertained and expanded upon to determine the likely coordinates of change in the near future.

In the opening chapter, Wallerstein traces the historical trajectory and dynamics of *pax Americana* from the enthronement of the hegemon in 1945 to today, and constructs his analyses around three clearly demarcated time peri-ods. The first period, from 1945 to 1967/1973, constituted the apogee of U.S. hegemony; the second, from 1967/1973 to 2001, its late summer glow, still luminescent but nonetheless devoid of the certitudes of the previous era; and the third, from 2001 forward, the onset of full-fledged decline. It was during the U.S. hegemony's late summer glow that the arrangements of its golden age were subjected to dramatic change, recorded in the push to cut back the level of wages worldwide, to reduce the level of taxes, and to restore the externalization of production costs.

Surely, it was the re-emergence of Europe, and later of Japan, that under-mined the arrangements put in place by U.S. hegemony. Wallerstein asserts that the European reconstruction will continue and that China, Japan, and Korea will begin to move closer, with great consequences. Yet, the waning of U.S. hegemony, although it is the central issue at hand, is treated accordingly as symptomatic of deep structural problems that have started to tax the world-system *qua* historical system. Wallerstein underlines the fact that the period we have entered is a period of transition. What looms in his account is not the transition from one hegemonic order to the next *per se*, but the pending sys-temic transition. It is this larger transition that contextualizes and informs his discussion of *pax Americana*'s passing.

Giovanni Arrighi, too, lays emphasis on the likely nature of this transi-tion: he maintains that this transition is not necessarily from one hegemonic order to another, but potentially a recentering of the world-economy. He main-tains that empire-building is not the only choice that confronts us; a "world-market society" centered on the East is a viable historical possibility. If the United States, as the late hegemon, fails to fine-tune its stratagems in tune with its diminishing powers, then a specter of a "universal empire" centered on the West may loom large. After all, it is not the strengthening of hegemonic rivals, but the perverse nature of the present conjuncture that challenges American rule, and the discussion of triadic rivalry is placed within this context. Surely, there are two contenders to the throne. Europe, now equipped with a strong currency, the euro, which has slowly been garnering the position as a world reserve currency, is seen as a *force majeure*. It is with the reconstruction of Europe that the consolidation of the euro as a world currency will inexorably unseat the dollar from its previously unchallenged position: the financial liberties the United States derives from seigniorage privileges will be severely curtailed.

Yet, the main theater of expansion will be in the East, Arrighi maintains, due to region-specific factors that undergird the centrality of China. The region's continuing economic expansion will be subversive of the global hierarchy of wealth, and upset the system's very stability. Growing U.S. dependence on the financial support of its competitors, Japan and China, only amplifies the problems that will plague the hegemon. There is now a high possibility of relocating the center of the world-economy in the East, with China serving as a potential substitute for the United States as the central market of the regional East Asian economy and beyond. Overall, Arrighi sees the emergence of a "world market society" centered in the East as a more likely path for the system.

Christopher Chase-Dunn, Thomas Reifer, and Andrew Jorgenson compare the trajectories of the British and American hegemonies, and lay out their distinct characteristics. They emphasize that the power that the United States commands in certain respects may appear to be beyond compare, but they also underscore the possibility that the attempts by the United States to turn its informal empire into a truly universal world-empire may encounter formidable resistance on many fronts. The growing allure of antisystemic movements in challenging transnational corporations and global elites is a testament to the change in world political dynamics. The dissolution of the system has so far failed to generate the kind of "nationalist" sentiment and alignment that characterized the first half of the twentieth century. That the forces opposing the latest military campaign by the United States have not been able to engender similar alignments and splits along national lines, but have taken the form of solidarity among different groups, they argue, may indicate a new dynamic dissimilar from the one that colored the interwar period.

These authors also argue that the semiperipheral states will start searching for new paths of development once they realize that all boats will not rise on the tide of globalization, thereby reversing the trend toward "free trade." The widening gap between the North and the South and the turbulence this creates is likely to force rival core states to reform the system of global governance in ways that do not fully serve the United States. At the least, the increasingly regressively financed military spending via borrowing on the global capital markets, they claim, will undermine the very underpinnings of the *pax,* for the military-industrial complex has been one of its most valued assets. They do not rule out the possibility that the widening disparity in incomes at home may play an important role in determining the future of the system.

Of the two rivals, Europe has been the most vocal in expressing its discord with the hegemon not only during the last military campaign but also on a wide range of economic issues since the 1980s; some of these contentious issues have been brought to the attention of, and adjudicated by, the World Trade Organization, mostly in favor of the European Union (EU). Peter Gowan argues that it would be a mistake to equate Europe's dissent only with reference to the recent turn of events, however significant they may be, and traces its origins back to the 1980s. He lays particular emphasis on Mitterand and Delors' *volte-face* in that decade because of growing Japanese challenges in select yet important branches of industry on the one hand and the pressures exerted by Reaganite policies on the other.

Gowan traces how the European Community underwent pivotal changes through the Single European Act and the treaties of Maastricht, Amsterdam, and Nice, and he pinpoints the tempestuous 1990s when events in Bosnia and the Balkans exposed the deep rift between Europe and the United States. Although the European Union may be momentarily weak militarily, politically its enshrinement of the human rights, democracy, and good governance diplomacy, Gowan stresses, has served the European Union well in its dealings with the South, for it has facilitated the makings of a "soft" imperial world order in comparison to the world order envisioned by the United States. This approach has invested the European Union with an ideological authority. These conditions place unbearable stresses on the trans-Atlantic alliance as the prevention of the emergence of a politically independent European entity remains an integral part of U.S. political strategy.

Çağlar Keyder entertains a scenario where empire-building, in one form or another, is emerging as an option available not only to the declining hegemon, but also to the European Union, for the latter will have to resort to it if it wants to rival the United States. The "soft" imperial order offered by the European Union then appears as a credible alternative to U.S. unilateralism. The "soft" empire rhetoric may be effective but not sufficient, Keyder maintains. He outlines two routes available to the European Union in its search for an empire: it either can opt for greater homogenization within the existing borders, a virtual fortress Europe, or it can expand outward, taking the form of a "civic and constitutional" empire, by incorporating new "provinces." Given the undesirability of the former option, which turns the European Union into a Christian "club" with little attraction to the barbarians at its gates, Keyder uses Turkey as a test-case for charting the European Union's future.

If the European Union were to facilitate the accession of Turkey to membership, the precedent this could set would allow it to enlarge its dominions in various directions. This inclusiveness, according to Keyder, will abet the transformation of the European Union into an empire, rivaling that of the United States. Equally important, it will confer by default a certain degree of credence and recognition to its second religion, Islam, thereby facilitating the social integration of groups hitherto confined to the bourgs of the European metropolises. For Keyder, the inclusion of Turkey will be of paramount significance in determining whether the European Union will have a defensive posture vis-à-vis the American empire, or a proactive role in giving birth to a polyglot, religiously diverse community that in the long run could pose a serious challenge to American designs.

Unfortunately, of the two rivals confronting the United States, Europe continues to receive more attention, especially since the bursting of the Japanese economic bubble and the deep crises that enmeshed other East Asian economies during the 1990s. The Japanese menace of the 1980s now seems to be a thing of the past, and has been supplanted by China. Yet, the emergence of China as a favored site for the relocation of the world's manufacturing activities portrays it as a low-cost locale with little proclivity toward serving as a market consonant with its population figures. Rather than broach the crisis as an end to an immature and unsustainable miracle, Ravi Arvind Palat views it as a period of restructuring for Japan and the region in general. He highlights the fact that new networks of trade and finance are being forged among eastern and Southeast Asian states, and that the emergence of China as a regional counterweight to Japan has led to greater willingness among the region's states to enter into bilateral and plurilateral trade agreements.

Crucially, Japan, dependent thus far on the whims of administrations in Washington, now finds itself in an enviable position, partly of its own making. The integration of China into regional and global economic flows has turned the erstwhile "Middle Kingdom" into a potential substitute for the United States. This new economic center of gravity richly endowed in capital resources and now invested with a huge market, poses a serious challenge for the United States. Palat demonstrates that the attendant increase in regional consumption will amplify the pressures placed on the dollar by the rise of the euro by shifting some of the region's capital resources away from the dollar, and thereby draining U.S. capital markets of their cheap and easily available credit. This would, in the short and medium run, unseat the United States from the privileged position it had carved for itself since the dismantling of the dollar standard.

If the economic renaissance ushered in by the reintegration of China into regional and global networks of production and trade offers the region opportunities to recycle its surplus, undermining the fragile foundations of U.S. dominance, this is a unity, John Gulick argues, the United States is more than willing to fracture so as to reproduce networks of dependency it diligently built in the post-1945 period. He emphasizes the fact that a dynamic similar to that in Europe has been at play in this quarter of the globe. As in the case of Europe, where one of the U.S. priorities since the onset of the Cold War was to prevent the emergence of an independent Europe, a similar policy, Gulick asserts, is in place in Asia. U.S. policies designed to wedge the rapprochement between China and Japan, the leading actors in the region, are expected to cushion the potential damage the rise of this new alliance could inflict on U.S. dominance and economic well-being.

Gulick argues that this strategy has become more pressing given the declining ability of the United States to prevent or subvert European unity, much less discourage growing adherence to the euro outside the Eurozone. The challenge posed by the euro to the dollar has made itself felt strongly in a field dear to U.S. policymakers and consumers alike: increasing talk of denominating oil prices in euros. This unsettles Washington, for the parking of oil receipts in euro accounts will undermine the dollar's suzerainty. Hence, the United States, in order to prolong its economic supremacy, has to derail the emerging union in the East before threats to its dominance become unmanageable. It is in this light that Gulick proposes we evaluate a wide range of issues stretching from North Korea's "rogue" status to the support given to Taiwan and the new missile system that includes Japan, but excludes China. He foresees that these issues are going to remain on the agenda for some time to come.

The apogee of American rule has had a deflationary effect on language capturing interstate conflict. The employment of terms like "tomato wars" to characterize relations between the United States and Canada, "banana wars" between the United States and the European Union, or "mushroom wars" between Japan and China, among others, have turned interstate conflict into harmless marketplace bickering devoid of any lasting influence on the existing balance of power. That these wars were fought in the 1970s and 1980s over agricultural commodities and not over industrial goods or services has further trimmed the significance of these medieval-sounding wars. Recently, however, issues surrounding agriculture have taken a pronounced if not ominous role in North-South negotiations, for example the controversy over genetically modified foods or the protracted war over banana imports, and have placed Europe and the United States at loggerheads in their dealings with each other.

Keith Nurse traces the evolution of banana wars, and how the struggle between U.S.-based transnational corporations, representing the dollar-zone banana exporters, and the European Union, offering preference to producers in the Caribbean, Africa, and the Pacific (its former colonies) as well as to those in its own overseas holdings and territories, shaped the final form of the single European market. He documents how the erosion of preferences, increased competition, and falling prices worked to the detriment of producers. Increasing concentration of capital into the hands of transnational corporations (supplying and distributing the bananas) and diminishing incomes for the producers signal a decline in the capacity of peripheral states that rely on the production and exportation of agricultural goods as their main source of revenue.

In the final chapter, John McNeill traces the environmental ramifications of imperial rivalry during the course of the twentieth century. He maintains that the twentieth century fared much worse than the nineteenth by highlighting two facts. First, the interstate system has come to cover the globe during the twentieth century, with all polities now subject to the same set of "national" security concerns. Secondly, even though the state of rivalry in the late nineteenth century was solved at the close of World War II, the Cold War that ensued did not lessen but furthered military mobilization. Security concerns that naturally flowed from the state of rivalry and later the Cold War provided immunity to a host of states to pursue ecologically imprudent policies. McNeill argues that the first round of rivalry between ascending and descending powers in the period from 1914 to 1945, and later the bipolar structure of the world-system in the 1945 to 1989 period, with the implications this had in terms of the wars taking place in the third world, deprived the world of a considerable proportion of its nonrenewable resources.

In addition to actual combat (and guerrilla warfare), military industrialization, building of large-scale transportation networks to move and deliver strategically important weapons, and the proliferation of military zones exempt from environmental scrutiny—not to mention pronatalism and nuclear weapons industry—all worked against the world's ecology by subjugating environmental concerns to security concerns and to the exigencies of rivalry. The current situation, by deepening the trends set in motion for most of the twentieth century, does not render future scenarios optimistic. Since the end of the Cold War, the rise in its stead of a full-fledged rivalry among contenders to the hegemonic post and the chaos that came to color the periphery of the system—symbolized in the debate about the possession of nuclear weapons—do not bode well for the future of the world and the environment. *Hic Rhodus, hic salta.*

# References

Amin, Samir. 1980. "Révolution ou décadence? La crise du système impérialiste contemporain et celle de l'Empire romain." *Review: A Journal of the Fernand Braudel Center* 4(1): 155–167.

Arrighi, Giovanni. 1994. *The Long Twentieth Century: Money, Power, and the Origins of Our Times.* New York: Verso.

Balakrishnan, Gopal, ed. 2003. *Debating Empire.* New York: Verso.

Braudel, Fernand. 1982. *Civilization and Capitalism, 15th–18th Century.* Vol. II: *The Wheels of Commerce.* New York: Harper and Row.

———. 1984. *Civilization and Capitalism, 15th–18th century.* Vol. III: *The Perspective of the World.* New York: Harper and Row.

Calleo, David. 2003. "Power, Wealth, and Wisdom: The United States and Europe after Iraq." *National Interest* 72 (Summer): 5–15.

Davis, Mike. 2004. "Planet of Slums." *New Left Review.* 2/26 (March–April): 5–34.

Debray, Régis. 2002. *L'Édit de Caracalla ou plaidoyer pour des États-Unis d'Occident.* Paris: Fayard.

Ferguson, Niall. 2003. *Empire: The Rise and Demise of the British World Order and the Lesson for Global Power.* New York: Basic Books.

Frank, Andre Gunder. 1998. *Reorient: Global Economy in the Asian Age.* Berkeley: University of California Press.

Gentil Da Silva, José. 1984. "De la modernité du XVIe siècle au sévère mais riche XVIIe." In John Day, ed., *Etudes d'histoire monétaire, XIIe–XIXe siècles.* Presses universitaire de Lille, pp. 397–421.

Goldstone, Jack. 1991. *Revolution and Rebellion in the Early Modern World.* Berkeley: University of California Press.

Gorz, André. 1997. *Misères du présent, richesse du possible.* Paris: Galilée.

Hardt, Michael, and Antonio Negri. 2000. *Empire*. Cambridge, MA: Harvard University Press.

Hopkins, T. K. 1990. "Note on the Concept of Hegemony." *Review: A Journal of the Fernand Braudel Center* 13(3): 409–411.

Howe, Stephen. 2002. *Empire: A Very Short Introduction*. New York: Oxford University Press.

Iriye, Akira. 2002. *Global Community: The Role of International Organizations in the Making of the Contemporary World*. Berkeley: University of California Press.

James, Harold. 2001. *The End of Globalization: Lessons from the Great Depression*. Cambridge, MA: Harvard University Press.

Johnson, Chalmers. 2004. *The Sorrows of Empire: Militarism, Secrecy, and the End of the Republic*. New York: Metropolitan Books.

Kagan, Robert. 2003. *Of Paradise and Power: America and Europe in the New World Order*. New York: Knopf.

Kasaba, Reşat, and Faruk Tabak. 1995. "Fatal Conjuncture: The Decline and Fall of the Modern Agrarian Order during the Bretton Woods Era." In Philip McMichael, ed., *Food and Agrarian Orders in the World-Economy*. Westport, CT: Praeger, pp. 79–93.

Kennedy, Paul. 1999. "The Next American Century?" *World Policy Journal* 16(1): 52–58.

Lane, Frederic. 1979. *Profits from Power*. Albany: State University of New York Press.

Mann, Michael. 2003. *Incoherent Empire*. New York: Verso.

Minc, Alain. 1993. *Le nouveaux moyen âge*. Paris: Gallimard.

Neal, Larry. 1990. *The Rise of Financial Capitalism: International Capital Markets in the Age of Reason*. New York: Cambridge University Press.

O'Brien, Patrick. 2003. "The Myth of Anglophone Succession." *New Left Review* 2/24 (November–December): 113–134.

O'Rourke, Kevin H., and Jeffrey G. Williamson. 1999. *Globalization and History: The Evolution of a Nineteenth-Century Atlantic Economy*. Cambridge, MA: MIT Press.

Pfaff, William. 2003. "Refusing to Treat Allies as Equals." *International Herald Tribune*, July 7.

Pomeranz, Kenneth. 2000. *The Great Divergence: Europe, China, and the Making of the Modern World-Economy*. Princeton, NJ: Princeton University Press.

Schama, Simon. 1987. *The Embarrassment of Riches*. New York: Fontana Press.

Stiglitz, Joseph. 2002. *Globalization and Its Discontents*. New York: W. W. Norton.

Tabak, Faruk. 2001. "Informalization and the Long Term." In F. Tabak and M. Critchlow, eds., *Informalization: Process and Structure*. Baltimore, MD: Johns Hopkins University Press.

Todd, Emmanuel. 2002. *Après l'empire. Essai sur la décomposition du système américain*. Paris: Gallimard.

Wallerstein, Immanuel. 1999. "States? Sovereignty? The Dilemmas of Capitalists in an Age of Transition." In David A. Smith, Dorothy J. Solinger, and Steven J. Topik, eds., *States and Sovereignty in the Global Economy*. London: Routledge, pp. 20–33.

# 2

# THE BUSH REGIME AND THE COLLAPSE OF THE POSTWAR GEOPOLITICAL STRUCTURES

## *Immanuel Wallerstein*

With the conquest of Iraq, the Bush regime has the wind in its sails. It thinks it can do anything, and it will most probably act on this belief for the foreseeable future. It is understandable that the U.S. hawks, having long preached that macho militarism would pay off, believe that they now have clear evidence of their thesis. It is also understandable that many of those around the world who have most strongly opposed the U.S. hawk vision for the world are not merely dismayed but depressed and gloomy, and fear that the U.S. hawks may be more successful than their opponents had anticipated. I believe that such assessments— whether made by the U.S. hawks or their fiercest opponents—miss the mark and fail to perceive what is actually happening in the geopolitical arena.

I shall build my analysis around three time periods: 1945–1967/1973, or the postwar apogee of U.S. hegemony; 1967/1973–2001, or the late summer glow; and 2001–2025/2050, or the anarchy the United States cannot control. I shall distinguish three axes in each period: the internal competitive struggles of the major loci of accumulation of the capitalist world-economy; the so-called North-South struggle; and the struggle to determine the future world-system between two groups whom I shall call metaphorically the camp of Davos and the camp of Porto Alegre.

# I. The Postwar Apogee of U.S. Hegemony

In the period from 1945 to 1967/1973, the United States was unquestionably the hegemonic power in the world-system. It combined economic, military, political, and cultural advantage over any and all others in the world-system.

When World War II ended, it was the only industrial power to have escaped wartime destruction, and even to have increased significantly its productive capacities over those considerable ones it already had when the war began. U.S. enterprises were therefore able to produce so much more efficiently than competitors that they could penetrate the markets of even the home territories of these competitors, at least at first. Indeed, the situation was so lopsided that the United States found it necessary to engage in the economic reconstruction of western Europe and Japan in order to have a reasonable world customer base.

This overwhelming economic edge was combined with a military edge. To be sure, U.S. public opinion insisted on an immediate downsizing of the size of the U.S. military after 1945 ("get the boys home"). But the United States had the atomic bomb and an air force capacity to use nuclear weapons anywhere. The only other military force of any serious consequence in the world, then and in the decades to come, was that of the Soviet Union, and by 1949 the Soviet Union also had nuclear weapons. So, there was only one thing for the United States to do—make a deal. And this is just what it did. We call the deal Yalta, although the actual Yalta accords were only a small part of the larger Yalta arrangements.

Yalta combined three clear clauses: status quo in Europe along the lines where the U.S. and Soviet troops stood in 1945; economic cloistering of two world zones; and freedom to use mutually denunciatory rhetoric. Each of the three clauses was respected more or less fully up to 1980 and very largely up until the collapse of the Soviet Union.

To be sure, the status quo was tested by the Berlin Blockade in 1949, but reaffirmed by its outcome. Subsequently, the United States rigorously abstained from assisting any rebellious uprisings in the Soviet zone, other than rhetorically. The two Soviet breakaways—Yugoslavia and Albania—were both countries in which no Soviet troops were stationed. Rather than becoming, however, part of the U.S. sphere, they were allowed by both sides in the Cold War to remain "neutral." Whether the Yalta arrangements were meant to apply to Korea was initially unclear. The Korean War tested this question, and its outcome—an armed truce at the line of departure—placed Korea squarely inside the arrangements.

Economic cloistering remained untouched during the first postwar period, but began to come unhinged in the post-1973 period. It was the persistence of the unmitigated rhetoric—the so-called Cold War—that persuaded most people that a serious conflict was occurring. No doubt, in the minds of many, and perhaps most people, it was a serious conflict. To many, even in retrospect, it seems to have been one. But a geopolitician from Mars might understandably have had the feeling that it seemed a choreographed conflict in which nothing really ever happened.

Politically, the Yalta arrangements allowed the two sides to line up a series of faithful allies. The allies of the Soviet Union have usually been thought of as satellites. But in this period, the allies of the United States—the members of NATO and Japan, South Korea, and Taiwan—acted for the most part as virtual satellites as well, with only one or two exceptions. Culturally, New York became the center of world high culture, and popular culture everywhere was "Americanized." Ideologically, the concept of the "free world" thrived at least as well as the concept of the "socialist camp."

So, within the North—the United States in relation to western Europe and Japan; the "West" in relation to the Soviet Union—the period 1945–1967/1973 was one in which the United States was able to impose its wishes on the rest of the North 95 percent of the time, 95 percent of the way. This was surely hegemony. The only sand in the machinery was a certain resistance in the South to this U.S.-defined world order. In theory, the United States preached the liberation of the South from colonial rule and the "development of the underdeveloped countries." The Soviet Union sang the same tune, in even screechier language. In practice, neither was in any rush to do too much to further these objectives.

It was left to the peoples of the South to take it upon themselves to advance their own cause. They did this with various degrees of political energy and militant tactics. There occurred some famous struggles that involved violent revolution—notably China, Vietnam, Cuba, and Algeria. None of these struggles had been in the agenda of the Yalta arrangements. The United States did what it could to suppress such movements, and it had some significant successes (Iran at the time of Mossadegh, Guatemala in 1954, and a long list of others), as did the Soviet Union (Greece). But the North also had a few very important failures—the Soviet Union in China, France in Algeria, the United States in Cuba, and first France and then the United States in Vietnam. What both the West and the Soviet Union did was try to adjust to these "realities"— that is, absorb these events into the ambit of their rhetoric, co-opt the new regimes, and thereby limit their impact on the geopolitical arena, and indeed on the world-economy as well.

In terms of what might be called the world class struggle, it seems as if it were a draw. On the one hand, there was a sweep of antisystemic sentiment during this period throughout the world, and especially throughout the South, which was very self-validating. Triumphalism was the order of the day. On the other hand, there was just enough accommodation of the demands of these forces by the North, and the accommodation was in fact sufficiently swift, that the antisystemic upsurge began to burn out, a bit like a phoenix.

## II. The Late Summer Glow

The period 1967/1973 represents the moment in which the *trentes glorieuses* came to an end, and the world-economy entered into a long Kondratieff B-phase downturn. Probably the biggest single immediate cause of the downturn was the economic rise of western Europe and Japan, which led inevitably to overproduction in the former leading industries in the world-economy. Politically and culturally, the world revolution of 1968 (actually 1966–1970) represented a challenge to everything that had happened in the previous period. It was triggered by the combination of resistance to U.S. hegemony and disillusionment with the traditional antisystemic movements. In the military arena, February 1968 saw the Tet offensive in Vietnam, which sounded the death knell of U.S. military action there, leading to an agonizing five more years of warfare consummated by U.S. withdrawal in 1973. The United States had actually lost a war against a small Third World nation. The triple occurrence—the downturn in the world-economy, the world revolution of 1968, and the U.S. defeat in Vietnam—transformed the world geopolitical scene and marked the onset of the slow decline of U.S. hegemony. It would no longer be true that the United States could realize its objectives 95 percent of the time, 95 percent of the way, even in the North. But one does not lose hegemonic control overnight. There was a late summer glow.

The economics of this late summer glow are really not that difficult to understand. Such a Kondratieff B-phase has certain standard economic characteristics:

1. A decline in the profitability of productive enterprises, especially those that had been most profitable previously, and consequently a shift in focus by capitalists in their search to accumulate capital from the arena of production to that of speculative financial activity;
2. A flight of industries whose profits were declining because their monopolistic advantages had disappeared from their loci in the core zones to semiperipheral countries—where wages are lower even if transactions costs are higher—these countries are thereupon proclaimed to be "developing";
3. A significant rise in world unemployment levels, and therefore an effort of the major loci of accumulation to "export" the unemployment to each other, in large part to minimize the political fallout.

All of this happened. The spectacular events (but not the causes) of this downturn were the oil price rises of 1973 and 1979 and the successive debt crises—that of the Third World and the socialist countries in the 1980s, that of the U.S. government and of transnational corporations in the early 1990s, that of U.S. consumers in the late 1990s (plus the East Asian and other devaluations), and another round of excessive U.S. government debt under the second Bush regime. As for the comparative well-being of the major loci of accumulation, it can be noted that Europe did best in the 1970s, Japan in the 1980s, the United States in the (late) 1990s, and all have been doing badly since 2000. In the rest of the world, the promise of national "development," so actively and optimistically pursued in the earlier period, was revealed to be the mirage it had always been, at least for the great majority of states.

Politically the U.S. order began to disintegrate. Western Europe and Japan wished to cease being satellites. They demanded to be partners. The United States tried to appease them with new structures—the Trilateral Commission and the G-7 (later G-8) meetings. The United States used two main arguments to hold their allies in line: the Soviet Union remained a menace to their interests, and a united position against a rising South was essential to maintain their collective advantages. These arguments were partially successful, but only partially. The Soviet zone also began to disintegrate after the spectacular rise of Solidarity in Poland and the not-so-quiet revolution of Gorbachev in the Soviet Union. The disintegration of the Soviet zone was accelerated by the collapse of developmentalism, parallel to that which had occurred in the Third World, revealing how the basic economic position of the states of the socialist bloc had always remained that of being peripheral and semiperipheral states in the capitalist world-economy. In the Third World, the weakened position of both the United States and the Soviet Union did seem to leave some space for the (quasi-)resolution of a number of long-standing conflicts in Central America, southern Africa, and southeast Asia, but all these resolutions represented political compromises.

The world revolution of 1968 combined with the collapse of developmentalism in the Kondratieff B-period undermined severely the moral legitimacy of the Old Left, the classical antisystemic movements, who now seemed to most of their erstwhile supporters to have little to offer other than a sort of defensive electoralism. The successor movements—in particular, the multiple Maoisms, and the so-called New Left (especially the Greens, the women's movements, and the multiple varieties of identity-based movements)—had short, brilliant impacts in various countries but never seemed to be able to acquire the dramatic centrality, either nationally or internationally, that the Old Left movements had displayed during the first postwar period.

In terms of the world class struggle, the weakening of the antisystemic movements (both Old and New) allowed the world establishment forces to launch a counteroffensive of considerable magnitude. This took the form first of all of the coming to power of neoliberal (actually fiercely conservative) regimes in Great Britain and the United States (Thatcher and Reagan); the so-called Washington Consensus, which buried the ideal of developmentalism and replaced it with the ideal of "globalization"; and the vigorous increase in the role and activity of the IMF, the World Bank, and the interstate newcomer, the World Trade Organization (WTO), all of which sought to defang the ability of non–core zone states to interfere with the free flow of goods and above all of capital.

This worldwide offensive had three main objectives: push back the level of wages throughout the world; restore the externalization of production costs by ending serious constraints on ecological abuses; reduce world tax levels by dismantling part or all of the welfare state provisions. At first, this offensive seemed magnificently successful, and Mrs. Thatcher's "there is no alternative" (TINA) slogan seemed to carry the day. But in fact, by the late 1990s, this offensive had reached its political limits.

The currency devaluations of the late 1990s in East and Southeast Asia, Russia, and Brazil brought to power rather rapidly Roh Moo-hyun in South Korea, Megawati Sukarnoputri in Indonesia, Vladimir Putin in Russia, and Luis Inácio (Lula) da Silva in Brazil. None of these leaders exactly met the expectations of the Washington Consensus. The collapse of Yugoslavia and the Soviet Union led to a long series of ethnic conflicts, resulting in a good deal of ethnic purification, large zones of political instability, and little political credit for either the United States or western Europe. The failed state phenomenon spread in Africa.

Most serious of all, the cultural/ideological sweep of the G-7, WTO, and Davos meetings met a stumbling-block in Seattle in 1999, when somewhat traditional, centrist U.S. trade-unionists joined forces with New Left groups to force the WTO into a standstill from which it has not been able to extricate itself since. The momentum thereafter fell to a loosely organized world coalition of multiple movements, these days called the alterglobalization movement, who have been able to hold a series of very successful meetings in Porto Alegre, and have established themselves as the other pole against the forces of Davos.

When George W. Bush pushed his way into the presidency of the United States under questionable conditions, the situation did not look good at all for the United States. One of the themes of his campaign had been the world policy failures of the Clinton administration, although any reasonable analyst would have observed that Clinton had merely been following the same basic policy of every U.S. president since Richard Nixon—trying to patch the leaking balloon of U.S. hegemony by repeated negotiations with its presumed allies as well as with Russia and China, combined with sporadic and limited use of force in the Third World. The primary objectives, since Nixon, had always been two: preventing the emergence of a politically independent European entity and maintaining the U.S. military edge by preventing the spread of nuclear weapons in the South. As of 2000, the scorecard for these two objectives was very mixed, and the future seemed very uncertain.

## III. The Anarchy the United States Cannot Control

It was at this point that George W. Bush came to power. His administration was divided between those who wished to continue the foreign policy of the 1973–2001 period, and those who argued vociferously that this was a failed policy, which had caused (not merely resulted from) the relative decline of U.S. hegemony. The latter were the U.S. hawks, who have three principal bases—the neoconservatives (Wolfowitz, Perle, et al.), the Christian right, and the "classical" macho militarists (Cheney and Rumsfeld, whose views were seconded by Senator McCain, even though he was personally on the outs with President Bush). Even though their motives, their detailed priorities, and their political strengths were quite different, these three groups formed a tight political bloc based on certain shared assumptions.

1. U.S. decline was a reality, but was eminently reversible. It had been caused by the unwise timidity of successive U.S. governments and could be rapidly reversed by frank, open, and speedy preemptive military actions in one zone after another;
2. Whatever the initial reluctance, even opposition, of the U.S. establishment, U.S. public opinion, and the "allies" of the United States in western Europe and East Asia, successful military action would have the consequence of getting them to fall into line;
3. The way to handle resisting, unfriendly regimes in the South is by intimidation, and if that fails, by conquest.

There was one more reading of history on which all the U.S. hawks agreed: They had never been able to get any U.S. administration to adopt their reasoning and follow their prescriptions to the degree they wanted, or persistently. They were quite a frustrated group. And when the Bush regime started, they were not at all sure they had the president on their side. Rather, they feared that he would be a replica of his father as well as (although they were careful never to say so) Ronald Reagan (who had committed the unforgivable sin of coming to terms with Gorbachev).

September 11 represented an incredible bonanza for the U.S. hawks. It catapulted George W. Bush into their camp, if only because being a war president in a "war against terrorism" seemed to guarantee his political future. It legitimated the use of military force against an ultraweak opponent, the Taliban, in an operation that commanded about as much worldwide legitimacy as any such action can ever acquire. And, now the hawks could go for broke—Iraq. They knew that Iraq would be more difficult politically, but they also knew that it was now or never, not only for the conquest of Iraq but for their entire geopolitical program.

They ran into far more difficulty than President Bush had anticipated. First, the so-called old Bushies (probably with the connivance of Bush's father) launched a campaign for a so-called multilateralist approach. Bush was persuaded to go down this path. But then, the warnings of the hawks seemed to materialize. France drew a line in the sand, and was able to get Germany and Russia to join it. This led to the humiliation of the United States, which had to withdraw its UN Security Council resolution in March 2003 because it was unable to get even a simple majority to vote for it, despite using all the pressures Bush could muster. Adding insult to injury, the forces of Porto Alegre were able to mobilize a worldwide antiwar protest on February 15, 2003, unmatched in previous world history. Finally even Turkey, faithful Turkey, failed the United States by refusing to open a northern front in the Iraq War despite being offered an incredibly large bribe.

Of course, as we know, the United States invaded Iraq nonetheless and the Saddam Hussein regime collapsed, militarily and politically. The hawks are now pursuing their policy by further threats to all and sundry—in the Middle

East, in Northeast Asia, and indeed in Latin America. The hawks are convinced they have won the gambit, and that U.S. hegemony is restored. They talk openly, and without shame, of the U.S. imperial role. But have they really intimidated everyone else? I do not think so. Of course, here we move into the uncertain immediate future. And, especially in moments of systemic anarchy, almost anything can happen. Still, there seem to be certain tendencies:

1. The present U.S. government is committed to a unilateralist and rather aggressive foreign policy;
2. European construction will move forward, no doubt with difficulty but unceasingly, and Europe will inevitably distance itself still further from the United States;
3. China, Korea, and Japan will begin to move closer together, a project more difficult than that of European integration, but one with greater consequence for the geopolitical arena;
4. Nuclear proliferation in the South will continue and probably expand;
5. Assuming the imperial mantle will further eviscerate the claims of the United States regime to moral legitimacy in the world-system;
6. The camp of Porto Alegre and the spirit of Porto Alegre will grow more solid and probably more militant;
7. The camp of Davos may well be increasingly split between those who will seek to survive by joining/coming to terms with/co-opting the camp of Porto Alegre and those who are determined to smash it;
8. The United States may soon start regretting the whirlwind it has unleashed with its action in Iraq.

We have entered an anarchic transition—from our existing world-system to a different one. In this transition, as in any such transition, no one controls the situation to any significant degree, least of all a declining hegemonic power like the United States. The U.S. hawks may think they have the wind in their sails, but in fact there are strong gales coming from all directions, and the major problem of all boats will be to not overturn—that of the U.S. hawks along with those of the rest of us. It will be a long time before the seas are calm again. Whether the ultimate outcome will portend a less or more egalitarian and democratic world is totally uncertain. On the other hand, the results will be a consequence of how we act collectively and concretely in the decades to come.

# 3

# ROUGH ROAD TO EMPIRE

## *Giovanni Arrighi*

The beginning of the twenty-first century has been marked by a renewed interest in empire-building. The purpose of this chapter is to examine this renewed interest in light of the interpretative scheme proposed in *The Long Twentieth Century* (Arrighi 1994) and in *Chaos and Governance in the Modern World System* (Arrighi and Silver 1999). After summing up the main features of this scheme, I will trace current U.S. imperial ambitions and the growing dependence of the United States on foreign capital to prop up its centrality in the global political economy. U.S. attempts to use its seemingly unchallengeable military supremacy to stave off economic decline have run into serious problems. My chapter analyzes these problems and then concludes by revisiting the contentions of *The Long Twentieth Century* and *Chaos and Governance* in light of recent trends and events.

## I. After U.S. Hegemony

A surprising number of readers have attributed to *The Long Twentieth Century* two contentions it never made. One is the contention, in the words of Michael Hardt and Antonio Negri, that "in the context of Arrighi's cyclical argument it is impossible to recognize a rupture of the system, a paradigm shift, an event. Instead, everything must always return, and the history of capitalism thus becomes the eternal return of the same" (2000, 239).[1] The other is the contention that Japan was poised to replace the United States as the new hegemonic power—a contention that in retrospect is dismissed in light of the Japanese economic crisis and U.S. economic resurgence of the 1990s.[2]

In reality, *The Long Twentieth Century* makes neither claim. The four systemic cycles of accumulation constructed in the book—each consisting of a phase of material expansion and a phase of financial expansion—neither prevent a recognition of systemic ruptures and paradigm shifts, nor describe the history of capitalism as an eternal return of the same. On the contrary, they show that systemic ruptures and paradigm shifts occur precisely when the "same" (in the form of recurrent system-wide financial expansions) appears to return. Moreover, by comparing successive periods of return/rupture, the book shows how the engine of restructuring and renewed expansion has changed over time, making the current crisis and financial expansion novel in key respects.

The novelty on which *The Long Twentieth Century* focused was an unprecedented bifurcation of financial and military power.

> What is new in the present configuration of power is that Japan has done so well by specializing in the pursuit of profit in the East Asian region and letting the U.S. specialize in the pursuit of world power . . . [so] as to wrest from the West one of the two most important ingredients of its fortunes over the preceding five hundred years: control over surplus capital. For each of the successive systemic cycles of accumulation that made the fortunes of the West has been premised on the formation of ever-more powerful territorialist-capitalist blocs of governmental and business organizations endowed with greater capabilities than the preceding bloc to widen or deepen the spatial and functional scope of the capitalist world-economy. The situation today seems to be such that this evolutionary process has reached, or is about to reach, its limits. (Arrighi 1994, 353–354)

The evolutionary process that underlies the recurrence of material and financial expansions is approaching its limits because "the state-and-war-making capabilities of the traditional power centers of the capitalist West have gone so far that they can increase further only through the formation of a truly global world-empire." Yet, the "realization [of such an empire] requires control over the most prolific sources of world surplus capital—sources which are now located in East Asia." It was not clear to me at the time—nor, as we shall see, is it clear to me today—"by what means the traditional power centers of the West can acquire and retain this control" (Arrighi 1994, 354–355).

I therefore concluded by sketching not one but three quite different scenarios as possible outcomes of the ongoing crisis of the U.S. regime of accumulation.

> First, the old centers may succeed in halting the course of capitalist history. The course of capitalist history over the last five hundred years has been a succession of financial expansions during which there occurred a change of guard at the commanding heights

of the capitalist world-economy. This outcome is present at the level of tendency also in the current financial expansion. But this tendency is countered by the very extent of the state-and-war-making capabilities of the old guard, which may well be in a position to appropriate through force, cunning, or persuasion the surplus capital that accumulates in the new centers and thereby terminate capitalist history through the formation of a truly global world-empire. Second, the old guard may fail to stop the course of capitalist history and East Asian capital may come to occupy a commanding position in systemic processes of capital accumulation. Capitalist history would then continue but under conditions that depart radically from what they have been since the formation of the modern interstate system. The new guard at the commanding heights of the capitalist world-economy would lack the state-and-war-making capabilities that, historically, have been associated with the enlarged reproduction of a capitalist layer on top of the market layer of the world-economy. If Adam Smith and Fernand Braudel were right in their contentions that capitalism would not survive such a disassociation, then . . . [c]apitalism . . . would wither away with the state power that has made its fortunes in the modern era, and the underlying layer of the market economy would revert to some kind of anarchic order. Finally—to paraphrase Schumpeter—before humanity chokes (or basks) in the dungeon (or paradise) of a postcapitalist world-empire or of a postcapitalist world-market society, it may well burn up in the horrors (or glories) of the escalating violence that has accompanied the liquidation of the Cold War world order. In this case, capitalist history would also come to an end but by reverting permanently to the systemic chaos from which it began six hundred years ago and which has been reproduced on an ever increasing scale with each transition. Whether this would mean the end just of capitalist history or of all human history, it is impossible to tell. (Arrighi 1994, 355–356)

These conclusions were reached on the basis of a research agenda that focused almost exclusively on state-capital relations in the European- and eventually U.S.-centered world capitalist system. *Chaos and Governance* confirmed the significance of the bifurcation of financial and military power identified in *The Long Twentieth Century*. But by investigating the role of social and intercivilizational conflicts in shaping hegemonic transitions, it added important new dimensions to the diagnosis of the ongoing crisis.

Regarding the continuing significance of the bifurcation of military and financial power, Silver and I argued that the inability of the Japanese economy to recover from the crash of 1990–1992 and the region-wide financial crisis of 1997–1998 in and of itself did not support the conclusion that the "rise of East Asia" had been a mirage. We noted that in previous hegemonic transitions, the newly emerging centers of world-scale processes of capital accumulation experienced the deepest financial crises as their financial prowess outstripped their institutional capacity to regulate the massive amounts of mobile capital flowing in and out of their jurisdictions. This was true of London, in the late eighteenth century and even more of New York in the 1930s. No one would use the Wall

Street crash of 1929–1931 and the subsequent Great Depression to argue that the epicenter of global processes of capital accumulation had *not* been shifting from the United Kingdom to the United States in the first half of the twentieth century. Nor should we draw any analogous conclusion from the East Asian financial crises of the 1990s (Arrighi and Silver 1999, especially Chapter 1 and Conclusion).

Nonetheless, throughout the 1990s the economic expansion of China at rates without parallel or precedent for a country of comparable demographic size had continued unabated.[3] We accordingly deemphasized the importance of the Japanese component of the rise of East Asia to underscore the deep roots of the Chinese ascent, not just in the social and political reconstitution of China in the Cold War era under communism, but also in the achievements of late imperial China in state-and-national-economy-making prior to its subordinate incorporation into the European-centered world system. From this standpoint, the increasing centrality of China and of the Chinese diaspora in promoting the region's economic integration and expansion was seen as building upon a long-standing East Asian practice of relying more heavily than the West on trade and markets to regulate relations among sovereigns and between sovereigns and subjects. This practice constituted a serious handicap in preventing the forcible subordination of the China-centered regional system within the structures of the European-centered globalizing system. Over time, however, it became the foundation of renewed competitiveness in the highly integrated global market that emerged under U.S. hegemony (Arrighi and Silver 1999, especially Chapter 3; see also Arrighi, Hamashita, and Selden 2003, especially Introduction and Chapter 7).

This interpretation of the increasing centrality of China in the East Asian economy and of East Asia in the global economy has two important implications for the prospective outcome of the ongoing crisis of U.S. hegemony. First, to the extent that these tendencies are indeed the expression of a region-specific historical heritage, they can be expected to be far more robust than if they were simply due to policies and behaviors that could be replicated elsewhere in the world. Second, China's demographic size means that its continuing economic expansion is far more subversive of the global hierarchy of wealth than all the previous East Asian economic "miracles" put together. For all these miracles (the Japanese included) were instances of upward mobility within a fundamentally stable hierarchy. The hierarchy could and did accommodate the upward mobility of a handful of East Asian states (two of them city-states) accounting for about one-twentieth of world population. But accommodating the upward mobility of a state that by itself accounts for about one-fifth of world population is an altogether different affair. It implies a fundamental subversion of the very pyramidal structure of the hierarchy.[4]

The subversive implication of the Chinese ascent is closely related to another dimension of the ongoing hegemonic crisis that was not explored in *The Long Twentieth Century,* but figures prominently in *Chaos and Governance*: the peculiar social character of the crisis in comparison with earlier hegemonic crises. In past hegemonic transitions, the massive redistribution of resources and the even greater social dislocations entailed by financial expansions provoked movements of resistance and rebellion by subordinate groups and communities whose established ways of life were coming under attack. Interacting with interstate power struggles, these movements eventually forced the dominant groups to form a new hegemonic social bloc that selectively included previously excluded groups and communities. In the transition from British to U.S. hegemony—under the joint impact of the revolt against the West and working-class rebellions—the hegemonic social bloc was expanded through the promise of security of employment and high mass consumption for the working classes of the wealthier countries of the West, and of rights to national self-determination and "development" for the elites of the nonwestern world. It soon became clear, however, that this package of promises could not be delivered. Moreover, it engendered expectations among the world's subordinate strata that seriously threatened the stability and eventually precipitated the crisis of U.S. hegemony (Arrighi and Silver 1999, 153–216; Silver 2003, 149–167).

Thus, although system-wide social conflict escalated in the wake of previous hegemonic crises, partly as a consequence of financial expansions, in the crisis of U.S. hegemony the system-wide explosion of social conflict of the late 1960s and early 1970s preceded and thoroughly shaped the subsequent financial expansion. Indeed, in a very real sense the current financial expansion has been primarily an instrument of the containment of the combined demands of the peoples of the nonwestern world and of the western working classes. Financialization and the associated restructuring of the global political economy have undoubtedly succeeded in disorganizing the social forces that were the bearers of these demands in the upheavals of the late 1960s and 1970s. At the same time, however, the underlying contradiction of a world capitalist system that promotes the formation of a world proletariat but cannot accommodate a generalized living wage (that is, the most basic of reproduction costs), far from being solved, is a constant source of tensions and conflicts within, between, and across political communities (Arrighi and Silver 1999, 282–286; Silver 2003, 20–25, 177–179).

It follows that the confrontation between the tendency toward the formation of a world-empire centered on the West and of a world-market society centered on the East is not occurring in a social void. Rather, the chances that one or the other tendency will prevail largely depend on whether the agencies of either tendency can provide feasible and credible solutions to the system-level problems left behind by U.S. hegemony. It seemed to us then, and it still seems to me now, that the most serious of these problems is "the seemingly unbridgeable gulf between the life-chances of a small minority of world population (between 10 and 20 percent) and the vast majority" (Arrighi and Silver 1999, 289). As noted above, the continuing rapid economic expansion of China was recognized as a major force beginning to close that seemingly unbridgeable gulf. *Chaos and Governance* nonetheless concluded on a cautionary note by identifying two major obstacles to a noncatastrophic transition to a more equitable world order.

The most immediate obstacle was traced to U.S. resistance to adjustment and accommodation. Paraphrasing David Calleo, we noted that the Dutch- and the British-centered world systems had broken down under the impact of two tendencies: the emergence of aggressive new powers and the attempt of the declining hegemonic power to avoid adjustment and accommodation by cementing its slipping preeminence into an exploitative domination (1987, 142). We maintained that

> There are no credible aggressive new powers that can provoke the breakdown of the U.S.-centered world system, but the United States has even greater capabilities than Britain did a century ago to convert its declining hegemony into an exploitative domination. If the system eventually breaks down, it will be primarily because of U.S. resistance to adjustment and accommodation. And conversely, U.S. adjustment and accommodation to the rising economic power of the East Asian region is an essential condition for a noncatastrophic transition to a new world order. (Arrighi and Silver 1999, 288–289)

Less immediate but equally important was the second obstacle: the still unverified capacity of the agencies of the East Asian economic expansion to "open up a new path of development for themselves and for the world that departs radically from the one that is now at a dead-end." This, we claimed "is an imposing task that the dominant groups of East Asian states have hardly begun to undertake."

> In past hegemonic transitions, dominant groups successfully took on the task of fashioning a new world order only after coming under intense pressure from movements of protest and self-protection from below. This pressure from below has widened and deepened from transition to transition, leading to enlarged social blocs with each new hegemony. Thus, we can expect social contradictions to play a far more decisive role than ever before in shaping both the unfolding transition and whatever new world order eventually emerges out of the impending systemic chaos. But whether the movements will largely follow and be shaped by the escalation of violence (as in past transitions) or precede and effectively work toward containing the systemic chaos is a question that is open. Its answer is ultimately in the hands of the movements. (Arrighi and Silver 1999, 289)

The issue raised in this passage is different from that raised at the end of *The Long Twentieth Century*. The three alternative scenarios sketched at the end of that book concerned possible developments of the global political economy *after* U.S. rule and accumulation had experienced its "terminal crisis." The United States was said to be living through one of those *belles époques* that historically had marked the closing phase of capitalist world hegemonies. That the U.S. regime would sooner or later experience its own terminal crisis was taken for granted. But nothing was said concerning the process of transition from the *belle époque* of the U.S. regime to the scenarios that were thought to be its most likely successors.

*Chaos and Governance,* in contrast, focused on the role that social conflict and systemic chaos—understood as a situation of severe and seemingly irremediable systemic disorganization—have played in the transition from one world order/hegemony to another. Like *The Long Twentieth Century,* it interpreted the revival of U.S. wealth and power of the 1980s and 1990s as the typical *belle époque* of closing phases of capitalist world hegemonies. Unlike *The Long Twentieth Century,* however, it raised the question of whether it was necessary for this particular *belle époque* to be followed, like previous *belles époques,* by a long period of systemic chaos and unspeakable human suffering. The answer given in the concluding passage quoted above was that this time around social movements of protest and self-protection had a better chance to act preemptively in the containment of chaos. Whether or not this was wishful thinking is an issue to which we shall return in the concluding section.

## II. Domination without Hegemony

One year after the publication of *Chaos and Governance,* the U.S.-centered "new economy" bubble burst. Shortly afterward came the shock of September 11, 2001. For a brief moment, through the war on Afghanistan, it seemed that the United States could strengthen its global hegemonic role by mobilizing a vast array of governmental and nongovernmental forces in the "war on terror." Within another year, however, the United States found itself almost completely isolated in waging a war on Iraq that was generally perceived to have little to do with the war on terror and to defy generally accepted rules and norms of interstate relations. What is the meaning of this sequence of events? Does it mark the end of the U.S. *belle époque* and, if so, what is the new condition of the global political economy?

Almost daily the media provide evidence that we may indeed be witnessing the terminal crisis of U.S. hegemony. One of the most telling pieces of evidence is a report in the *New York Times* on the eve of the Asia-Pacific Economic Cooperation (APEC) meeting in Bangkok. According to the report, political and business leaders in Asia see U.S. hegemony "subtly but unmistakably eroding as Asian countries look toward China as the increasingly vital regional power." Although the United States remains the region's biggest trading partner, China is rapidly catching up, especially vis-à-vis the two most important strategic U.S. allies, Japan and South Korea. More important, over the last year the politics of the situation has experienced a radical turnabout. As an illustration, the report quotes the assessment of a prominent Singaporean businessman, who a year earlier gave speeches in Hong Kong and London accusing China of being a juggernaut poised to smother the weaker economies of Southeast Asia. Now he draws an altogether different picture. "The perception is that China is trying its best to please, assist, [and] accommodate its neighbors while the United States is perceived as a country involved more and more in its own foreign policy, and strong-arming everyone onto that agenda" (Perlez 2003a, 1; see also Pan 2003; Perlez 2003b).

This perception of the United States is not limited to Asian countries. In the United States itself, prominent foreign policy scholars and analysts across the political spectrum see the doctrine underpinning the invasion of Iraq as having backfired. Inspired by the Project for the New American Century of 1997 and officially adopted by the Bush administration with the National Security Strategy document issued in September 2002, the doctrine rests on and propagates the belief that the United States can retain its predominant position in the world, and that it should do so virtually at all costs and by any means. These include preemptive wars waged against would-be rivals and the reshaping of world regions to fit U.S. interests and values. Moreover, the doctrine maintains that the more uncompromisingly the United States pursues these policies, the greater are the chances that the rest of the world will follow along. As it turns out, one year after the doctrine became official policy, far from following along, the rest of the world rejected U.S. leadership to an extent that has no precedent in the annals of U.S. hegemony. In the words of Scott McConnell, chief editor of the *American Conservative* magazine, "We are more isolated from general opinions of mankind than at any time in history" (quoted in Lobe 2003).

This may well be an exaggeration. But it is probably true that at this time the United States is exercising not hegemony, but what Ranajit Guha has called "domination without hegemony" (1992, 231–232).[5] If this is indeed the case, have we entered the worst case scenario foreseen in *Chaos and Governance*—the scenario, that is, in which U.S. resistance to adjustment and accommodation plunges the world into a long period of systemic chaos? U.S. policies since September 11 certainly constitute an extreme form of resistance to adjustment and accommodation. But it is not yet clear whether the plunge into systemic chaos is irreversible.

Two related considerations may help in clarifying the issues involved. The first is that, as William Raspberry (2003) has put it, "the president's mind has been the battleground for the fighting between pragmatists and ideologues— between those who see America's interests in more or less traditional terms . . . and those who see America's unchallenged power as a heaven-sent opportunity to reorder the world." Although the ideologues have managed to drag Bush into a mess the pragmatists had warned him about, the pragmatists may still convince him to do what it takes to get out of it.

The second consideration is that the adventurism of the ideologues on the West Asian front has strengthened the hand of the pragmatists on the East Asian front. Bush himself, on his way to and from the APEC meeting in Bangkok, geographically and rhetorically skirted China, the country that once was at the center of his administration's national security policy. This is "a significant shift," note James Harding and Peter Spiegel, "for a president who came into office touting his break from Clintonian policies of engagement with China, insisting in the first weeks of his presidency that China was a 'strategic competitor' to the United States." Thus, although before September 11 the Bush administration stepped up overtures to India in an attempt to create a counterweight to China, after September 11 balance-of-power politics took a back seat to the war on terrorism. The more security issues in Afghanistan, Iraq, and West Asia in general weighed down the U.S. government, the more warnings of the Chinese threat gave way to an even greater engagement with China than under Clinton. Indeed, the turnabout has been so complete that the Bush administration now boasts that it has better relations with China than any administration since Richard Nixon resumed relations with the PRC (Harding and Spiegel 2003).

To be sure, in its latest evaluation of China's military strength, the Pentagon still warned that "Beijing has greatly expanded its arsenal of increasingly accurate and lethal ballistic missiles and long-range strike aircraft that are ready for immediate application should the [People's Liberation Army] be called on to conduct war before its modernization aspirations are fully realized." More important, as John Gershman has underscored, the war on terrorism has helped the United States to "prepare for China" through the development of a network of military bases in Central Asia unimaginable before September 11, the strengthening of frayed military ties with the Philippines, a greatly expanded defense budget, and the revival of Reagan's defunct strategic defense initiative. "If China is the enemy of the future," concludes Gershman, "then the U.S. got a lot of what it wanted, without saying that China is the enemy" (quoted in Harding and Spiegel 2003).

Be that as it may, in order to assess the likely trajectory of U.S. policies in the long run, we must situate the struggle between pragmatists and ideologues and the present truce in U.S.-Chinese rivalry in the broader context of the contradictions that underlay the crisis of U.S. hegemony before and after September 11 and the Wall Street crash of 2000–2001. This brings us back to the growing dependence of the United States on foreign capital. In spite of persistent recession in Japan and economic revival in the United States, the reversal of positions between the two countries in the international credit system continued unabated throughout the 1990s. Writing in the midst of the Wall Street crash, but before September 11, Eamonn Fingleton underscored how Japan was then exporting "more capital in real terms than any nation since America's days of global economic dominance in the 1950s" (2001, 6). As a result, "in the first nine years of the 1990s Japan's net external assets jumped from $294 billion to $1,153 billion. Meanwhile, U.S. net external liabilities rocketed from $49 billion to $1,537 billion. In the long run this changing balance of financial power will be about the only thing that historians will remember about U.S.-Japanese economic rivalry in the last decade" (6).

Two years later, as U.S. troops were invading Iraq, historian Niall Ferguson (2003) pointed out a fundamental difference between the financial position of the United States today and that of Britain a century ago. In Britain's case, hegemony "also meant hege*money.*" As the world's banker, during its imperial heyday Britain "never had to worry about a run on the pound." The United States, in contrast, as it "overthrows 'rogue regimes,' first in Afghanistan and now in Iraq, is the world's biggest debtor. . . . Foreign investors now have claims on the United States amounting to about $8 trillion of its financial assets." This staggering indebtedness is the result of ever-larger deficits in the current account of the U.S. balance of payments, totaling nearly $3 trillion since 1982 and now surpassing $1.5 billion a day.[6] Ferguson concludes: "Thus President Bush's vision of a world recast by military force to suit American tastes has a piquant corollary: the military effort involved will be (unwillingly) financed by the Europeans—including the much reviled French—and the Japanese. Does that not give them just a little leverage over American policy, on the principle that he who pays the piper calls the tune? Balzac once said that if a debtor was big enough then he had power over his creditors; the fatal thing was to be a small debtor. It seems that Mr. Bush and his men have taken this lesson to heart" (Ferguson 2003).

This is a restatement of the bifurcation thesis advanced in *The Long Twentieth Century* and further elaborated in *Chaos and Governance*. Ferguson's version of the thesis, however, misses three key aspects of the bifurcation. First, the main financiers of the huge U.S. current account deficit are not the Europeans, let alone "the much reviled French." European private investment did play a major role in financing the U.S. deficit in the closing years of the new economy financial bubble. But before and after the bubble, by far the most important financiers of the U.S. current account deficits have been East Asian governments engaged in massive purchases of U.S. government securities and in building up dollar-denominated foreign exchange reserves—first and foremost the Japanese but to an increasingly significant extent the Chinese and other "China Circle" governments. Suffice it to mention that, in the first half of 2003 Japan and China alone bought $95 billion worth of U.S. Treasury bonds (Denny 2003). According to one estimate, between them China and Japan now hold more than $1 trillion in U.S. Treasury bonds (Ignatius 2003). Moreover, of the $870 billion increase in world foreign exchange reserves between December 1999 and June 2003, $665 billion occurred in Asia alone (Woolf 2003). And in the second half of 2003, China is said to be adding $10 billion a month to its huge dollar reserves of $346 billion (Sperling 2003).

Second, the main motivations of the governmental institutions that finance the escalating U.S. current account deficit are not strictly economic but political. Ferguson himself quotes the chief economist of the International Monetary Fund (IMF), Kenneth S. Rogoff, to the effect that he would be "pretty concerned" about "a developing country that had gaping current account deficits year after year, as far as the eye can see, of 5 per cent or more [of GDP], with budget ink spinning from black into red." Of course, as Rogoff hastened to add, the United States is not a "developing" country. As neither Rogoff nor Ferguson noticed, however, the United States is no ordinary "developed" country either. It is a country that expects and obtains from other governments and intergovernmental institutions—first and foremost the IMF—preferential treatment in the handling of its finances that no other state, no matter how "developed," either expects or would obtain if it did. And this preferential treatment is expected and granted not so much because of the Balzac effect noted by

Ferguson but because of the declining but still unparalleled centrality of the United States in the global economy and of the quasi-monopoly over means of mass destruction of the U.S. military apparatus.[7]

Finally, Ferguson misses the single most important reason why the financial position of the United States today is fundamentally different from that of Britain one century ago—the fact, that is, that Britain had a territorial empire from which it could extract financial and military resources almost at will, whereas the United States has no such thing. Suffice it to mention that India was, in Lord Salisbury's words, "an English barrack in the Oriental Seas from which we may draw any number of troops without paying for them" (Tomlinson 1975, 341). Paid for entirely by the Indian taxpayers, these troops were organized in a European-style colonial army deployed regularly in the endless series of wars through which Britain opened up Asia and Africa to western trade, investment, and influence.[8] At the same time, the infamous Home Charges and the Bank of England's control over India's foreign exchange reserves jointly turned India into the "pivot" of Britain's global financial and commercial supremacy. India's balance of payments deficit with Britain and surplus with the rest of the world enabled Britain to settle its deficit on current account with the rest of the world. Without India's forced contribution to the balance of payments of imperial Britain, it would have been impossible for Britain "to use the income from her overseas investment for further investment abroad and to give back to the international monetary system the liquidity she absorbed as investment income" (de Cecco 1984, 62–63).

We may sum up what Ferguson says and does not say about the present condition of U.S. domination without "hege*money*" as follows. As in Britain's case at a comparable stage of hegemonic decline, escalating U.S. current account deficits reflect deterioration in the competitive position of U.S. business at home and abroad. As in Britain's case, although less successfully, U.S. capital has partially countered this deterioration by specializing in global financial intermediation. Unlike Britain, however, the United States has no territorial empire from which to extract the resources needed to retain its politico-military preeminence in an increasingly competitive world.

Britain did, of course, eventually lose its politico-military preeminence. As competition from old and new empire-building rivals intensified, creating a favorable environment for the rebellion of colonial subjects, the costs of empire escalated over and above its benefits. As Britain found it increasingly difficult to make empire pay for itself, let alone provide a surplus, it became increasingly indebted to the United States, which combined lower protection costs and greater proficiency in industrialized warfare than Britain or any of its rivals. Over time, this situation forced Britain to liquidate its overseas empire and to settle for the position of junior partner of the new hegemonic power. It nonetheless took two world wars, both of which Britain won militarily but lost financially, for Britain to lose its prior position as the world's leading creditor nation (Arrighi and Silver 1999, 72–87).

The United States, in contrast, has become the world's leading *debtor* nation without fighting a single war against actual or potential "strategic competitors," as Britain did in World Wars I and II. For throughout its hegemony the United States has had no "barrack in the Oriental Seas" from which to draw, without paying for them, all the troops it needed to wage in the global South as endless a series of wars as Britain did during its own hegemony. Not only has the United States had to pay for those troops and their highly capital-intensive weaponry but also instead of extracting tribute from an overseas empire, it has had to compete aggressively in world financial markets to attract the capital needed to balance the explosive growth of its current account deficit. Although the United States has been extremely successful in this competition, the capital it has attracted has not come for "free," as Indian "contributions" to the British balance of payments did. On the contrary, it has generated a self-expanding flow of incomes to foreign residents that makes the U.S. current account deficit increasingly hard to balance, and the more so, as Martin Wolf notes (2003), because the inflow of capital has financed primarily government and private consumption rather than investment.

It follows that the United States has plunged into a protracted and costly war on multiple fronts under financial constraints far greater than those faced by Britain on the eve of World War I. How does the United States expect to pay for the protracted and costly war in Iraq? And how realistic are these expectations in light of the present situation of U.S. domination with neither hegemony nor hege*money*?

## III. The Political Economy of U.S. Financial Irresponsibility

There are two possible answers to these questions. One is that U.S. policymakers, like many of their critics, believe that seigniorage privileges—due to the generalized acceptance of the U.S. dollar as international currency—will set the United States free from financial constraints. The other is that they expect the war on terror itself to generate the financial resources needed to reestablish U.S. world hegemony on new foundations.

Writing in the columns of the *Financial Times*, Wolf provides a good illustration of the first answer. After noticing how foreign countries have provided the United States with goods, services, and assets in return for overpriced pieces of paper, thereby enabling it to consume far beyond its means, he points out that a cynic might view what is happening "as a brilliant U.S. conspiracy."

> In the 1980s and 1990s, its policymakers persuaded a host of economies to liberalize their financial markets. Such liberalizations generally ended with financial crises, currency crises, or a combination of the two. These disasters lowered domestic investment in the afflicted countries, instilled deep fear of current account deficits, and engendered a strong desire to accumulate foreign exchange reserves.

The safest way was to invest surplus funds in the country with the world's biggest economy and most liquid capital markets. When gullible foreigners can no longer be persuaded to finance the U.S., the dollar will decline. Since U.S. liabilities are dollar-denominated, the bigger the decline, the smaller net U.S. liabilities to the rest of the world will then turn out to be. In this way, the last stage of the "conspiracy" will be partial default through dollar depreciation. (Wolf 2003)

In a letter to the *Financial Times* of October 10, 2003, John Incledon echoes this view and reckons that a 10 percent devaluation of the U.S. dollar—which is roughly what occurred in 2003—reduces the real value of the total external obligations of the United States by $500–700 billion.[9] "The Bush administration," he goes on to claim, "looks at this decline as the contribution to the defense of the free world from terrorism; as a fair contribution to be made by the coalition of the unwilling." Leaving aside the fact that the main victim of the "conspiracy" would be Japan (a member of the "coalition of the willing"), U.S. exploitation of its seigniorage privileges in order to consume both guns and butter far beyond its means can postpone but not avoid indefinitely a fundamental structural adjustment of the United States to the new realities of the global economy. As Wolf himself underscores, the question is not whether but when and how the adjustment will occur.

Adjustment will involve some combination of further depreciation of the U.S. dollar, appreciation of the currencies of the countries with the largest current account surpluses, and a rerouting of these surpluses from the financing of U.S. deficits to the creation of demand elsewhere, especially in East Asia. As Wolf (2003) suggests, this eventual adjustment may be "brutal," through a dollar rout, or "smooth." The greater the U.S. exploitation of seigniorage privileges, we may add, the greater are the chances that the adjustment will be brutal and that the United States will lose those privileges earlier than might otherwise be the case. But whether brutal or smooth, the adjustment will further decrease U.S. command over world economic resources and undermine both the centrality of the U.S. market in the global economy and the role of the U.S. dollar as international means of payment and reserve currency.

In short, the freedom from financial constraints that the United States derives from seigniorage privileges has limits; and the more that freedom is abused, the greater the chances that those privileges will be lost. The Bush administration has shown some awareness of the risks involved in relying too heavily on a depreciating dollar to buttress U.S. competitiveness at home and abroad and to default on U.S. liabilities to foreigners. Thus, at the Doha meeting in June 2003, U.S. Treasury Secretary John Snow persuaded the finance ministers of the other G-7 countries to sign a joint statement arguing that the determination of exchange rates should be left to the market. The statement was taken as a signal that Washington was officially abandoning its strong dollar policy, and the dollar promptly dipped against all major currencies. But whenever the dive threatens to become a rout, "Mr. Snow repeats the familiar mantra about the importance of a strong currency. Nobody in the markets quite knows what [that] means any-more, but just in case it could signal a burst of intervention, they take cover and stop selling greenbacks" (Denny 2003).

Confusion in the markets is fully justified in light of the contradiction between rhetorical adherence to the importance of a strong currency and the practice of extreme monetary and fiscal laxity (see, among others, Ignatius 2003). Dictated partly by the escalating costs of the war on terrorism, and partly by the attempt to revive the U.S. economy after the bursting of the new economy bubble, this extreme laxity is reminiscent of the U.S. experience of the 1970s, when serious abuses of U.S. seigniorage privileges eventually re-sulted in a devastating run on the U.S. currency. For a brief moment in January 1980, the rise of the price of gold to an all-time high of $875 an ounce seemed to signal an imminent end of the de facto dollar standard inaugurated in 1971, when the United States finally abandoned its commitment to buy gold at the fixed price of $35 an ounce. As it turned out, the dollar quickly recovered from the rout and the de facto dollar standard has remained in place ever since. In light of this experience, the Bush administration's willingness to push to its limits the abuse of U.S. seigniorage privileges may be due to the belief that, if worse comes to worst, the United States can pull back from the brink and enjoy another 20 years of uncontested seigniorage privileges. If so, a rude awakening may be in store for either the Bush or a successor administration.

As argued elsewhere, in the 1980s the U.S. dollar recouped its position as the world's money by virtue of a sudden and radical reversal of U.S. monetary policies from extreme laxity to extreme tightness, accompanied by stepping up U.S. competition for capital worldwide through record-high interest rates, tax breaks, and increasing freedom of action for capitalist producers and specula-tors (Arrighi 2003, 42–43, 63–67). In the event of a new dollar rout compa-rable to that of the late 1970s, however, it would be far more difficult, if at all possible, for the United States to regain the upper hand in the world monetary system. U.S. creditors may pause—as they certainly do—at the idea of pulling the rug from under the feet of such a big debtor nation. *Pace* Balzac, it would nonetheless make no sense at all for them to redouble their lending to a debtor that has partially defaulted on its debt through massive currency depreciation. Moreover, having already granted extraordinary incentives to capital, the United States has little left to offer in case of a new dollar rout. Under these circumstances of unprecedented indebtedness and exhaustion of incentives, a hike in interest rates like the one engineered under Reagan would provoke a far more severe domestic contraction, without any guarantee that the contraction would be fol-lowed by a robust recovery. It would thereby aggravate rather than alleviate the relative downsizing of the U.S. economy that would ensue from the dollar rout.

To this we should add that at the time of the dollar rout of the late 1970s there were few, if any, viable alternatives to the U.S. dollar as international currency. The euro was still a project rather than a reality. The rapidly appreci-ating German mark and Japanese yen had neither the global economic weight nor the national institutional support needed to become significant means of international payment and reserve currencies. Having nowhere else to go, capital taking flight from the dollar thus went primarily into gold. But no major capitalist power had any interest in a remonetization of gold at a time of world economic stagnation, especially in view of the leverage that such a remonetization would have put in the hands of the Soviet Union. Under these circumstances, U.S. attempts to preserve the dollar standard could count on the active cooperation of all the governments that mattered in world monetary regulation. Also in this respect the situation today is quite different. The governments that matter are still willing to cooperate with the U.S. government in preserving the U.S. dollar standard. But should U.S. abuses of seigniorage privileges once again result in a dollar rout, European and East Asian governments are in a far better position than they were 25 years ago to create viable alternatives to that standard.

In light of these considerations, it is plausible to suppose that the Bush administration is willing to take quite a few risks in exploiting U.S. seigniorage privileges as a partial and temporary solution to the economic problems involved in recasting the world by military force to suit U.S. interests and values. But for the Project for the New American Century and the National Security Strategy of 2002 to make any economic sense at all, their promoters must assume that the open-ended war on terror can itself generate the financial resources needed to reestablish U.S. world hegemony on new foundations. From this standpoint, the conquest and remaking of Iraq promised to be an ideal starting point. Politically and militarily, Afghanistan had to come first. But even before invading Afghanistan, the Bush administration had put coercive regime change in Iraq at the top of its priority list. As a tactical move in the war on terror, a war on Iraq made no sense at all. But as a tactical move in a longer term strategy of using military might to recoup economic might, it had some plausibility. As David Harvey has argued, if the United States could install a friendly regime in Iraq, move on to do the same in Iran, consolidate its strategic presence in Central Asia, and so dominate Caspian Basin oil reserves— "then it might, through control of the global oil spigot, hope to keep effective control over the global economy for the next fifty years." Since all the economic competitors of the United States, both in Europe and in East Asia, are heavily dependent on West Asian oil, "What better way for the United States to ward off that competition and secure its own hegemonic position than to control the price, conditions, and distribution of the key economic resource upon which those competitors rely? And what better way to do that than to use the one line of force where the U.S. still remains all-powerful—military might?" (Harvey 2003, 24–25).

There can be little doubt that in deciding to wage war on Iraq virtually alone and in defiance of the express will of the UN Security Council, the Bush administration was thinking along these lines. In doing so, however, it may have disregarded other, less rhetorical questions that are nonetheless crucial in determining the viability of the emerging U.S. strategy. These questions are best formulated in terms of Charles Tilly's conceptualization of state activities as complementary facets of the organization and monopolization of violence. The conceptualization refers to the organization and monopolization of violence within the territorial domains of nation states. But it can be easily recast to encompass the contemporary U.S. case of a state that is aiming at organizing and monopolizing violence at the global level.

Whatever else they might do, argues Tilly, governments "stand out from other organizations by their tendency to monopolize the concentrated means of violence." This tendency materializes through four different kinds of activity: protection, state-making, war-making, and extraction. Protection is the most distinctive "product" of governmental activities, and as we shall see, it has a double meaning that has some bearing on the legitimacy of governments. But whether legitimate or not, the credibility of, and difficulty to resist, a particular government's claim to provide protection increase with that government's success in monopolizing concentrated means of violence within its territorial domains. This involves the elimination or neutralization of rivals both inside those domains (state-making) and outside (war-making). Since protection, state-making, and war-making all require financial and material resources, extraction consists of the activities through which governments procure those resources. If carried out effectively, each of these four activities "generally reinforces the others" (Tilly 1985, 171, 181).

Tilly's conceptualization emphasizes the synergy among state-making, war-making, and extraction activities in ensuring governmental success in monopolizing concentrated means of violence at the national level. Current U.S. attempts to monopolize concentrated means of violence at the world level blur the distinction between state-making and war-making, as witnessed by the anomalous nature of the war on terror (which is a war *sui generis* combining war-making and state-making) and by the war on Iraq (which was ostensibly undertaken as a first step in the remaking of the entire West Asian region to suit the interests and values of the United States). This blurring creates two major problems for the synergy envisaged by Tilly at the national level.

For one thing, U.S. capabilities in state-making and war-making as distinct activities at the national level may be seriously impaired when deployed as indistinct activities at the world level. A good illustration of this possibility is the contrast between the ease with which the United States has formally won the wars on the Taliban and Hussein regimes, and the difficulties it is encountering in attaining the substantive objectives for which the wars were fought. This problem is compounded by a second: the difficulty of carrying out extraction activities minimally commensurate to the scale and scope of the state- and-war-making activities involved in monopolizing concentrated means of violence on a world scale. As we have seen, the inadequacy of the U.S. extractive apparatus is the single most important reason why the U.S. position in the international credit system has deteriorated far more rapidly than that of Britain at a comparable stage of hegemonic decline. Moreover, anticipation that the stepped-up deployment of U.S. military power would solve this problem by generating a *net* surplus of resources has not materialized. Indeed, judging from the first two main engagements of the war on terror—the wars on Afghanistan and Iraq—the chances are that it will generate a huge net *deficit*, as witnessed, among other things, by the $87.5 billion that the Bush administration had to request in October 2003 over and above the $65 billion originally authorized by Congress.

In short, no matter how unparalleled and unprecedented U.S. military power is, it may not be up to the task of establishing U.S. control over global oil supplies, as opposed to scoring victories that take control out of some hands without putting it in U.S. hands. And even if it is up to that task, it may be able to do so only by further increasing U.S. dependence on the financial support of the very competitors against whom control over global oil supplies is directed. Would not that heightened dependence seriously limit U.S. capacity to close the oil spigot on these competitors-financiers lest they close the money spigot on the United States?

## IV. The Protection That Few Would Buy

This brings us to the issue of the legitimacy of U.S. efforts to recast the world by military force to suit U.S. interests. Tilly follows Arthur Stinchcombe in claiming that the legitimacy of power-holders depends far less on the assent of those on whom power is exercised than on the assent of other power-holders (Stinchcombe 1968, 150). To this Tilly adds that other authorities "are much more likely to confirm the decisions of a challenged authority that controls substantial force; not only fear of retaliation, but also desire to maintain a stable environment recommend that general rule" (Tilly 1985, 171). This general rule applies with even greater force in a social system divided into multiple political jurisdictions, each controlled by a formally sovereign governmental authority. In such a system the importance of the assent of the governed for the legitimacy of governmental actions is limited and mediated by interstate relations. These relations, in turn, are thoroughly shaped by fears of retaliation and of systemic instability—what we earlier called systemic chaos.

This double fear plays a major role in shaping relations between the United States and its competitors-financiers. The Balzac effect noted earlier is one particular source of the fear of retaliation and systemic chaos that restrains the competitors-financiers of the United States from closing the money spigot that enables the United States to go on consuming well beyond its means. But the United States wields powers of retaliation and systemic destabilization that are much more threatening than the power to default on its colossal debt. These powers, as well as their limits, have to do with the issue of protection.

As Tilly notes, "the word 'protection' sounds two contrasting tones." With one tone, it evokes the comforting image of a powerful friend or organization that provides shelter against danger. With the other, it evokes the ominous image of a racket in which a bully forces merchants to pay tribute in order to avoid damage that the bully himself tacitly or openly threatens to deliver.

> Which image the word "protection" brings to mind depends mainly on our assessment of the reality and externality of the threat. Someone who produces both the danger and, at a price, the shield against it is a racketeer. Someone who provides a needed shield but has little control over the danger's appearance qualifies as a legitimate protector, especially if his price is no higher than his competitors.' Someone who supplies reliable, low-priced shielding from local racketeers and from outside marauders makes the best offer of all. (Tilly 1985, 170–171)

By this standard, Tilly goes on to argue, the provision of protection by governments often qualifies as racketeering.

> To the extent that the threats against which a given government protects its citizens are imaginary or are consequences of its activities, the government has organized a protection racket. Since governments themselves commonly simulate, or even fabricate, threats of external war and the repressive and extractive activities of governments often constitute the largest current threats to the livelihoods of their own citizens, many governments operate in essentially the same way as racketeers. There is, of course, a difference: Racketeers, by the conventional definition, operate without the sanctity of governments. (Tilly 1985, 171)

Also in this respect, Tilly's considerations concerning governmental activities at the national level apply with even greater force at the level of a global system in which the "sanctity of governments" is a much fuzzier reality. Interestingly, U.S. secretary of state Colin Powell himself evoked the ominous image of protection when he said that the United States ought "to be the bully on the block." The rest of the world would happily accept this role—he went on to assert, calling up the comforting image of protection—because the United States "can be trusted not to abuse that power" (quoted in Harvey 2003, 80).

Trust is a highly elusive entity. We do not know on what grounds Powell based his belief that the rest of the world trusted the United States not to abuse its power as "the bully on the block." But if the reports from Bangkok cited earlier are at all accurate, less than a year after Powell professed this belief, even in the friendly environment of APEC the comforting image of U.S. protection against a real or imaginary Chinese threat had given way to the ominous image of a United States strong-arming everyone onto its own foreign policy agenda. Whatever the extent and immediate reasons of the change, the massive swing of governmental dispositions toward U.S. policies from assent to resistance since the promulgation of the National Security Strategy of September 2002 has little to do with whether or not other governments trust the United States not to abuse its power. Rather, it has to do with two related but distinct perceptions. One is the generalized perception that the deployment of U.S. military might along the lines envisaged by the National Security Strategy is likely to produce, directly or indirectly, far greater dangers for the rest of the world than the terrorist threat against which it is ostensibly directed. In Tilly's terms, this is the perception that the U.S. government is behaving like a global racketeer who is producing both the danger and, at a price, the shield against it. Equally important is the other, less general, but quite widespread perception that the costs and risks of supporting U.S. policies are greater than the costs and risks of not supporting it. In Tilly's terms, this is the perception that U.S. shielding from local racketeers worldwide is neither reliable nor low-priced.

The vicissitudes of the war on terror have validated these perceptions much faster than any government might have feared or hoped. As events are showing daily, the most technologically sophisticated and destructive war machine in history is not fit to provide minimal protection "on the block." Local bullies wielding comparatively primitive means of violence, but a better sociological understanding of the block, seem capable of holding in check the global bully's pretensions to be in a position to offer superior protection on their turf. Indeed, they seem capable of forcing him to concentrate his energies on protecting himself, starkly revealing his incapacity of protecting anybody else. The global bully can, of course, subcontract protection to local bullies. But this would reduce the resources that the global bully can extract locally or undermine the credibility of his claims to be able to provide protection anywhere he chooses to.

Thus, two years after the United States ousted the Taliban regime, the executive director of the UN Office on Drugs and Crime writes that there is "a palpable risk that Afghanistan will again turn into a failed state, this time in the hands of drug cartels and narco-terrorists." In 2001, after the Taliban had banned opium production, the annual crop had dropped to 185 metric tons. But in 2003, a crop that UN estimates put at 3,600 tons will be the second largest in Afghan history and will account for 75 percent of the poppies grown for narcotics worldwide. "The crop is worth twice the Afghan government's annual budget," notes Nicholas Kristof, "and much of the profit will support warlords and the Taliban." Not surprisingly, a representative of a U.S. aid group that has operated in Afghanistan for 15 years feels that "we've never had the insecurity that we have now" (Kristof 2003).

In Iraq—where the need to extract resources to sustain the strategy to stave off economic decline through the use of military might makes the effective provision of protection far more imperative than in Afghanistan—the situation is evolving in the same direction or worse. As a UK official told *The Observer*, the U.S.-led coalition no longer faces a "monolithic organization with a clear command, [which] would be far easier . . . to deal with." Instead, it faces "lots of different groups with different agendas." According to a former colonel in the Iraqi security services, some of the people involved "are criminals, who under other circumstances few people would have anything to do with." But most are involved "for religious and nationalist reasons." This facilitates recruitment and the mobilization of support not just locally but also among foreign Muslims (Beaumont and Graham 2003).

Although Iraq is not Vietnam, and 2003 is not 1968, the ever more frequent use of images like "quagmire," "attrition," "credibility gap," "Iraqification," and so on makes "parts of the current debate seem to be almost as much about Vietnam as about Iraq" (Whitney 2003). As Senator John McCain has pointed out, contrary to what many thought, victory in the first Gulf war "did not end the hold of the Vietnam syndrome over [the American] national consciousness." In his view, the reason is that Saddam Hussein was not removed from power (quoted in Whitney 2003). Yet ironically, the U.S. ousting of Hussein from power is now making the Vietnam syndrome more visible than it had been in the preceding 20 years. This is probably the reason why in November 2003 the Bush administration suddenly revised its original plan to keep control of post-Hussein Iraq firmly in U.S. hands. Commenting on this change, an editorial of the *New York Times* stated the "grim truth" that there are no attractive options for the United States in Iraq. "The Bush Administration would clearly love to be able to remove American troops from the line of fire . . . Yet a rushed American withdrawal without an orderly handoff to the United Nations would leave Iraq open to just the kind of mixture of misgovernment and terrorism that the White House waged this war to prevent" (*New York Times* 2003).

The "orderly handoff to the United Nations" advocated by the *New York Times* is not that easy to achieve. From the standpoint of the Bush administration, it would involve a more or less open recognition of the political failure of the Project for the New American Century, of the National Security Strategy of 2002, and of the assumption underlying both that the United States could effectively use its military might to stave off economic decline. It would also involve a fundamental adjustment to a less exalted position in world politics, something that at the moment seems to be entirely beyond the horizon not just of the ideologues but also of the pragmatists within the administration.

This problem is compounded by the widespread reluctance of other governments to put up the resources needed to bail the United States out of the Iraqi quagmire. To be sure, many among the foreign critics of the U.S. war on Iraq—including the reviled French—do not find much to rejoice in the U.S. predicament. As a senior adviser at the French Institute for International Relations put it, the current situation "has given a new meaning to the formula 'When America sneezes, the entire world catches a cold.'"

> When the U.S. finds itself bogged down abroad it poses a big challenge to the rest of the world. If America simply pulled out now, other countries would find themselves in the strange position of having to put pressure on the Americans to stay, having previously begged them not to risk invasion without a United Nations resolution. In the aftermath of a rapid withdrawal, the focus of international concern would quickly switch from the perils of U.S. global domination, to the dangers of a world deprived of U.S. international engagement. The problem is that if the present strategy in Iraq does not really work, there is no convincing alternative. It is unlikely that sending more U.S. troops or handing over power to the Iraqis would make a serious difference. America is in a mess, but so are we. (Moisi 2003)

Leaving aside for now the question of whether there really is no convincing alternative to the U.S. occupation of Iraq, reasoning along the above lines probably motivated the unanimous UN Security Council resolution of October 16, 2003, that provided the U.S.-led occupation with some juridical legitimacy and called on governments to lend a helping hand. Juridical legitimacy as such, however, was not what the United States was after. Rather, juridical legitimacy mattered primarily if not exclusively as a means of extracting resources from other governments to cover the escalating human and financial costs of the Iraqi occupation. Indeed, the main purpose of rushing the resolution through the UN Security Council was to ensure the success of the "donors conference" the United States had convened in Madrid for the following week. It is precisely the poor results of this conference that provided a good measure of U.S. inability to extract protection payments commensurate to costs even from its best customers.

Despite Colin Powell's attempt to put up a brave front by declaring the conference a success, its most conspicuous outcome was how little money it raised relative to expectations, and especially in comparison with what the United States raised for the 1991 Gulf War. Actual donations (that is, grants) were less than one-eighth of the $36 billion target and considerably less than one-fourth of the U.S. $20 billion pledge. These poor results are all the more striking in view of the fact that, in order to encourage generosity, three days before the conference the United States had reluctantly agreed to set up a fund handled independently from the United States by the World Bank and the United Nations. "We had to act because the international community was stonewalling us on aid," declared a U.S. official who went on to quote Paul Bremer, U.S. chief administrator in Iraq, as saying "I need the money so bad we have to move off our principled opposition to the international community being in charge" (Docena 2003; Weisman 2003).

The contrast with the financing of the 1991 Gulf War is even more revealing than the contrast with expectations. One of the most striking aspects of the 1991 Gulf War is how the United States managed to persuade other countries— most notably, Japan, Germany, and Saudi Arabia—to pay entirely for the war (see, among others, Hobsbawm 1994, 242). One of the most striking features of the war on Iraq, in contrast, is how other countries managed to leave the United States holding the bag. Germany and Saudi Arabia gave virtually nothing—half of the $100 million pledged by Germany in Madrid was its share of the modest European Union contribution. But even Japan's $1.5 billion pledge— by far the largest at the Madrid conference—pales in comparison with Japan's payments for the 1991 Gulf War, which were at least four times as large in nominal (that is, current dollars) terms and many more times as large in real terms. Although the dangers against which the United States offers protection are at least as great as 12 years ago, the price that even the best clients are willing to pay for that protection has contracted sharply.

In part, this sharp contraction is due to the perception that U.S. protection has become counterproductive, either because the United States squeezes some of its clients dry and then leaves them exposed to even greater dangers than the ones from which they have been protected—as in the case of Saudi Arabia—or because U.S. actions are projected to create greater long-term dangers than the present dangers against which it offers protection—as has probably been the case with Germany. In part, however, the sharp contraction in the price that even the best clients are willing to pay for U.S. protection is due to a perception that the need to pay tribute to the United States is less compelling than it was 12 years ago. This perception is far more widespread than the ritualistic respect still paid to U.S. power lets on. But it is probably most important in the case of Japan and other U.S. clients in the East Asian region.

For up to very recently many states in the region still perceived U.S. protection as essential for countering the real or imagined threat that China posed to their security. Today, in contrast, the PRC is no longer perceived as a serious threat, and even if such a threat were to re-emerge, U.S. protection is perceived as unreliable. Moreover, the capacity of the United States to extract protection payments from its East Asian clients has been curtailed by the combination of growing U.S. dependence on East Asian money to finance its huge current account deficit and the reduced dependence of East Asian countries on the U.S. market. Not only is China perceived to be less of a threat to the security of its neighbors; equally important, it is increasingly perceived as an alternative to excessive dependence on the U.S. market (Perlez 2003b).

## V. Tipping the Scales of Global Turbulence

If we now return to the issues raised in *The Long Twentieth Century* and in *Chaos and Governance*, three main conclusions emerge from the analysis of recent tendencies. First, as both books envisaged, the U.S. *belle époque* seems to have come to an end, and U.S. world hegemony has probably experienced its terminal crisis. The United States does remain by far the most powerful state but its relationship to the rest of the world is best described as one of domination without hegemony.

Second, as *Chaos and Governance* envisaged, the terminal crisis of U.S. hegemony—assuming that is what we are actually witnessing—has been brought about not by the emergence of aggressive new powers but by U.S. resistance to adjustment and accommodation. U.S. attempts to depict Hussein's Iraq as an aggressive new power never had much credibility, whereas the national security strategy adopted by the Bush administration in September 2002 is a far more extreme form of U.S. resistance to adjustment and accommodation than anything envisaged in *The Long Twentieth Century* or in *Chaos and Governance*. To a far greater extent than in previous hegemonic transitions, the terminal crisis of U.S. hegemony has been a case of great power (attempted) "suicide."

Third, assessments like Moisi's that "America is in a mess, but so are we," can be taken as symptomatic of an emergent situation of systemic chaos. It is nonetheless not at all clear whether this emergent situation is a permanent state—as in one of the three possible scenarios envisaged in *The Long Twentieth Century*—or a transitional state—as in the past hegemonic transitions analyzed in *Chaos and Governance*—or yet a far less severe and protracted state than experienced in past hegemonic transitions. Particularly significant in countering the tendency toward systemic chaos is the consolidation of the East Asian economic renaissance through the emergence of China as its most dynamic center—a tendency that has been strengthened rather than weakened by U.S. resistance to adjustment and accommodation.

These conclusions do not fundamentally alter the three post–U.S. hegemony scenarios envisaged at the end of *The Long Twentieth Century*. All three scenarios remain within the realm of historical possibilities. True, the world-empire project is at the moment in the midst of a serious crisis. The project that is in crisis, however, is not the one envisaged in that book. The world-empire envisaged there as a possible post–U.S. hegemony scenario was a *collective* western construction. The idea that the United States would embark on such a construction virtually alone, in opposition to the political and economic core of the European Union, was deemed too unrealistic to be worth considering. Although not surprising, the crisis of this unrealistic course of action does not rule out the possibility that a reconstituted western alliance will engage in the more realistic multilateral imperial project envisaged in *The Long Twentieth Century*. Indeed, the very failure of the U.S. unilateral project may create more favorable conditions for such an engagement both in the United States and in western Europe.

Although a western-dominated universal empire remains a historical possibility, an East Asia–centered world-market society appears today a far more likely outcome of ongoing transformations of the global political economy than it did 10 years ago. The most important changes are the stunning economic expansion of China through the East Asian crisis of 1997–1998, the bursting of the new economy bubble, and the crisis of the unilateral U.S. imperial project. As we cautioned in *Chaos and Governance,* such a rapid economic expansion is bound to be punctuated by one or more of those crises that are typical of emerging economic centers. Whether such a crisis (or crises) will undermine or eventually consolidate the regional economic expansion remains an open question. Moreover, there are still few signs that East Asian elites, the Chinese included, are up to the task of opening a path of regional and global development that would be ecologically less destructive and sociologically more sustainable than the U.S.-sponsored path that is now at a dead end.

These reservations notwithstanding, China already appears to be a potential substitute for the United States as the central market of the regional East Asian economy and beyond. As previously noted, China is rapidly catching up with the United States as the biggest trading partner of the East Asian region. But its importance relative to the United States is growing rapidly even outside the East Asian region. The European Union, for example, forecasts that by 2010 China will probably overtake the United States as its biggest trade partner. A former Merrill Lynch chief economist sees China already playing the role of "global locomotive" along with the United States. Similarly, Nicholas Lardy sees no one else coming close to the Chinese as "global customers." "They've been a big driver of global trade expansion and a significant force in promoting the recovery" (Pine 2003).

Equally important, China has begun to overshadow the United States in the promotion of multilateral trade liberalization. Regionally, it has sought integration with the Asia-Pacific Economic Cooperation (ASEAN) by agreeing to a Treaty of Amity and Cooperation, simultaneously seeking economic ties with Japan, South Korea, and India. Globally, it joined Brazil and India in leading the global South's attack at the 2003 WTO meeting in Cancun against the northern practice of imposing market opening on the South, although remaining fiercely protectionist in lines of production where the South has the greatest comparative advantage, first and foremost agriculture. China's stance contrasts sharply with the U.S. abandonment of multilateral trade negotiations in favor of bilateral free trade agreements aimed at breaking up the southern alliance that emerged at Cancun, or at gaining support for the Bush administration's war on terror (Kwa 2003; Smith and Cooper 2003).

An East Asia–centered world-market society thus appears today a far more likely post–U.S. hegemony scenario than it did 10 or even 5 years ago. This greater likelihood, however, does not rule out either one of the other two scenarios envisaged in *The Long Twentieth Century.* On the contrary, the very success of East Asia under Chinese leadership to recenter upon itself the global political economy, and to provide the global South with a more equitable alternative to continuing western domination, may well become the catalyst of renewed western cohesion in the pursuit of a western-dominated universal empire. And this reaction, in turn, may succeed or may end up plunging the world into a period of protracted and severe systemic chaos with or without a light at the end of the tunnel.

In this respect, the contention of *Chaos and Governance* that social forces are likely to play a far more decisive role than ever before in shaping both the unfolding hegemonic transition and its ultimate (still unknown) destination, remains valid. As Beverly Silver (2004) has pointed out, the massive antiwar protests of February 2003—"the biggest demonstrations in world history," according to some observers—appear "as an almost intuitive recognition by people around the world (including many in the United States) that what amounts to a new U.S. imperial project risks precipitating major worldwide chaos." This unprecedented transnational demonstration of popular antiwar sentiment failed in its immediate objective of stopping the war on Iraq. Yet, as Gary Younge notes, it had a lasting impact on how the world's elites and governments themselves came to perceive the war and its aftermath. For one thing,

> the anti-war movement had a decisive impact on exposing the bankrupt rationale of attacking Iraq. . . . Neither Bush nor Blair would have bothered trying to persuade the UN to give its blessing were it not for the pressure they were under.

The fact that they failed showed the war for what it was—a criminal act of military violence expressly executed against the global will. The implications of this exposure are anything but abstract. It explains the reluctance of other nations to relieve America of the burden of clearing up its mistakes, and has left Blair and Bush isolated on the world stage. It contributed significantly to the critical climate that produced the Hutton inquiry and the row over Bush's misleading comments in his state of the union speech. The anti-war movement got the German chancellor, Gerhard Schröder, re-elected, and has pushed the centre of gravity in the Democratic primaries in [an anti-war] direction. . . . True, none of this has saved Iraqi lives. But with ratings for Bush and Blair plummeting, it may keep Iranians, North Koreans, or whoever else they are considering bombing out of harm's way. (Younge 2003)

Moreover, the antiwar movement's perception about the war on terror has proved correct. It claimed that "the bombing would not stamp out terrorism—the atrocities in Bali, Jakarta, and Mombasa show it hasn't—but fuel resentment that would create more terrorists; and Iraq is a far greater threat to global security than six months ago." It claimed that "the war was a bad idea, even if Saddam did have weapons of mass destruction—given enough time the inspectors would have found them. News that he didn't have them blows away the final fig leaf and leaves the emperors naked." Not one national poll, including in the United States, supported a U.S.-led war without UN support. That it happened "exposed the global crisis in democratic legitimacy" (Younge 2003). In short, *pace* Stinchcombe, even at the level of the global system, the legitimacy of power-holders depends in critical ways not just on the assent of other power-holders, but also on the assent of those on whom power is exercised. True, the impact of the assent or dissent of the governed is mediated and filtered by the perceptions and actions of power-holders. But at least in the case under examination, the mediation and the filtering have not prevented the dissent of the governed from making it much harder for the United States to embark on new wars as means of staving off economic decline. Indeed, to return to the question that we left open at the end of *Chaos and Governance*, the mass antiwar protests of 2003 augur well for the possibility that social movements will preemptively work toward containing systemic chaos, rather than largely following and being shaped by the escalation of violence as was the case in past hegemonic transitions.

## Notes

1. For the most recent criticism along the same lines, see Detti (2003, 551–552).
2. Most recently Benigno (2003, 557) and Maione (2003, 564–565). See also Hardt (1996).
3. Suffice it to mention that China's GNP per capita as a percentage of the world average, which had increased by 28 percent in the 1970s and by 84 percent in the 1980s,

rose by 95 percent in the 1990s (calculated from World Bank 1984 and 2002). As we shall see, the Chinese ascent has in fact been even more significant than these figures imply. Persistent current account surpluses in the balance of payments of the "China Circle" (Mainland China, Singapore, Hong Kong, and Taiwan) on the one side, and large and growing U.S. current account deficits on the other, have turned the China Circle, and the PRC in particular, into the second main financier after Japan of the escalating U.S. deficit.

4. Indeed, to the extent that recent research on world income inequality has detected a statistical trend toward declining intercountry inequality in the 1990s, this is due *entirely* to the rapid economic growth of China (Arrighi, Silver, and Brewer 2003).

5. This notion is based on the Gramscian understanding of hegemony as the additional power that accrues to a dominant group by virtue of its capacity to lead society in a direction that serves the dominant group's interests but is perceived by subordinate groups as serving also a more general interest (Gramsci 1971, 181–182). When that *additional power* wanes—as it seems to have done in the case of the United States in the aftermath of the Iraqi war—hegemony turns into sheer domination.

6. The latest projection at the time of writing puts the U.S. current account deficit for 2003 at $570 billion (Major and Swann 2003, 1).

7. This issue is explored further in the next section of the chapter.

8. If we take Asia and Africa together, there were as many as 72 separate British military campaigns between 1837 and 1900 (Bond 1967, 309–311). By a different count, between 1803 and 1901 Britain fought 50 major colonial wars (Giddens 1987, 223).

9. If Ferguson's estimate that foreigners now have claims on the United States amounting to $8 trillion is right, then this figure should be raised to $800 billion. Estimates of U.S. obligations to foreigners vary widely depending on the sources, but the order of magnitude is not in dispute.

# References

Arrighi, Giovanni. 1994. *The Long Twentieth Century: Money, Power, and the Origins of Our Times.* London: Verso.

———. 2003. "The Social and Political Economy of Global Turbulence." *New Left Review* 2/20 (March–April): 5–71.

Arrighi, Giovanni, Takeshi Hamashita, and Mark Selden, eds. 2003. *The Resurgence of East Asia: 500, 150, and 50 Year Perspectives.* New York: Routledge.

Arrighi, Giovanni, and Beverly J. Silver. 1999. *Chaos and Governance in the Modern World System.* Minneapolis: University of Minnesota Press.

Arrighi, Giovanni, Beverly J. Silver, and Benjamin Brewer. 2003. "Industrial Convergence and the Persistence of the North-South Divide." *Studies in Comparative International Development* 38(1): 3–31.

Beaumont, Peter, and Patrick Graham. 2003. "Rebel War Spirals Out of Control as U.S. Intelligence Loses the Plot." *Observer*, November 2.

Benigno, Francesco. 2003. "Braudel in America ovvero le radici lunghe del presente." *Contemporanea* 6(3): 554–558.

Bond, Brian, ed. 1967. *Victorian Military Campaigns.* London: Hutchinson.

Calleo, David. 1987. *Beyond American Hegemony: The Future of the Western Alliance.* New York: Basic Books.

de Cecco, Marcello. 1984. *The International Gold Standard: Money and Empire.* 2nd ed. New York: St. Martin's Press.

Denny, Charlotte. 2003. "Trap a Dragon, Mr. Bush, and Lose an Election." *Guardian*, November 3.

Detti, Tommaso. 2003. "L'avventura di ripensare il passato." *Contemporanea* 6(3): 549–553.

Docena, Herbert. 2003. "Madrid's Donor's Conference: The Pending Bonanza." *Focus on Trade* 94 (November). Available at N.Bullard@focusweb.org.

Ferguson, Niall. 2003. "The True Cost of Hegemony." *New York Times*, April 20.

Fingleton, Eamonn. 2001. "Quibble All You Like, Japan Still Looks Like a Strong Winner." *International Herald Tribune*, January 2, p. 6.

Giddens, Anthony. 1987. *The Nation-State and Violence*. Berkeley: University of California Press.

Gramsci, Antonio. 1971. *Selections from the Prison Notebooks*. New York: International Publishers.

Guha, Ranajit. 1992. "Dominance without Hegemony and Its Historiography." In R. Gupta, ed., *Subaltern Studies IV.* New York: Oxford University Press, pp. 210–305.

Harding, James, and Peter Spiegel. 2003. "Beijing Looms Large in the White House's Defence Strategy." *Financial Times* (London), October 17, p. 19.

Hardt, Michael, and Antonio Negri. 2000. *Empire*. Cambridge, MA: Harvard University Press.

Harvey, David. 2003. *The New Imperialism*. Oxford, UK: Oxford University Press.

Hobsbawm, Eric J. 1994. *The Age of Extremes: A History of the World, 1914–1991*. New York: Vintage.

Ignatius, David. 2003. "Fiddling while the Dollar Drops." *Washington Post*, December 5.

Kristof, Nicholas D. 2003. "A Scary Afghan Road." *New York Times*, November 15.

Kwa, Aileen. 2003. "The Post-Cancun Backlash and Seven Strategies to Keep the WTO Off the Tracks." *Focus on Trade* 95 (November). Available at N.Bullard@focusweb.com.

Lobe, Jim. 2003. "Foreign Policy Experts Target U.S. 'Empire-Building.'" Available at www.OneWorld.net, accessed October 17.

Maione, Giuseppe. 2003. "Fragilita' dei modelli e profezie smentite." *Contemporanea* 6(3): 562–567.

Major, Tony, and Christopher Swann. 2003. "Euro Highs Spark Fears for Exports." *Financial Times*, October 8, p. 1.

Moisi, Dominique. 2003. "The World Is Trapped in the Iraqi Quagmire." *Financial Times*, November 14, p. 21.

New York Times. 2003. "America's Iraq Policy in Crisis." *International Herald Tribune*, November 14.

Pan, Philip P. 2003. "China's Improving Image Challenges U.S. in Asia." *Washington Post*, November 15.

Perlez, Jane. 2003a. "Asian Leaders Find China a More Cordial Neighbor." *New York Times*, October 18, p. A1.

———. 2003b. "With U.S. Busy, China Is Romping with Neighbors." *New York Times*, December 3.

Pine, Art. 2003. "The World's New Import Power." *International Herald Tribune*, November 3.

Raspberry, William. 2003. "The Iraqi Monkey Trap." *Washington Post*, October 20.

Silver, Beverly J. 2003. *Forces of Labor: Workers' Movements and Globalization since 1870*. New York: Cambridge University Press.

———. 2004. "Labor, War and World Politics: Contemporary Dynamics in World-Historical Perspective." In B. Unfried, M. Van der Linden, and C. Schindler, eds., *Labour and New Social Movements in a Globalizing World System*. Leipzig: Akademische Verlagsanstalt (in press).

Smith, Russell L., and Caroline G. Cooper. 2003. "The U.S. and Economic Stability in Asia." *Asia Times Online,* December 6.
Sperling, Gene. 2003. "U.S. and China Are on a Collision Course." *International Herald Tribune,* November 4.
Stinchcombe, Arthur L. 1968. *Constructing Social Theories.* New York: Harcourt, Brace and World.
Tilly, Charles. 1985. "War-Making and State-Making as Organized Crime." In P. B. Evans, D. Rueschemeyer, and T. Skocpol, eds., *Bringing the State Back In.* Cambridge, UK: Cambridge University Press.
Tomlinson, B. R. 1975. "India and the British Empire, 1880–1935." *Indian Economic and Social History Review* 12(4): 337–380.
Weisman, Steven R. 2003. "U.S. Set to Cede Part of Control over Aid to Iraq." *New York Times,* October 20.
Whitney, Craig R. 2003. "Watching Iraq, and Seeing Vietnam." *New York Times,* November 9.
Wolf, Martin. 2003. "A Very Dangerous Game." *Financial Times,* September 30.
World Bank. 1984. *World Tables.* Vols. 1 and 2. Washington DC: World Bank.
——— 2002. *World Development Indicators.* CD-ROM. Washington, DC: World Bank.
Younge, Gary. 2003. "For Better—Or Worse." *Guardian,* October 6.

# 4

# THE U.S. TRAJECTORY: QUANTITATIVE AND HISTORICAL REFLECTIONS

*Thomas Reifer, Christopher Chase-Dunn, and Andrew Jorgenson*

## Theoretical Perspectives on Rise and Fall

There has been vociferous debate over terminology that reflects underlying theoretical and disciplinary differences among those who have sought to compare the power processes of recent centuries. As David Wilkinson has said, our concepts contain the bones of our disciplinary ancestors. Some historians and historical sociologists, although making the requisite comparisons between Dutch, British, and American histories, reject the idea that these histories should be considered instances of a single phenomenon (e.g., Mann 1993; O'Brien 2002). In other words, they stress the differences to the extent of trivializing the similarities, although the particular differences they stress are themselves different. Both Mann and O'Brien refuse to characterize the role of Britain during the *pax Britannica* as hegemonic, especially as compared with the superpowerdom of the United States in the post–World War II period. Britain is seen as leading the world in the ways of industrialization and democracy, but not as a controller or exploiter of other countries. The question of the relative size of the British economy in the larger world economy during the nineteenth century compared with relative size of the U.S. economy during the twentieth century is a matter that we shall investigate below.

Among those who are more willing to analyze structural similarities across different historical periods, the ways in which these similarities are defined vary greatly. Several dimensions are at play in these differences. One important distinction among theorists is between the functionalists (who see emergent global hierarchies as serving a need for global order), and conflict theorists (who dwell more intently on the ways in which hierarchies serve the privileged, the powerful, and the wealthy). The term "hegemony" usually corresponds with the conflict approach, and the functionalists tend to employ the idea of "leadership," although several analysts occasionally use both of these terms (Arrighi and Silver et al. 1999). Another difference occurs between those who stress the importance of political/military power versus what we shall call "economic power." This issue is confused by disciplinary traditions (e.g., differences between economics, political science, and sociology). Most economists entirely reject the notion of economic power, assuming that market exchanges occur among equals. Most political scientists and sociologists would agree that economic power has become more important than it formerly was. Some of the literature on recent globalization goes so far as to argue that states and military organizations have been largely subsumed by the power of transnational corporations and global market dynamics, although the resurgence of U.S. military intervention, most recently in the Anglo-American invasion of Iraq, has raised profound questions about these arguments (Robinson 1998; Ross 1995).

Rather than reviewing the entire social science corpus of theories, we will describe four contrasting and overlapping approaches in some detail—those of Wallerstein (1984; 2002), Modelski and Thompson (1994), Arrighi (1994), and Rennstich (2001; 2002). Wallerstein defines hegemony as comparative advantages in profitable types of production. This economic advantage is what serves as the basis of the hegemon's politico-cultural influence and military power. Hegemonic production is the most profitable kind of core production, and hegemony is just the top end of the global hierarchy that constitutes the modern core/periphery division of labor. Hegemonies are unstable and tend to devolve into hegemonic rivalry.

Wallerstein posits a Dutch seventeenth-century hegemony, a British hegemony in the nineteenth century, and U.S. hegemony in the twentieth century. He perceives three stages within each hegemony, based on successive supremacy in agroindustrial production, in global commerce, and eventually in finance, with the process of decline following the same sequence.

George Modelski and William R. Thompson (1994) are political scientists whose theoretical perspective contains a strong dose of Parsonsian structural functionalism as applied to international systems. They allege that the world needs order and so world powers rise to fill this need. World powers rise on the basis of economic comparative advantage in new lead industries that allow them to acquire the resources needed to win wars among the great powers and to mobilize coalitions that keep the peace. World wars function as selection mechanisms for global leadership. But the comparative advantages of the leaders diffuse to competitors and new challengers emerge. Successful challengers are those who ally with the declining world leader against another challenger (e.g., the United States and Britain against Germany).

Modelski and Thompson (1994) measured the rise of certain key trades and industries, so-called new lead industries, that are seen as important components of the rise of world powers. They also have measured the degree of concentration of naval power in the European interstate system since the fifteenth century (Modelski and Thompson 1988). Their "twin peaks" model posits that each "power cycle" includes two Kondratieff waves.[1] Their list of world powers begins with Portugal in the fifteenth century. They include the Dutch period of world leadership in the seventeenth century, and they see the British as having successfully performed the role of world leader twice, once in the eighteenth century and then again in the nineteenth century. Thus they introduce the possibility that a world leader can succeed itself. They designate the United States as the world leader of the twentieth century.

Giovanni Arrighi's *The Long Twentieth Century* (1994) employs a Marxist and Braudelian approach to the analysis of what he terms "systemic cycles of accumulation." Arrighi rejects any consideration of Kondratieff waves as he perceives them to be unrelated to theories of capitalist accumulation.[2] He sees hegemonies as successful collaborations between capitalists and wielders of state power. His tour of systemic cycles of accumulation begins with Genoese financiers who allied with Spanish and Portuguese statesmen in the fifteenth century, and by launching the great discoveries helped provide for a vast material expansion of trade and production in the capitalist world-economy. In Arrighi's approach the role of hegemon itself evolves, becoming more deeply entwined with the organizational and economic institutional spheres that allow for successful capitalist accumulation. He posits a Dutch hegemony of the seventeenth century, then a period of contention between Britain and France in the eighteenth century, and a British hegemony in the nineteenth century, followed by U.S. hegemony in the twentieth century. A distinctive element of Arrighi's approach is his contention that profit-making from trade and production becomes more difficult toward the end of a systemic cycle of accumulation, and so big capital becomes increasingly focused on making profits through financial manipulations. Arrighi's approach is compatible with the idea that new lead industries are important in the rise of a hegemon, but he sees the economic activities of big capital during the declining years in terms of speculative financial activities. The latter often correspond with a period of "growth" in which incomes are rising during a latter-day *belle époque* of the systemic cycle of accumulation. But this period of accumulation is based on the economic power of *haute finance* and the centering of world markets in the global cities of the hegemons rather than on their ability to produce real products that people will buy, and so these *belles époques* are unsustainable and are followed by increased global polarization and continued hegemonic decline.

Recent research by Joachim Rennstich (2001) retools Arrighi's (1994) formulation of the reorganizations of the institutional structures that connect capital with states to facilitate the emergence of larger and larger hegemons over the last six centuries. Modelski and Thompson (1996) argued that the British successfully managed to enjoy two "power cycles,"[3] one in the eighteenth and another in the nineteenth century. With this precedent in mind, Rennstich considers the possibility that the United States might succeed itself in the twenty-first century. Rennstich's analysis of the organizational, cultural, and political requisites of the contemporary new lead industries—information technology and biotechnology—imply that the United States has a large comparative advantage that will most probably lead to another round of U.S. preeminence in the world-system. He argues that a hegemon can succeed itself if the rising industrial sectors within the hegemon are able to separate themselves sufficiently from the old declining industrial sectors. Rennstich focuses on the regional and institutional differences between old and new sectors of the U.S. economy.

## Previous Research

Earlier studies have most often proceeded by designating a country as hegemonic during a certain period and dividing this period up into subperiods based on a narrative of events. Only a few studies have quantitatively compared the hypothesized hegemons with other core powers or subjected the subperiodizations to quantitative analysis. Modelski and Thompson (1988) examined the distribution of naval power among the "great powers" of the European interstate system since the fifteenth century. This is the most thorough and comprehensive quantitative study that actually measures hegemony by comparing contending countries over a long period of time. Modelski and Thompson's (1996) quantitative study of new lead industries does not break these down by country.

Using economic (total GDP and per capita GDP) and military indicators (military expenditures) to create composite measures of power in the world-economy, Kentor (2000) explores the changes in core power and hegemony by providing snap-shot profiles for core countries in 1820, 1900, 1930, 1950, 1970, and 1990. Results indicate that in 1820, the United Kingdom was the dominant core power with an overall standardized composite score twice that of its nearest rival, France (Kentor 2000). The United Kingdom's relative strength came primarily from its level of capital intensity (as indicated by GDP per capita) and military strength. By 1900, relationships between core powers had changed dramatically. The United Kingdom still possessed the highest overall score, but its strength was based primarily upon its military power. The United States and China had surpassed the United Kingdom in output, and the United States was approaching the United Kingdom's level of capital intensity (Kentor 2000). The shift in hegemony was quite evident by 1930 when the United States achieved dominance through its advantage in national output. In 1950, national output for the United States had grown to more than three times that of its nearest rival (the Soviet Union), its relative level of capital intensity was twice that of the United Kingdom, and its relative level of military power increased to an almost identical level with the Soviet Union (Kentor 2000). By 1970, U.S. relative military strength had increased, although its advantages in output and capital intensity had declined. By 1990, the Soviet Union lost its military dominance, Japan continued its rise in the world-economy with increases in all areas, China had grown to the second largest producer in the world-economy, and the United States had increased its global dominance with relative growth in all three power dimensions (Kentor 2000).

## New Quantitative Data on Economic Hegemony

Angus Maddison (2001) has published a revision and extension of his long-range estimates of populations, gross domestic products, and levels of economic development of countries and world regions. His most recent endeavor presents quantitative snapshots of economic and demographic change over the past 2000 years. In this article we combine the more detailed estimates from Maddison's (1995) earlier publication with the more recent and revised estimates published in 2001 to paint a quantitative and comparative historical picture of the trajectories of economic hegemony in the modern world-system.

Maddison's estimates make it possible to examine the relative sizes and levels of development of the national states and how these have changed over time. The necessary methodological operation for these economic estimates has been to transform statistical evidence from all over the world and from earlier centuries into a single comparable metric—1990 "international dollars." Maddison carefully explains and justifies his use of purchasing power parity (PPP) estimates rather than currency exchange rates to convert country currency data into constant dollars (2001, 171–175). Purchasing power parity estimates convert GDP estimates denominated in country currencies into one another by estimating comparable purchasing power for consumer goods and the other elements that compose the GDP. Maddison has worked for years on efforts to produce comparable estimates for very different kinds of accounting systems (e.g., the Net Material Product of centrally planned economies) and for different kinds of economies (e.g., highly monetized versus the partially monetized economies in the periphery of the world-system). Maddison applies all this experience to the most difficult task he has yet undertaken—the valuing of the economic activity of premodern world regions. These quantitative estimates shed important light on the various contentions of the social scientists and historians who have made comparisons of the modern hegemons.

## Shares of World Gross Domestic Product

Total gross domestic product (GDP) combines both economic development and economic size. It rises simply because there are more people. Thus a graph of shares of world GDP over the last two millennia looks quite similar to a

60 *Thomas Reifer, Christopher Chase-Dunn, and Andrew Jorgenson*

population graph until the beginning of the nineteenth century. This is to say that India and China contained most of the world's GDP because they contained most of the world's population. But after 1800 this began to change because of the rapid increase in GDP per capita in certain European countries and the United States. Figure 4-1 shows the shares of world GDP held by the core countries of the European interstate system since 1820. Maddison (1995) provides estimates for 1820 and 1850, and then yearly estimates from 1870 on. We have interpolated his estimates of total world GDP in order to calculate the yearly shares after 1870, and we have added data from Maddison (2001) for the years after 1994.

The first question is whether or not shares of world GDP are really a good indicator of hegemony. Obviously GDP does not capture the military, political, or cultural aspects of hegemony. It is perhaps not the best indicator even for economic hegemony because, as we have pointed out above, a strong component of GDP is merely demographic. With these qualifications in mind let us discuss the features revealed in Figure 4-1.

The most striking feature is the rapid ascent of the U.S. economy in its relationship with the world economy as a whole from less than 2 percent in 1820 to a peak of 35 percent in 1944. The U.S. share slumped precipitously from 1929 to 1933, and then rapidly ascended again to its highest point in 1944. A rapid post–World War II decline was followed by a slight recovery that began in 1949, and then beginning in 1951, a decline until 1958, then a plateau until 1968, then another decline until 1982, followed by another plateau until

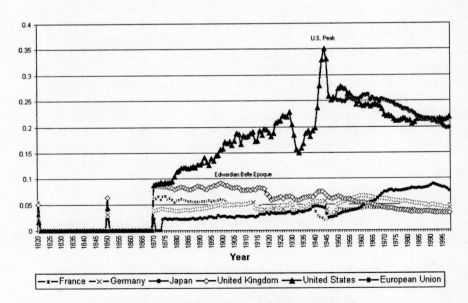

**Figure 4-1. Shares of World GDP, 1820–1998**

1998 at between 21 and 22 percent. The U.S. GDP share trajectory supports discussions of U.S. hegemonic rise and decline in the world economy, but the details contradict some versions of this trajectory. By the measure of share of world GDP, the U.S. decline began in 1944, not in 1970 as some world-systems analysts have claimed. There were three steps of U.S. decline, the first beginning in 1944, the second in 1951, and the third in 1968.

What are the implications of Figure 4-1 for our understanding of the British hegemony? The figure shows the British ascent from 5 percent in 1820 to a peak of almost 9 percent in 1870, then some wobbling, and then a full 9 percent in 1899, followed by a slow decline to 3.3 percent in 1998. Those observers who have emphasized the difference in scale between the huge U.S. primacy and much smaller British component of the world economy would seem to be correct based on this measure (Mann 1992; O'Brien 2002). At its highest peak in 1899, during the Edwardian *belle époque,* the British economy only constituted 9 percent of the world economy. Recall that the U.S. peak in 1944 was 35 percent. The United States passed Britain in 1870 with respect to share of the world GDP.

Of course the British GDP does not include the great economic mass of the British Empire, which included India and many other colonies during most of the period portrayed in this figure. But neither does the U.S. GDP include its "neocolonial" dependencies, those countries that have been economically and politically dominated by the United States since its rise to world power. If both formal and informal imperialism were taken into account we surmise that the British hegemony would be more prominent than it appears in the figure, but it would still not be such a huge portion of the world economy as the U.S. hegemony has been. A related issue to keep in mind here is that both England and the United States combined formal and informal empire; the British amassed the largest territorial empire the world had ever seen, whereas the U.S. trajectory has been largely based on informal empire (Arrighi 1994).

The French economy peaked in 1872 and then entered a slow decline. The German economy fluctuated between 3 and 5.5 percent, with its most recent peak in 1962. The Japanese economy rose from 1820 to a peak of 4.6 percent in 1941, then fell after World War II and rose again to a peak of 8.8 percent in 1991, from whence it fell back to 7.5 percent in 1998.

Of interest for the question of hegemony is the size of the European Union (EU),[4] an emergent core polity that has changed the terrain of global geopolitics (Boswell forthcoming). The emergence of the European Union transformed the world economy from a unicentric structure dominated by the United States into a bipolar structure with two very large states at the center, albeit with one in only an embryonic stage of formation. The countries that were to become the European Union contained 26 percent of the world's GDP in 1963, but have declined since then to slightly less than 20 percent in 1998. The trajectories since 1992 of Japan and the European Union have been down, while the United States has remained on a plateau since 1974. These differences may have implications for future trajectories and for the question of possible hege-monic rivalry among core states. We will return to this issue after considering another measure of economic hegemony, the ratio of national GDP per capita to the average world GDP per capita.


## Ratio of National Economic Development to World Average

As we have mentioned above, shares of world GDP indicate a combination of size and economic power. Large and populous countries such as China and India are high on this measure, and this is why we consider them to be in the semiperiphery. But power status in the modern world-system is more than just a matter of size. It is fundamentally a matter of economic development, mean-ing the ability to produce capital-intensive products and to specialize in types of production that employ highly skilled labor. A better indicator of this is GDP per capita, though GDP per capita is not ideal. A better estimate of average capital intensity is GDP per worker or per labor hour. GDP per capita is a fair proxy for capital intensity in cross-national comparisons. Some countries have high per capita GDP because they hold great natural resource wealth. Thus Saudi Arabia and Libya have relatively high per capita GDPs because of their huge oil exports. In order to indicate this important difference the World Bank and the United Nations often present data for the oil-exporting countries sepa-rately. For the countries we are examining in Figure 4-2—the upper tier of the core—this is not an issue. Figure 4-2 shows the scores of countries based on the ratio between their national GDP per capita and the average world GDP per capita based on Maddison's revised estimates (2001). Figure 4-2 begins in 1500, but again beware that the horizontal axis does not have equal temporal intervals. As with Figure 4-3, the earlier time intervals are allotted less space on the horizontal axis than are the later intervals. Keep this in mind as you inter-pret Figure 4-2.

The first thing we can notice about Figure 4-2 is that all the core coun-tries show a general upward trend in the ratio of their national GDP per capita to the world average GDP per capita. This is an indication that the trend to-ward greater inequality between the core and the periphery that has been noted in recent decades is in fact of long standing. But this is not our main concern in this chapter. Rather we are investigating changes in relative differences among countries within the core and upwardly mobile semiperipheral challengers.[5]

The seventeenth-century economic hegemony of the Netherlands is indi-cated by its peak ratio of 3.4 in 1700. Interestingly, the Netherlands has re-turned to this same high point in 1998. The difference is that in 1700 the Netherlands was far ahead of its closest competitor, the United Kingdom, while in 1998 it was bunched together with all the other countries save the United States, which was much higher.

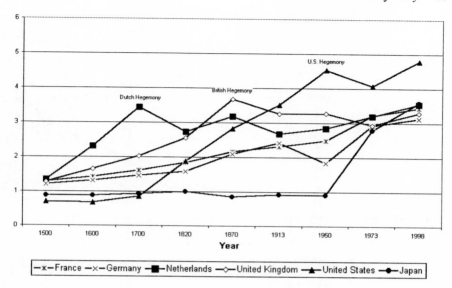

**Figure 4-2. Country GDP Per Capita as a Ratio to Average World GDP Per Capita, 1500–1998**

The British hegemony of the nineteenth century is much more evident in Figure 4-2 than it was in Figure 4-1, and its high point appears to have been in 1870 (but see Figure 4-3). Maddison's books do not contain estimates of British GDP per capita between 1700 and 1820 and so we are not able to see if Modelski and Thompson's contention that there was a British "power cycle" in the eighteenth century would be borne out by comparative economic data.

Figure 4-2 indicates the long ascent of the United States to an apparent peak in 1950 (ratio = 4.52), and then a decline to 4.06 in 1973, and rise back to 4.78 in 1998 (but see Figure 4-3). The U.S. ratio in 1998 is significantly larger than that of the second country, Japan, as gauged by the GDP per capita ratio (3.57). The story of Germany and France is a similar long rise, except for Germany's dip in 1950. In Figure 4-2, Japan shows no rise in the GDP per capita ratio until after 1950, contradicting all the literature about Japanese development after the Meiji restoration (but see Figure 4-3). Japan's ascent after 1950 is quite rapid and in 1998 it is higher than any of the other core countries, save the United States.

In order to more closely examine the temporality of the changes indicated in Figure 4-2 we have combined estimates from Maddison's (1995) earlier presentation with his updated estimates (2001) to produce Figure 4-3.[6]

Figure 4-3 can be compared with Figure 4-1 to see the differences between shares of world GDP and the ratios of country GDP per capita to world GDP per capita. Figure 4-3 shows that British capital intensity was already significantly higher than French capital intensity in 1820, whereas its share of

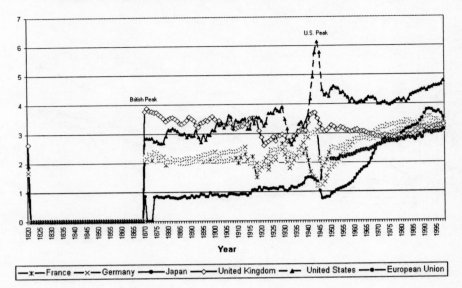

**Figure 4-3. Country GDP Per Capita as a Ratio to World GDP Per Capita, 1820–1998**

world GDP was nearly the same (see Figure 4–1). The French economy was demographically and territorially larger than the British economy, and this accounts for the similar size and share of world GDP. But the British GDP per capita ratio to average world GDP per capita was 2.6, whereas the French ratio was 1.8. This indicates a significant advantage in average capital intensity for the British. Figure 4–3 shows that the British economic hegemony as indicated by relative capital intensity peaked in 1871, when the British ratio was nearly 3.9. The British ratio then declined slowly until 1918, when it took a dive to a low point of 2.6 in 1921, from whence it wobbled around below 3 until 1932, then experienced a revival to 3.7 in 1943, and then another slow decline to 2.8 in 1977 followed by a slow rise to 3.3 in 1998.

The trajectory of U.S. relative capital intensity is similar in many respects to U.S. GDP share as shown in Figure 4-1, but there are also some interesting differences. The U.S. rise during the nineteenth century was steeper by the GDP share measure than by the relative capital intensity ratio. This is because the U.S. population and territory were growing as fast as was its relative capital intensity during the nineteenth century. The capital intensity ratio shows the same peak in 1944 as was revealed in the GDP shares in Figure 4-1. But after that the U.S. trajectory is a bit different. The postwar plummet is followed by a recovery, as was the GDP share indicator, but the successive plateaus and declines after that are less evident, and there is a new upward movement that begins in 1982 and reaches a rather high level of 4.8 in 1998. This last might be interpreted as indicating a renewal of U.S. economic hegemony as hypothesized by Rennstich, but another aspect of Figure 4-3 needs to be noted. Since the middle of the 1970s all the core powers have been increasing their relative capital intensities. This is because global inequality has been increasing for the last three decades, with the core countries experiencing greater growth in GDP per capita than most of peripheral and semiperipheral countries. The rise in relative capital intensivity for the core countries shown in Figure 4-3 is probably due to increasing global inequality of development (Jorgenson 2003b).

## Conclusion

Maddison's new estimates are not the best possible measures of relative economic power of core countries, as discussed above. But they do make it possible to make some long-run and large-scale historical and quantitative comparisons, the results of which have implications for future research on the problem of hegemony. It should be noted that the hegemonic rise of the Dutch, British, and American power constitutes a continuation of the phenomenon of semiperipheral development in which a formerly semiperipheral society transforms institutional structures and ascends to the top of the world-system. All of the hegemons were former semiperipheral countries before they rose to hegemony.

The shares of world GDP (Figure 4-1) give us a way to analyze the rise of economic hegemony in the global system. The United States became the heavyweight of the world-economy in a rapid ascent after 1850. Figure 4-1 supports those who emphasize the important difference in scale between the *pax Britannica* and the *pax Americana* (Mann 1993; O'Brien 2002). This difference may have significant implications for the possibilities of future hegemonic developments. Market size is clearly a valuable advantage that might facilitate the possibility of another round of U.S. hegemony. Figure 4-3 shows a milder difference between the British and U.S. hegemonies in terms of relative capital intensity. The British peak in 1871 was 3.9, and the U.S. peak in 1944 was 6.1. This is a sizeable difference, but the U.S. peak was an unusual spike due to the extremities of World War II. The U.S. plateau varied between 4 and 4.8, a level that was higher than that of the British in the nineteenth century, but not greatly higher. Figure 4-3 shows a slow Japanese ascent from 1820 to 1942, a collapse, and then a rapid Japanese ascent after 1949. Since 1992 the Japanese capital intensity ratio has declined from 3.8 to 3.5, reflecting the East Asian economic crisis.

The big question raised by our analysis of Maddison's data is the future trajectory of the United States. The Maddison GDP data indicate that the U.S. decline after World War II reached a plateau and turned up a bit in the 1990s. The question is whether or not this is a hiatus in the U.S. decline that might turn out to be the beginning of a new phase of U.S. hegemony, or is only a temporary phenomenon similar to the Edwardian *belle époque* of British hegemony in the last decade of the nineteenth century.

Ultimately, only the future will tell. But in the meantime a close examination of other indicators of the U.S. position in the world-economy can shed more light on this question. Trends in the U.S. balance of trade and balance of payments are germane. It is well known that the U.S. economy has increasingly imported more goods than it has exported. There has been a huge increase in the amount of foreign direct and portfolio investment in the U.S. economy since the early 1990s. Proponents of the *belle époque* thesis contend that slowing of decline of general indicators of U.S. position such as those found in the Maddison data may be the result of stock bubbles and overinvestment in housing and commercial real estate created by the influx of foreign capital. Much of the recent foreign investment is coming from East Asian investors seeking greater returns than the ailing East Asian economies have been able to generate recently.

What are the implications of this study for our understanding of the potentialities of the contemporary globalization backlash? An important part of the last globalization backlash was an increase in hegemonic rivalry that was only resolved by the long world war between 1913 and 1945. A potential renewed period of U.S. economic primacy might be understood as good news regarding its implications for future violent conflict among core states resulting from hegemonic rivalry. Such a potential future conflict among core states is only likely if U.S. economic hegemony continues to decline. The current situation of a single military superpower is eminently stable as regards the problem of conflict within the core.

But the nineteenth- and twentieth-century globalization backlash had another major component—the rise of antisystemic movements that challenged the domination of core capital. These rebellions against increasing inequalities resulted in a global revolutionary wave, including the Mexican revolution, the Bolshevik revolution, the Chinese revolution, and anticolonial movements that eventually succeeded in decolonizing almost all of Asia and Africa. The phenomenon of increasing intranational and international (North-South) inequalities is also an important dimension of the contemporary emerging globalization backlash, and we can expect important antisystemic movements to emerge that will challenge the power of transnational corporations and global elites. Semiperipheral countries with strong labor movements will probably develop democratically elected regimes that pursue self-reliant models of development once it becomes clearer that all boats will not rise on the tide of capitalist globalization. Here, the electoral victory of Lula, the candidate of the Workers Party in Brazil, is perhaps one indication of what may be a growing trend. Recent protests against Lula's proposals for reforming the Brazilian pension system and related protests may indicate an increasing mobilization of lower strata to ensure that politicians represent their interests.

On the question of U.S. hegemony versus domination, although some analysts argue there has already been a transformation from the former to the latter, others stress the advantages that the United States has been able to develop in new lead industries such as information technology and biotechnology.

Rennstich (2001; 2002) argues that the huge size of the U.S. economy has made it possible for these new lead technologies to become relatively autonomous from the older declining industries within the United States, and that these will be the basis for a new round of U.S. economic leadership and another power cycle in which the United States will renew its predominance in the global economy. Indeed, bubbles are often incubators of new lead industries and, although most of these businesses fail, the few successful firms that survive can become the basis for hegemonic leadership (see Chase-Dunn and Reifer 2002).

Here, it is important to consider a critical difference between the U.S. and the Dutch and British hegemonic cycles, namely the much greater extent to which the United States has been able to manage the global interstate system through its military alliances, related forms of military Keynesianism, and overseas power projection, within which it has contained both enemies and allies, the latter as semisovereign states. Although some argue that much of this postwar geopolitical structure, as the title of Immanuel Wallerstein's chapter intimates, has collapsed, whatever the current geopolitical restructuring, many path-dependent aspects of this "postwar" structure arguably still endure.

The deep structural features of the present trajectory of the U.S. and intracore ties in the world-system come from the particular role of militarized state-corporate capitalism in the U.S. hegemony cycle and systemic cycle of accumulation. Specifically, Cold War techniques for managing the domestic and global aspects of U.S. hegemony came at the cost of a pronounced path dependency on militarization. Recognition of this is crucial to understanding the still great residual strengths of the United States in the military-industrial and monetary realms, the overseas projection of geopolitical power, and the exchange of petrodollar payments for "protection," central in privileges of seigniorage, the right to mint the coin of the realm (see Spiro 1999).

Yet far from being merely a World War II or Cold War phenomena, new research indicates that the emergence of the U.S. military-corporate complex in embryo during the nineteenth century was a central part of what Giovanni Arrighi calls the "organization revolutions" in the strategies and structures of hegemonic powers that have accompanied all financial expansions and the autumns of systemic cycles of accumulation and larger hegemonic structures of which they are a part (1994, 14). The adumbration of the U.S. military-corporate complex in the late nineteenth century, which culminated in the militarized state-corporate capitalism of World War I, served as a model to which U.S. elites returned during World War II and the Cold War and once again today. Yet here there are dramatic differences that must be underscored.

The centrality of military spending in U.S. hegemony after World War II emanated from the realization by U.S. power elites that the internalization of allied protection costs could give the U.S. military-corporate complex global economies of scale. The subsequent synthesis of violence, profits, and power in U.S. hegemony has given it a virtual monopoly in the global projection of geopolitical military power in the early twenty-first century. Yet there are major structural differences here between the functions of U.S. military spending at different points in its hegemonic cycle. Whereas during the early years of the Cold War, military Keynesianism and developmentalism functioned as part of the New Deal, however watered down from its original vision, today increasingly regressively financed military spending, via borrowing on the global capital markets, is part and parcel of the reconstitution of U.S. power on increasingly narrow and militarized social foundations (see Reifer 2002).

Moreover, the politics of the world-system today are notably different from the late nineteenth and early twentieth century. The main characteristic of that period was the turn toward overseas empire and related ideologies of social imperialism by all the great powers. Here, states sought to incorporate workers as junior partners in overseas expansion so as to curb struggles for domestic and international working class solidarity. In contrast, today we are witnessing the massive leap forward in global social justice and antiwar movements, but one in which the great powers, rather than pursuing overseas imperial expansion themselves, instead have largely lined up to oppose the United States in the invasion of Iraq and its aggressive unilateralist foreign policy more generally.

Although this augurs well for the question of intracore war in the near- to medium-term future, the aggressive expansionism of the United States is a poor substitute for the decline of its formerly unrivalled position in all relevant power indicators, and will likely increase global chaos. If such U.S. behavior continues, it will thus also likely increase, rather than decrease, the potential for the emergence of future hegemonic challengers, both on the politico-economic and military planes. Thus, despite the ostensible monopoly of U.S. power in the last few decades, challenges to hegemonic leadership can be expected to increase, especially if the United States continues to try and transform its up to now largely informal empire into a truly universal world-empire, with tightly linked formal and informal aspects, as trends may indicate. This is especially likely if the United States continues to block reform on addressing pressing problems of the global system: poverty reduction, human-induced climate change, environmental degradation, growing politico-economic instability, and deadly conflict (Jorgenson 2003a, 2003b, 2004; Jorgenson and Burns 2003; Jorgenson and Kick 2003; Reifer 2002).

The increasing backlash against globalization has already generated a global justice movement and a global resurgence of Islamic activism as well, the vast majority nonviolent as well as extremist movements against U.S. power such as al-Qaeda (Lubeck and Reifer forthcoming). The growing economic chasm between North and South along with U.S. unilateralism in the use of military superiority to gain advantages (such as the conquest of Iraq) could conceivably create enough world-economic and politico-military turbulence so as to become an impetus for U.S. core allies to initiate efforts to provide for their own security. They might also support reforming the system of global governance in ways that challenge the policies of the United States (e.g., Camilleri, Malhotra, and Tehranian 2000). It might be supposed that a still-powerful United

States would automatically resist and suppress such developments. But it is also possible that political struggles resulting from increasing inequalities within the United States and resistance to the illegal use of force abroad will challenge the use of U.S. power to suppress democratic movements in the semiperiphery and efforts to democratize global governance. The people of the United States may decide to live up to the discourse about equality and democracy that has been promulgated by their leaders for so long, albeit on both a global and a national scale.

## Notes

1. The Kondratieff Wave (K-wave) is a 40 to 60 year business cycle. The "A-phase" is a 20 to 30 year period of higher average growth rates in the world economy, and the "B-phase" is a 20 to 30 year period of lower average growth rates. The best evidence for the existence of the K-wave is found in price histories, but considerable evidence also exists for a temporally similar production long wave (Goldstein 1988).

2. Many of the political scientists who analyze K-waves spurn any analysis of capitalism (e.g., Goldstein 1988; Modelski and Thompson 1994), but Marxist economists such as Ernest Mandel (1980) and David Gordon (1980) have provided important theorizations of the K-wave.

3. "Power cycle" is Modelski and Thompson's term for what Arrighi (1994) calls "systemic cycles of accumulation" and Chase-Dunn (1998) calls the "hegemonic sequence."

4. The "European Union" in Figure 4-1 is composed of France, Germany, Greece, Ireland, Italy, Netherlands, Portugal, Spain, Sweden, and the United Kingdom. The share of world GDP of these countries is calculated from 1950–1998 despite the fact that the European Union only emerged as an effective confederation in the last decade. This is to show the trajectory of this emergent state's position in the world economy.

5. For an empirical analysis (using Maddison's data) and discussion of economic inequality between countries and zones in the world-system over the last five centuries, see Jorgenson (2003b).

6. Figure 4-3 uses Maddison's new estimates (2001) from 1950 to 1998 and his yearly estimates (1995) from 1870 to 1950 to calculate the ratio of country GDP per capita to the average world GDP per capita.

## References

Arrighi, Giovanni. 1994. *The Long Twentieth Century.* New York: Verso.

Arrighi, Giovanni, and Beverly Silver, et al. 1999. *Chaos and Governance.* Minneapolis: University of Minnesota Press.

Boswell, Terry. Forthcoming. "Hegemonic Decline and World Revolution: When the World Is Up for Grabs." In Thomas Ehrlich Reifer, ed., *Globalization, Hegemony, and Power: Antisystemic Movements and the Global System.* Boulder, CO: Paradigm Publishers.

Boswell, Terry, and Albert Bergesen, eds. 1987. *America's Changing Role in the World-System.* New York: Praeger.

Boswell, Terry, and Christopher Chase-Dunn. 2000. *The Spiral of Capitalism and Socialism: Toward Global Democracy.* Boulder, CO: Lynne Rienner.

Boswell, Terry, and Mike Sweat. 1991. "Hegemony, Long Waves, and Major Wars: A Time Series Analysis of Systemic Dynamics, 1496–1967." *International Studies Quarterly* 35(2): 123–150.

Camilleri, Joseph A., Kamal Malhotra, and Majid Tehranian. 2000. *Reimagining the Future: Towards Democratic Governance.* Bundoora, Australia: Department of Politics, LaTrobe University.

Chase-Dunn, Christopher. 1998. *Global Formation: Structures of the World-Economy.* Lanham, MD: Rowman and Littlefield.

Chase-Dunn, Christopher, and Terry Boswell. 2002. "Transnational Social Movements and Democratic Socialist Parties in the Semiperiphery." Paper presented at the Annual Conference of the California Sociological Association, Riverside, CA: October 19. Available at http://www.irows.ucr.edu/papers/csa02/csa02.htm.

Chase-Dunn, Christopher, and Thomas E. Reifer. 2002. "U.S. Hegemony and Biotechnology." Paper presented at the ISA Research Committee on Environment and Society RC24, XV. ISA World Congress of Sociology, Brisbane, Australia, July 7–13.

Goldstein, Joshua. 1988. *Long Cycles: Prosperity and War in the Modern Age.* New Haven, CT: Yale University Press.

Gordon, David M. 1980. "Stages of Accumulation and Long Economic Cycles." In Terence K. Hopkins and Immanuel Wallerstein, eds., *Processes of the World-System.* Beverly Hills, CA: Sage, pp. 9–45.

Jorgenson, Andrew. 2003a. "Consumption and Environmental Degradation: A Cross-National Analysis of the Ecological Footprint." *Social Problems* 50(3): 374–394.

———. 2003b. "International Inequality in the Capitalist World-Economy, 1500–2000: A Quantitative Cross-National Analysis." Paper presented at the Annual Meetings of the American Sociological Association, Atlanta, Georgia, August 16–19.

Jorgenson, Andrew K. 2004. "Global Inequalities, Water Pollution, and Infant Mortality." *Social Science Journal* 41: 279–288.

Jorgenson, Andrew K., and Edward Kick. 2004. "Globalization and the Environment." *Journal of World-System Research* 9: 195–203.

Jorgenson, Andrew K., and Thomas J. Burns. 2004. "Globalization, the Environment, and Infant Mortality: A Cross-National Study." *Humboldt Journal of Social Relations* 28: 7–52.

Kentor, Jeffrey. 2000. *Capital and Coercion: The Economic and Military Processes That Have Shaped the World Economy, 1800–1990.* New York: Garland.

Lubeck, Paul, and Thomas Reifer. Forthcoming. "The Politics of Global Islam: U.S. Hegemony, Globalization, and Islamist Social Movements." In Thomas Ehrlich Reifer, ed., *Globalization, Hegemony, and Power: Antisystemic Movements and the Global System.* Boulder, CO: Paradigm Publishers.

Maddison, Angus. 1995. *Monitoring the World Economy, 1820–1992.* Paris: Organization for Economic Cooperation and Development.

———. 2001. *The World Economy: A Millennial Perspective.* Paris: Organization of Economic Cooperation and Development.

Mandel, Ernest. 1980. *Long Waves of Capitalist Development: The Marxist Interpretation.* New York: Cambridge University Press.

Mann, Michael. 1993. *The Sources of Social Power.* Vol. 2. New York: Cambridge University Press.

Modelski, George, and William R. Thompson. 1988. *Seapower in Global Politics, 1494–1993.* Seattle: University of Washington Press.

―――. 1996. *Leading Sectors and World Powers: The Coevolution of Global Economics and Politics.* Columbia: University of South Carolina Press.

O'Brien, Patrick K. 2002. "The Pax Britannica, American Hegemony, and the International Economic Order, 1846–1914 and 1941–2001." Paper presented at the annual PEWS Conference, University of California, Riverside, May 3–4.

Rennstich, Joachim K. 2001. "The Future of Great Power Rivalries." In Wilma Dunaway, ed., *New Theoretical Directions for the 21st Century World-System.* Westport, CT: Greenwood.

―――. 2002. "The Phoenix Cycle: Global Leadership Transition in a Long-Wave Perspective." Paper presented at the annual PEWS Conference, University of California, Riverside, May 3–4.

Reifer, Thomas E. 2002. "Globalization and the National Security State Corporate Complex (NSSCC) in the Long Twentieth Century." In Ramon Grosfoguel and Margarita Rodriguez, eds., *The Modern/Colonial Capitalist World-System in the 20th Century.* Westport, CT: Greenwood.

Robinson, William I. 1998. "Beyond Nation-State Paradigms: Globalization, Sociology, and the Challenge of Transnational Studies." *Sociological Forum* 13: 561–594.

Ross, Robert J. S. 1995. "The Theory of Global Capitalism: State Theory and Variants of Capitalism on a World Scale." In David Smith and Jozsef Borocz, eds., *A New World Order? Global Transformations in the Late Twentieth Century.* Westport, CT: Praeger, 19–36.

Spiro, David E. 1999. *The Hidden Hand of American Hegemony: Petrodollar Recycling and International Markets.* Ithaca: Cornell University Press.

Wallerstein, Immanuel. 1984. "The Three Instances of Hegemony in the History of the Capitalist World-Economy." In Gerhard Lenski, ed., *Current Issues and Research in Macrosociology.* Leiden: E. J. Brill, 100–108.

Wallerstein, Immanuel. 2002. "The Eagle Has Crash-Landed." *Foreign Policy* 131 (July–August): 60–68.

# 5

# THE TRANS-ATLANTIC
# CONFLICT OVER PRIMACY

*Peter Gowan*

## Introduction

The open trans-Atlantic rupture over the Bush administration's decision to attack and occupy Iraq has generated a variety of contingency theories. Some of these focus on chance configurations of leadership: Bush's supposed neoconservative cabal, Chirac's ability to capture control of the French government in the spring of 2002, and Schroeder's use of Iraq for supposedly purely electoral reasons in the autumn of 2002. Other contingency theorists stress party ideologies: the Republican coalition of militarists and Christian fundamentalists, the pacifism of the German left, and Gaullist anti-Americanism. Yet others stress the specific, localized clashes of interests in Iraq: U.S. determination to get rid of Saddam versus French and Russian economic interests there, and the clashes on Israeli occupation and colonization of Palestinian lands. Then, of course, there is the patronizing European view that the American people and leaders understandably lost their balance and became overwrought because of the insecurities produced by September 11—a view that clashes with the Bush administration's response to September 11 as a great *strategic opportunity* for the United States (Lehmann 2002; Woodward 2002; Woodward

73

and Balz 2002), and in particular Cheney's view that the United States now had the world in its hands.

Contingencies did of course shape the forms of the trans-Atlantic splits over the Iraq war as over any major international political event. But the flip side of the contingency theories is the claim, implied or explicit, that the structural unity of the Atlantic Alliance remains solid. This chapter argues that this claim is false and that there is a genuine structural crisis in the alliance, centered on the *power structure* of the alliance itself. The direct source of this conflict was the Soviet Bloc collapse, which destabilized the old power structure. Since then, no agreement has been reached on a new power structure, and tensions and conflicts have mounted as a result. We should see the way that the Bush administration articulated its whole strategy after September 11 and the way it prepared its war against Iraq diplomatically as an *effect* of this structural crisis in trans-Atlantic relations rather than as a contingent *cause* of the trans-Atlantic rupture.

Robert Kagan has also claimed that the alliance faces a structural crisis, but he locates its source in a cultural divide (Kagan 2002). This is misleading. In many respects it would be more accurate to say that the attempts in western European business and governing elites to bring western Europe into line with the sociocultural model of the United States—that of a "market state" (Bobbitt 2002)—have impelled these same elites to raise the European Union's political profile internationally to strengthen its domestic authority. These efforts to raise the European Union's profile have exacerbated the trans-Atlantic crisis.

The tensions became endemic during the 1990s, yet they remained largely contained within the closed institutions of the alliance. Thus when they finally burst through the integuments of these structures into public conflict during the Iraq crisis, they struck many, understandably but wrongly, as a sudden and unexpected development.

To trace the sources of the trans-Atlantic crisis, I will first explore the peculiarities of the Cold War trans-Atlantic political structures. This will enable readers to understand the impact of the Soviet Bloc collapse on those structures. I will then examine some features of the new project of western European integration since the mid-1980s relevant to trans-Atlantic relations. Against these backgrounds I will trace the development of the conflicts in trans-Atlantic relations since the start of the 1990s. I will then suggest various possible variants of future evolution in this relationship.

# I. Western Europe under U.S. Primacy

The Cold War Atlantic Alliance is conventionally presented as that of a cooperative, collegial power structure of "partners" bound together by common values and a shared mission. There was, of course, cooperation, shared values, and a shared mission of confronting the Soviet Union. But there was also a power structure within which that cooperation took place. This was a unipolar Atlantic Alliance dominated by a United States that had the right to make unilateral decisions in a crisis. The armed forces of the NATO members were integrated directly under U.S. command—an extraordinary arrangement for a peacetime alliance, from which the French state broke away in the 1960s. Each western European member of NATO was tied into the U.S. center in a hub-and-spokes system: western Europe had no collective, autonomous role whatsoever in the Atlantic alliance system. Attempts at various times by western European leaders to form such caucuses were firmly slapped down by Washington: the de Gaulle-Adenauer attempt in the early 1960s; the efforts by Brandt, Pompidou, and Heath vis-à-vis the Middle East crisis in the early 1970s; and the attempt, led by the French, to revive the Western European Union in 1984.

The European pattern was repeated in East Asia, in relation to Japan, South Korea, and Taiwan. The levels of U.S. control were greatest in the two main centers of industrial capitalism outside the United States itself: Japan and Germany. Both these powers were kept non-nuclear, lacked seats in the United Nations Security Council (UNSC), and had intrusive internal invigilation by the United States. This was the formidable system of U.S. political power upon which cooperation, partnership, and consensual relations rested.

The conventional orthodoxy can hardly deny the unipolar, hub-and-spokes power structure. But it regards it as incidental and secondary: a derivative *result* of the East-West confrontation. Given that confrontation, such a disciplined military-political subordination of western Europe to American leadership was, on this theory, inevitable. Yet there have been dissenting voices on these matters. One such dissident voice has been that of Paul Nitze, the lieutenant of Dean Acheson, the real architect of the alliance system. Nitze wrote the key document spelling out the system, NSC-68.

In an essay called "Coalition Policy and the Concept of World Order," which he wrote for a book by Arnold Wolfers at the end of the 1950s, Nitze criticized the idea that America's postwar alliances were negatively generated by the Soviet threat (Wolfers 1959). He accused John Foster Dulles of being "sometimes but not always a member" of that negative school. Nitze stressed that there was a second school of which he was a member. This school believed that "United States foreign policy is, or should be, positive and not merely negative and defensive. It maintains that United States interests and United States security have become directly dependent on the creation of some form of world order compatible with our continued development as the kind of nation we are." He explained that the construction of this positive world order began in 1946 and continued until it was completed in 1953. It centered on the construction of a system of regional alliances. In this reading, the militarized confrontation with the Soviet Union should be seen as the *means* for constructing a positive U.S. world order.

Nitze's view has the merit of being, so to speak, from the horse's mouth. But it also corresponds to what we now know about perceptions and motivations among the trans-Atlantic leaders when the alliance system was being constructed. As Melvyn Leffler has shown, none of these leaders believed there was a threat of Soviet attack against western Europe (Leffler 1992). He even shows how Acheson's push against the Soviet Union's sphere was conducted with scant regard for military realities and possibilities in the event of a war with the Soviet Union, much to the concern of U.S. military planners.

If Nitze was right, then the unipolar power structure established by Acheson and persisting throughout the Cold War was not an incidental effect of the Soviet confrontation at all: it was the telos of U.S. postwar outward expansion and could persist as the telos of American grand strategy with or without a Soviet Bloc.

An important article by Samuel Huntington in 1973 gives us a sense of the *social substance* encased within the U.S.-led postwar security alliances. As he put it:

> Throughout the two decades after World War II, the power of the United States government in world politics, and its interests in developing a system of alliances with other governments against the Soviet Union, China, and communism, produced the underlying political condition which made the rise of [business] transnationalism possible. Western Europe, Latin America, East Asia and much of South Asia, the Middle East, and Africa fell within what was euphemistically referred to as "the Free World" and what was in fact a security zone. The governments of countries within this zone found it in their interests: (a) to accept an explicit or implicit guarantee by Washington of the independence of their country and, in some cases, of the authority of the government; and (b) to permit access to their territory by a variety of U.S. governmental and nongovernmental organizations pursuing goals which those organizations considered important. "The 'Pax Americana,'" as I. F. Stone put it, "is the 'internationalism' of Standard Oil, Chase Manhattan, and the Pentagon." (Huntington 1973)

If we place Nitze's and Huntington's conceptions together, we can see a distinctive kind of U.S. imperial order embracing the entire capitalist core at both ends of Eurasia. The European empires had largely covered the noncapitalist world, societies without the distinctive capitalist differentiation between a property-owning class exploiting wage labor and a separated state institution using legal-coercive mechanisms to enforce property rights. Expanding the system into these regions required some kind of colonial state. American Fordist capitalism was configured for penetrating other *advanced capitalisms,* and its political methods and requirements for restructuring the domestic political economies of other capitalisms were correspondingly different. One of the distinctive requirements of Fordist expansionism was that since Fordism was geared to mass consumption and not just sales to small middle classes, it required buoyant, expanding mass markets in other capitalist centers. It thus required these other centers to flourish as industrial growth centers. But this carried a risk:

such industrial growth could revive the political capacities of the other centers, and these political capacities could be used to generate new regional geopolitical "spheres of influence," which could then be organized independently of, and possibly antagonistically toward, U.S. international capitalist expansion. Hub-and-spokes security alliances led by the United States could enable it to directly manage and invigilate the geopolitical strategies of the other main centers, hence nullifying that political, and ultimately that capitalist, economic risk.

In this context, the Achesonian design was extraordinarily elegant because it both privileged (West) Germany and Japan as being the designated industrial hubs of their respective regions, seeking to facilitate their revival as the strongest industrial economies outside the United States, and it simultaneously ensured that these two centers would have absolutely minimal autonomy from the United States in their geopolitical orientations and even to a considerable degree in their internal orientations.

None of this is meant to suggest either that the American-Soviet antagonism was artificial as far as Washington was concerned. Such antagonism was absolutely inevitable because these two centers represented alternative, rival modernization projects. America, after all, was uniquely a business state, celebrating and accepting the worldview and values of only one class, the business class (Kolko 1976; Lindblom 1977; McCormick 1995). The American dream is one-dimensional: the core American value is freedom-defined-as-free-market opportunities leading to business success. Insofar as individual enrichment leaves a deficit in the lives of Americans, the resources of Christianities of various kinds are offered as spiritual supplements. It is thus hard to imagine an amicable cohabitation with Communism, even though both systems did emerge from some common western modernist historical source.

But such inevitable antagonism did not necessarily have to take the militarized form that emerged at the end of the 1940s. That emerged only with NSC-68 in 1950 and the thinking of its author Paul Nitze and his boss, Dean Acheson. Like Leffler (1992), some have viewed NSC-68 as merely a quantitative intensification of pre-existing trends: the anticommunism and the NATO alliance against the Soviet Union along with the containment doctrine. They point out that there was no new geopolitical orientation or new policy direction, but just intensification of what went before. But as Kennan (architect of the containment doctrine but strong opponent of the Acheson-Nitze project) saw at the time, this misses the point. The intensification turned quantity into quality. By calling for a tripling of the U.S. military budget and sweeping rearmament of the allies, it constituted a huge threat to the Soviet Bloc, impelling it to adopt the only deterrent option available to it at the time: the threat to overrun western Europe. This, in turn, bound the western European allies, utterly dependent on U.S. strategic nuclear forces, to the United States, justified an integrated military command structure, mobilized the American population for a permanent commitment of resources to U.S. world leadership, and provided the U.S. economy not only with a strongly militarized component but with a brand of military Keynesianism after the serious recession of 1949. NSC-68 also ensured that anticommunism and anti-Sovietism would become what Brzezinski has called a quasi-religious ideology of the West cementing the new U.S.-centered world order (Brzezinski 1998).

This Cold War cleavage structure transformed not only the geopolitical field but also the internal sociopolitical systems of the subordinate allies, for the cleavage was also a sociopolitical one against domestic political forces seeking to introduce state socialism or seeking to change the external alliances of the states concerned. Officially legitimate political forces within the allies were only those based upon the U.S. side of the Cold War cleavage (with Gaullism being the only sustained, though still partial, exception). This largely ensured that the domestic political systems of the allies would at a basic programmatic level want what Washington wanted. Left or right political leaders within the mainstream would quickly find if they sought to swing policy squarely against American strategy the political structure of their own domestic party and media systems would react strongly against them. Furthermore U.S. geopolitical maneuvers and thrusts against the Soviet Bloc, provided they were successful, would strengthen the parties of the right and their business-class backers against the left-oriented parties of labor. Where liberal democratic political systems could not securely achieve a stable pro-American/anticommunist based order, then U.S. power was dedicated to ensuring that liberal democracy would be modified accordingly or kept off the agenda—as in much of the north Mediterranean, from Turkey through Greece, Italy, and Spain to Portugal during much of the postwar period. This domestic sociopolitical dimension ensured that the capitalist parties and mass medias of the allies remained strongly loyal to the United States.

The Achesonian conception became the accepted consensus within the U.S. governing class. With the U.S. defeat in Vietnam and the success of Willy Brandt's Ostpolitik in the 1970s, the primacy system in Europe came under serious strain. Brandt had opened Germany's door to a new relationship with the Soviet Bloc and there were serious efforts to make the European detente "irreversible," decoupling interbloc relations in Europe from the more general superpower relationship. This raised serious concerns in Washington. With Paul Nitze coming forward again at the head of the so-called Committee on the Present Danger, a major effort was made to reestablish the Cold War cleavage on a world scale and most particularly in Europe. Raising the slogan of the danger of the Finlandization of western Europe, Washington easily drew the French and the British into its project of reining back Germany under alliance discipline through planting Pershing Missiles in the Federal Republic of Germany (FRG). Then the Reagan administration greatly intensified the cleavage, entirely destroying the European detente. In this effort, Washington could, on the whole, rely upon the loyalty of the German right and the German business class. Thus the primacy system held right up to 1989.

## The Cold War System and Political Concepts

Various terms and concepts are deployed today to try to capture the shape of the U.S.-centered system in the Cold War. One such notion is that of hegemony, another is that of grand strategy discourse, and a third empires and imperialism. Our analysis can be related to each of the debates concerning these concepts.

In some ways the most general concept is that of hegemony in the sense of a dominant capitalist state within a world-system theorists usefully call the capitalist core. The Achesonian political form is evidently one type of hegemony in this sense and not the only possible type of hegemony. But to call the Achesonian system simply a form of hegemony like other supposed hegemonies in the past is far too general: it misses the unique character of this "hegemony," in which one state effectively took over the strategic defense functions of all other core states and laid down the parameters of their domestic sociopolitical cleavages. This was historically unparalleled. Secondly, too much of the discussion about hegemony in international relations debates focuses abstractly on quantitative resource comparisons between states and fails to take account of how the United States could use its resources to configure the environments of other core states.

Neo-Gramscian concepts of hegemony are superior in their emphases on both ideational factors and the basic linkage between the ideational dimension and class and social production systems (Anderson 1977; Cox 1987). Ideational factors were crucial and so too were class factors. But too often Gramscian concepts are used in a way that conflates two quite separate issues: the capacity of the hegemonic state to consolidate a political form, and the extent to which that political form results in subsequent capitalist development or not. Class issues were central to the construction of the Achesonian system. But when that system was established, the class issues were specific and highly political: the German and Japanese capitalist classes wanted the revival of their strength and were entirely dependent upon the United States for this. The class issues for Britain had everything to do with preserving its empire; empire was also important for France along with confronting communism at home and the prospect of (American-sponsored) West German revival. By 1953, the Achesonian political system had been established and confronted all these dominant classes as an objective framework for its activities. The neo-Gramscians are right to stress that subsequently the system became developmental, as the postwar boom and Fordism took hold. U.S. capitalism was the bearer of a social development project within capitalism and this did make the Achesonian system "organic"; thus it was experienced as a "consensual" development. But this does not absolve us from the task of spelling out what the political form was.

Debates on grand strategy provide another source of concepts. In the jargon of American grand strategy, the Achesonian Cold War concept corresponds to the idea of "primacy." U.S. primacy is counterposed to other ways of organizing U.S. hegemony, such as offshore balancing—the British way in the nineteenth century vis-à-vis Europe and a way also favored by Kennan in the late 1940s (Harper 1996)—or "selective engagement," cooperative security, or indeed isolationism, which can also generate a kind of hegemony, but in a "soft power" form (Hoffman 1978; Huntington 1993; Jervis 1994; Posen and Ross 1996).

One feature of this grand strategy view is its stress on the fact that for U.S. capitalism the main potential challenge derives not from "rogue states" or from other social deviants, mainly in the South, or indeed from the Soviet Bloc countries during the Cold War, but from the other most advanced capitalist centers. This is because these centers could acquire the capital power to pull other economies under their influence, along with the technological capacities and resources for mounting serious regionalist spheres of influence and challenges, particularly if they formed regional political centers. The Cold War primacy system decisively neutralized such potential challenges when the United States took direct control over the geopolitical orientations of the other main capitalist centers and bound each of the core capitalisms to itself through hub-and-spokes arrangements, maintaining their internal fragmentation within their regions. This would not have happened if the United States had chosen to operationalize its hegemony through offshore balancing arrangements.

But the concept of primacy does not capture the territorial and formal-institutional system of U.S. power adequately. To do so, we can draw upon debates about empire. But much of the actual literature on American empire both on the right and the left does not capture the central imperial form of institutionalized security zones covering the advanced capitalist core. The left has focused above all on U.S. policies toward the South in its theories of U.S. imperialism. These policies, with their stress on regime change against dissident regimes, sometimes entailing support for brutally regressive regimes defending U.S. capitalist property, have indeed been imperialist—coercively imposing internal regimes on other states. But the programmatic core of U.S. foreign policy has not been directed toward the South; rather, it has been directed toward the capitalist core. Indeed, outside Latin America, control over the core has given the United States the jumping-off point for power projection into the rest of the South. But more importantly, the consolidated U.S. ascendancy over other core capitalisms has been at the very heart of the U.S. imperial project.

U.S. imperialism has often been described as informal. Yet this is not correct as far as the U.S. relationship to the core capitalisms is concerned. It has been formalized in juridical agreements regarding certain institutions. The forms have not been those of colonies, but those of security treaties. They legitimated the deployment of U.S. military and intelligence agencies on the territories of the allies. They enabled the United States to invigilate and effectively control the geopolitical orientations of the allies. Also, they legitimated a common effort by the United States and the state security agencies of the allies to take action both against the external enemies of the alliances and against internal threats to the given capitalist systems and their alliances with the United States.

This system then ensured that the allies did not group together or strike out individually to create their own geopolitical spheres of influence and "coprosperity." Secondly, as the protector of the core, the United States could claim the right to special privileges, for example, in the monetary field, since its economic prosperity was the basis of the defense resources of the security zones. Thirdly, political ascendancy over the core formed the basis for a series of other regimes and institutions regulating the world capitalist economy, in which the United States was able to exercise disproportionate degrees of control.

## The Collapse of the Main Foundations of U.S.-European Primacy and the U.S. Elite Consensus on the Need to Build New Ones

The Soviet Bloc collapse had many beneficial effects for the United States, but once we appreciate the specific political form of U.S. dominance within the capitalist world during the Cold War, we can equally appreciate some rather serious negative consequences of the collapse.

The most serious consequence was that the underpinnings of U.S. primacy, although retained in East Asia, almost entirely collapsed in western Europe. The security and survival of the Federal Republic of Germany no longer depended on decisions taken in Washington and Moscow. And the need for iron discipline under U.S. control in the face of the Soviet Bloc no longer applied to the other main European powers. Furthermore, as a result of these changes it was by no means obvious that the overriding governing external relationship of each of the main European powers was with Washington as opposed to with other major European players. The hub-and-spokes system of the Cold War was placed under threat: the spokes could recombine into a wheel of their own alongside the admittedly still much more powerful American wheel. The western European states might try to turn the alliance into a bicycle.

Indeed, the Reagan administration assertion of primacy in the "Second Cold War" in the early 1980s, although successful at the level of the state policies of the western European states, generated substantial opposition in the political systems of western Europe, including proliferating initiatives on both the left and the right for moves to "Europeanize" NATO both by generating a western European pillar within it and by ending its unipolar decisionmaking structure (Garton Ash 1994; Laird 1991). These would rise more strongly as the Soviet Bloc collapsed. Furthermore, the collapse opened a great opportunity in eastern Europe for western European expansion. The Cold War homogenization of political values in western European states in support of American leadership against communism also evaporated. It was by no means certain that the dominant social classes of western Europe and their main parties would construct new value systems fitting with U.S. primacy.

## *The Continued Elite Consensus for U.S. Primacy after the Soviet Bloc Collapse*

The collapse of the Soviet Bloc did not end the commitment of the United States to a world order based on primacy and hub-and-spokes security zones. Both scholarly and journalistic literature suggests that a commitment to U.S. primacy runs very deep in American state-business establishment circles (Gowan 2002b). A lengthy and detailed study in the late 1990s by Posen and Ross notes that primacy was the programmatic goal for the elder Bush administration and also a platform of the Dole candidacy (Posen and Ross 1997). But they also note that key figures among strategic thinkers associated with the Democrats also share the goal of primacy. They add that despite the presence of some opponents of primacy, notably amongst Department of Defense civilian officials, the basic direction of the Clinton administration was also that of primacy, albeit wrapped up in the language of cooperative security. National Security Adviser Anthony Lake made this very clear in his first major keynote speech on U.S. grand strategy. Lake stressed that the fundamental "feature of this era is that we are its dominant power. Those who say otherwise sell America short. ... Around the world, America's power, authority, and example provide unparalleled opportunities to lead. ... Our interests and ideals compel us not only to be engaged, but to lead." The word "lead" here is code for protectoratism. He continued: "The successor to a doctrine of containment must be a strategy of enlargement—enlargement of the world's free community of market democracies" (Lake 1993). Secretary of State Warren Christopher also left little room for doubt as to where he stood on this issue. As he declared after his retirement, "by the end of the [first Clinton] term, 'should the United States lead?' was no longer a serious question" (Christopher 1998). The Clinton NSC's chief analyst Philip Bobbitt also leaves us in no doubt about his own passionate commitment to U.S. primacy in his book *The Shield of Achilles*. Primacy was also strongly supported by Madeleine Albright and her mentor, Zbigniew Brzezinski (Brzezinski 1997).

Paul Wolfowitz, a leading architect of the contemporary doctrine of primacy, acknowledged before the second Bush administration came to office that the Clinton administration had espoused the doctrine. Wolfowitz claimed that the doctrine had by 2000 become the consensus, questioned only by Pat Buchanan on the right (Wolfowitz 2000). Wolfowitz's criticism of the Clinton administration was not that it rejected his goal of primacy (or *pax Americana*). It was that Clinton did not pursue it vigorously and boldly enough. As Wolfowitz puts it: "in reality today's consensus is facile and complacent. ... Still, one should not look a gift horse in the mouth." William Pfaff, from a different political standpoint than Wolfowitz's, nevertheless concurs on the broad consensus for primacy. He points out that Al Gore shares the same programmatic goal of U.S. primacy or unipolar hegemony as the neoconservatives (Pfaff 2001). He adds that the U.S. coalition for this programmatic goal is very wide, including the leadership of the U.S. business class.

## II. The Uses of Europeanism

The primacy challenge was exacerbated by the uses of Europeanism in the late 1980s. Europeanism is simply a spatial "container" of political identity. It can be filled with practically any sociopolitical substance and can be counterposed to almost any other sociopolitical substance. The Comintern, western European liberal imperialists, and Nazi Germany all used Europeanism, filling it with their own sociopolitical substances. Postwar western European "Europeanism" was shaped by the Truman administration, and for Washington it always presupposed U.S. political dominance. Between 1945 and 1947, the Truman administration repudiated the Europeanist banner, viewing it correctly as the banner of those in western Europe seeking to build an independent "third force" between the United States and the Soviet Union. Only as the United States assumed political leadership over western Europe through polarization against the Soviet Union did it fashion a Europeanist politics of its own. It was this American version of Europeanism that was established.

American Europeanism yoked together two quite distinct elements: one was the Europeanist banner—the idea of European unity—an inspiring form of identity politics for popular politics with the social substance of capitalism; and the other was a novel kind of political-economy machinery involving an ingenious use of international law to achieve certain political economy goals. Cold War Europeanism was a specific combination of these two elements.

### The Europeanist Banner in American Hands

From 1947 forward, Washington began using the Europeanist concept as a rallying banner for anticommunist forces and to counter the old nationalism and militarism of the European right. As the Truman administration drove to split Germany, it feared the revival of German nationalism in moves to negotiate German unity with the Soviets. Europeanism within Atlantic capitalism gave an alternative identity for West Germans. But the slogan was also important for reorganizing the anticommunist forces in France and Italy. Third, a European identity could prepare the ground for the revival of a (West) German state and its acceptance in the rest of western Europe (Beloff 1976).

But finally and no less importantly, American Europeanism was to materialize within a distinctive set of political-economy institutions that were designed both to integrate western Europe and to facilitate the expansion thereto of American capital. The creation was what became the European Economic Community (EEC).

## International Law for a New Western European Political-Economy Regime

The American institutional concept derived from the distinctive structure of western law. States are sovereign and their domestic ("municipal") law reigns supreme internally. Yet insofar as states voluntarily enter internationally binding treaties, the resulting international law trumps and overrides the state's domestic law. The consequence of this legal structure has been that states (and most paradigmatically, the United States) have historically been reluctant to enter into any binding treaties, especially treaties that constrain their room for domestic policy maneuvers. But the American idea for western European integration was to achieve just that: to cajole western European states into entering binding international treaty commitments structuring and constraining their domestic political-economy frameworks.

The first U.S. attempt at this was the Marshall Plan, using U.S. aid to tempt the western Europeans into a binding political-economy regime. But the British would have none of this and sabotaged the effort. Acheson then agreed to keep the British empire alive and give Britain an extra-European orientation, much to the satisfaction of the British. Then, he proceeded to sideline London and work through Paris to put in place his political-economy regime for western Europe. (When the British discovered what Acheson was up to with the French, they were, of course, furious, but could do nothing: they were presented with a *fait accompli* in the form of the Schuman Plan.)

In Paris, Washington had a key ally in the person of Jean Monnet, a former Wall Street banker, in charge of the French planning secretariat. This largely hidden but very close collaboration between Monnet (and others like the Belgian, Spaak) and a group of policy makers in Washington throughout the 1950s and early 1960s ensured that the United States got the political-economy regime that met its needs at that time (Winand 1993).

During the war, Washington policy makers had often focused on trade and exports in their thinking about U.S. expansion into Europe. But as Acheson and others grasped, the crucial strategy was increasingly the export of U.S. capital to Europe in the form of direct investment. The 1955 U.S.-German economic agreement laying the political-economy basis for the end of the U.S. occupation of Germany gave U.S. capital free entry into the German Federal Republic. The EEC then gave these U.S. subsidiaries based in Germany free access to the whole EEC product market. It was also agreed that U.S. capital with operations in the EEC would be treated as European—a key gain for the United States, not, of course, extended to other states such as Japan. American sacrifices in agricultural trade as a result of the Common Agricultural Policy (CAP), created in the 1960s, were a small price to pay relative to the far greater gains to American industrial capital from the EEC arrangements. Trade issues could be handled through the GATT rounds of tariff reductions.

Among U.S. policy elites, there were always conflicting emphases on how to handle this Europeanist subsystem of the U.S. primacy order. The network linked to Monnet wanted to enhance the Europeanist dimension, but others wanted to stress the "Atlantic Community" as the primary focus of institution-building, downgrading the Europeanist stress; and yet others—the "internationalists"—sought to stress the entire range of the U.S. community-under-primacy, including the centers in East Asia, above all the Japanese (Cleveland 1966; Winand 1993).

As Alan Milward has shown, the European integration efforts of the 1950s and early 1960s were also about strengthening the domestic bases of the western European states, notably through the CAP (Milward 1993). The EEC also gave West German capitalism a secure basis for strong industrial growth. Some European political forces, notably but not exclusively Gaullism in France, sought to maintain and develop a Europeanist *politics* different from the American Europeanist concept: one that sought to build Europe as a semiautonomous political center within the Atlantic Alliance. This Europeanism did not necessarily support the development of the legal-economic path laid out in the treaties of Rome. De Gaulle's confrontation with the EEC Commission in the 1960s dealt its authority a severe blow and halted its ambitious legislative plans. In addition, the language of the EEC Treaty, influenced both by American lawyers and by German economic liberals on the right, was strongly in favor of free markets and against the Keynesian statist industrial development paradigm of the 1960s and early 1970s.

In reality, the outcome of these contrasts and conflicts was a large measure of deadlock from the mid-1960s to the mid-1980s. On the one hand, the Gaullist Europeanist political project was blocked by the failure of the de Gaulle-Adenauer initiative in this direction in 1963, and the implementation of much of the promises for juridical integration contained in the 1957 treaty was also blocked.

But a number of international developments combined to impel European business and political elites to transform the EEC in the 1980s. The first was the U.S. decision to destroy any rule-based international monetary regime and establish a unipolar dollar system under unilateral U.S. management. These U.S. moves, all too reminiscent to the western Europeans of how they imposed their imperial monetary orders on their colonies (and ex-colonies), generated a determination to construct their own regional monetary shield.

The Anglo-American drive to liberalize international finance and the new Reagan trade agenda (for opening up services, public procurement, etc.) along with the strong Japanese challenge in cars and electronics—all these developments further focused the minds of western European business and political leaders in the early 1980s. And looming over everything was the Anglo-American right's insistence that Keynesian prioritizing of industrial growth and full employment had to be abandoned in favor of a new priority of targeting inflation and allowing unemployment to rise.

The crucial political shift that made the new European Union construction possible was the Mitterrand government's dramatic turn toward neoliberalism after 1983 and its decision to process the new policy strategy through a transformed

EEC (Featherstone and Dyson 1999). Mitterrand's finance minister, Jacques Delors, was then made president of the European Commission and, with the full backing of France and Germany, launched the new path for the political economies of western Europe, a path that would also radically transform the European Commission.

## The European Turn to Neoliberalism and the New European Integration Project

From 1985, when agreement was reached on the Single European Act, the states participating in "European integration" have repeatedly used the international law mechanism of treaty-amending conferences to lock each other into political and economic changes (something they had avoided for almost 30 years): first the Single European Act, then the Maastricht Treaty on European Union, then the Amsterdam Treaty, then the Nice Treaty, and finally the current Inter-Governmental Conference (IGC) to provide a "constitution" for the European Union (Moravcsik 2000).

Both the social substance and the policy mechanisms of the new drive have been "owned" by the executives of the member states, the commission, and Europe's big, internationally oriented business groups. The transformations have been controlled and directed by these elite actors from above, unconstrained by any popular democratic mandate; the EU parliamentary elections do not supply the executive leadership—the commission is appointed by the executives of member states. It has a monopoly on legislative initiatives in the EC part of the European Union, and the crucial deliberating body on legislation is the Council of Ministers (the state executives again) meeting in secret session with no minutes published. The commission interacts constantly with European business groups, who have multiple points of privileged access and who form a kind of transnational big business coalition with its own program for change. Once legislation is passed by EC institutions, it binds the member states. This machinery is thus both very powerful and lacking in secure normative foundations of liberal democratic legitimacy, with important consequences to which we will return.

The social substance of the transformation is easily summarized by the term "neoliberalism." Yet this term is vague and does not capture the complexities of the changes. It is valuable for signalling a general trend toward weakening the social power and security of labor and strengthening the power of capital. But it does not necessarily mean that the western European states have accepted the Anglo-American program for a "market state" in which the financial sector rules. Many of the institutional forms of neoliberalism are rather those of German capitalism, notably in the role of the central bank. But German capitalism remains predominantly an industrial capitalism. Thus the neoliberal turn is in substance a hybrid set of policies, albeit all converging on the weakening of labor rights.

At the same time, the new integration program is not just about the relationship between labor and capital within member states. It also has transformed other social relationships inside the European Union and between the European Union and social forces outside it. A major effort has been devoted to fostering the concentration of European capital and scale economies in European businesses. It has also made the expansion of European business operations across the European Union much easier and provided exchange rate security for such expansion. It has provided a whole battery of new protectionist and trade policy instruments to the commission, thus giving the European Union much greater clout in international economic diplomacy and much greater capacity to shape the flows between the European Union and the rest of the world. These changes in turn have also provided the European Union with a whole battery of economic statecraft instruments for use vis-à-vis the South and for potential use vis-à-vis other advanced capitalist states. In practice they have been used mostly for what we could call the purposes of soft imperialism: soft because they did not include military statecraft; imperial, because they did involve reshaping the domestic political economies of other states in the interests of EU-based capital.

What the changes have not been used for is engaging in a tough rivalry between a European capitalism and American transnational corporations. On the contrary, in practice the new arrangements accommodated U.S. economic interests and gave great benefits to U.S. companies operating in Europe. More, the whole transformation set the scene for harmonizing the political economy programs of both sides of the Atlantic in relation to the rest of the world in the 1990s: the whole trans-Atlantic "globalization" formula agreed upon between the Clinton administration and the European Union in their World Trade Organization deal. Finally, the western European business and political elites had no coherent collective program for organizing capitalism in Europe *differently* from the U.S. model. Some national leaderships had national platforms for resisting various European-wide neoliberal projects for change. But the only European-wide project for strengthening the international position of European capitalism was so-called *negative integration:* in other words, U.S.-style neoliberalism.

The new integration program changed western Europe into a genuine concert of capitalisms, in which all big international businesses in the member states gained a far greater stake in the European Union than they had at the start of the 1980s. Many strategic functions for capital accumulation have remained at the national level: above all the link between states and commercial banking (lender of last resort functions), the great bulk of tax powers and policies, budgetary resources, export policy, foreign direct investment policy, inward investment policy, research and development policy, etc. But the integration that has taken place has real significance for Europe's internal and external political economy relations.

Yet this result was full of paradoxes. It was legitimated as a drive to unite Europe politically, but without any genuine will among the owners of the project to gain that political goal, that is, a federal democracy. It produced a concert of European capitalisms with a strong and diverse set of instruments for shaping relations between western Europe and the rest of the world economy, yet these were harmonized closely with the interests of U.S. capital operating in Europe and were closely aligned both with U.S. models and with U.S. approaches to the reorganization of the world economy. As a result, the European Union became the key transmission belt for driving the new U.S. approaches to world-economy regimes across the capitalist world as a whole.

These paradoxes might seem, then, to fit with U.S. global interests. Yet Washington was evidently nervous about the development, demanding without success a seat at the table when the Single Act was being negotiated and legislated. If Washington's worries concerning the substance of policy were to prove groundless, at least up to the formation of the single currency at the end of the 1990s, it had other grounds for concern. One was that the socioeconomic basis for European unity was greatly strengthened; another was that a set of powerful instruments for European "soft imperialism" toward the South had been constructed, and some of these instruments could, in principle, be used against the United States. A further cause for anxiety was the fact that the European Council, involving heads of state and government, was playing a high-profile and increasingly important collective role in managing the European Union (despite the fact that this had not been envisaged in the original treaty) and might give itself increasing powers in international politics. Finally, the new construction was occurring in the late 1980s against a background of powerful dissatisfaction with the behavior of the Reagan administration in the second Cold War, seen by many, including European capitalist elites, as an American effort to treat western European states as simply vassals. As the Soviet Bloc crumbled, the idea of building a stronger European political role in international affairs became more pronounced and merged with the efforts to build the new European capitalist concert. Then, to cap it all off, the Soviet Bloc collapsed.

## III. U.S. Efforts to Restore Primacy in the 1990s

Even before the formal collapse of the Soviet Union in December 1991, Washington was trying to work out its path for restoring U.S. primacy over western Europe. The basic origins of the eventual open trans-Atlantic split over Iraq has lain in the efforts of Washington to rebuild its European primacy in the 1990s, the failure of these efforts, and the concurrent failure of the main western European states to mount a cohesive response to these U.S. efforts to reimpose primacy.

George H. W. Bush announced the U.S. programmatic goal rather clearly: the United States was dedicated to making Europe "whole and free." Wholeness referred to NATO. The key goal of the Bush administration during the 1989–1990 collapse was to ensure that Germany remained in the NATO security alliance. The administration then envisaged NATO eventually expanding up against the Soviet Union and, after its collapse, up against Russia. Through the newly enlarged NATO, as the central political institution of the new Europe, the United States would retain its political control over the continent. "Freedom" referred to the European Union as a free-market regime. The European Union was also to be enlarged across the continent and thereby lose its political coherence and become simply a single-market regime. The western European states, in Bush Senior's vision, should not be allowed to construct a cohesive "political identity" as a caucus within NATO.

U.S. leadership of western Europe would thus involve restructuring NATO as Europe's political center. This would involve more than just its enlargement. NATO would be restructured as Europe's political-military enforcer of a new free-market order for the East. Instead of being a Cold War defender of its western European members' territory against the Soviet Union, it must be an aggressive enforcer of the new free-market order in eastern Europe and beyond. Thus, Washington's slogan for NATO in the early 1990s was: "[Striking] Out of Area, or Out of Business!"

In this project, Washington hoped to use Britain as its Trojan horse and spoiler within the European Union as well as its adjutant in NATO. The Major government was eager, in principle, to oblige, pushing for the European Union to be no more than a single market and pushing also for NATO to be the central political institution in the new Europe. At the same time, the British were ready for feverish competition as usual with the French. The Anglo-Americans hoped to coax Germany away from the French, thus maintaining the isolation of Paris that had existed for so long during the Cold War.

But the immediate problems the first Bush administration and its successor, the Clinton administration, faced were those of derailing western Europe's attempts to manage the breakdown in Yugoslavia. On the one hand, Washington was not ready to risk its own troops on the ground in Yugoslavia to impose a solution to the crisis. But on the other hand, it was determined to ensure that the western European states' efforts to impose their own solution on Europe's most important crisis bear no fruit.

As Yugoslavia moved toward breakdown and war in the summer of 1991, the Bush administration could see that the German Foreign Office was backing Croatia's and Slovenia's drive for independence, and the French government was backing Belgrade. It thus chose to stand back from the conflict and let European divisions open wide, perhaps to the point of a proxy war between the two main western European powers. But in December, to the surprise and alarm of Washington, the western Europeans rallied around the German position: for recognizing Croatia, Slovenia, and Macedonia, but keeping the rest of Yugoslavia together (Gowan 1999b). The Bush administration responded in January and February 1992 by playing its Bosnia card: calling for an independent, unitary Bosnian state. At the same time, the Wolfowitz-Lewis-Libby Defense Policy Guidelines were leaked to the *New York Times,* indicating that the United States saw regionalist challenges to U.S. power among advanced capitalist countries as the single greatest threat to U.S. national security interests—a clear warning to the western Europeans to fall into line.

As the Bush administration well knew, the idea of an independent, unitary Bosnia was a complete nonstarter: it was a formula for civil war that was bound to be an atrocious one given the history and the social geography of Bosnia. The Bosnian Muslims were a minority within the state, though the largest minority. The Bosnian Serbs had lived since 1918 in the same state as the rest of the Serb nation and were totally opposed to being separated from them in a state dominated, presumably, by the Muslim minority. And the Bosnian Croats wanted to join Croatia. The fourth minority, those who transcended the Bosnian ethnic divisions, did not define themselves as Bosnians either, but as Yugoslavs. By calling for a unitary Bosnia when there was no Bosnian political identity, the Bush administration was plunging the country into a bloodbath (Gowan 1999c). But it was simultaneously regaining leverage over the entire Yugoslav crisis, seizing the initiative from the western Europeans.

As the Bosnian war began and deepened, the western Europeans attempted to resolve the conflict through the so-called Vance-Owen peace plan. But as the Clinton administration came into office, one of its first acts in early 1993 was to sabotage the Vance-Owen plan. It was simultaneously supplying and steering the Muslim government in Sarajevo and threatening the operations of the British- and French-led forces, operating under UN auspices in Bosnia. The Clinton administration's slogan of "lift and strike," if implemented, would have opened the way to British forces being captured and held hostage by the Bosnian Serbs.

The result of these Bosnian maneuvers by the United States was to produce a deep crisis in NATO and not least between Washington and London. The British found that their supposedly special relationship with Washington counted for nothing: their vital interests were threatened; the United States had closed down intelligence cooperation with Britain on the conflict and indeed was using its intelligence apparatus against the British there. Only by the Major government threatening to pull out of NATO altogether could it block the Clinton administration's threat to implement lift-and-strike. Anglo-American relations suffered lasting damage from this confrontation in Bosnia, leading influential players within the British state to start looking differently toward providing Europe with its own more autonomous military-political capacities.

The Clinton administration developed a powerful public diplomacy in the Bosnian war, likening the Serbs to the Nazis and likening the British, French, and other western Europeans to Chamberlain and the appeasers. On this basis, Washington sabotaged a series of western European peace attempts on the grounds that they gave too much to the Serbs. But in reality, what concerned Washington was not the detail of any deal but who imposed the deal. By finally using the Croatian army along with NATO air strikes to drive back the Bosnian Serbs, Washington gained the basis for the Dayton Agreement, which ended the war (now granting the Bosnian Serbs their own "entity," splitting Bosnia while leaving it as unviable as ever).

The confrontation between the United States and Europe over Bosnia thus resulted in a U.S. victory. The western Europeans accepted the centrality of NATO and its enlargement eastward. But simultaneously, at the Berlin North Atlantic Council of 1996, the Clinton administration found itself confronted with an organized western European caucus demanding an "identity" within NATO.

In response to this challenge, the Clinton administration persisted in its drive for hegemony, and the result was the 1999 NATO war against Yugoslavia (Gowan 2000). In this war as in the Bosnian War, Washington's basic justification was that it was serving German interests in clearing southeastern Europe of the last surviving communist leaders (Milosevic and the Serbian Socialists), who, if allowed to remain, could generate a wider backlash against the German-led drive to consolidate the transition to capitalism. This no doubt had an appeal in Berlin, yet on the other side of the ledger, Washington was simultaneously creating an extremely costly long-term mess in the western Balkans. The NATO war on Yugoslavia was viewed both in Germany and in the other capitals of western Europe as the last straw. The war was very nearly a military failure and a political catastrophe. German diplomacy played the central role in bringing it to an end, the war was declared over at an EU council meeting in Cologne (with the U.S. administration falling into line a week later), and the same Cologne meeting that ended the war announced a new European Security and Defense Policy (ESDP) with an autonomous military force and planning and command structure. This was precisely the opposite of what the Clinton administration had intended.

Yet other dimensions of the NATO war against Yugoslavia were extremely favorable to Washington. Through that war, the United States greatly strengthened its political links with state executives in eastern, central, and southeastern Europe (despite the war's great unpopularity in that region) and it began to develop its own political caucus among these states, which felt excluded from any early prospect of membership in the European Union and treated harshly by a mean-spirited EU trade regime, which lectured them on human rights issues. Furthermore, the chaotic situation in southeastern Europe required some big economic initiative on the part of the European Union to offer the region a bright future. Yet southeastern Europe could not be offered a better regime of economic links with the European Union than the other, more stable states of east central Europe. Under these conditions, the EU states finally decided that they had to move toward allowing the bulk of the east central European states into the European Union itself.

Thus, by the time George W. Bush was taking office, there was a tense standoff between the bulk of the western European states and Washington. The supposedly neat new European order of an enlarged NATO and an enlarged European Union with a clear division of labor and harmony between them was a fiction. From an American angle, NATO had a large and malign lump inside it in the form of the ESDP, and at the same time NATO's chief function for Washington was increasingly that of blocking western European autonomy and building a pro-American caucus in eastern Europe. On the other side, the European Union was committed to an enlargement that could result in its effective disintegration as a cohesive political body. Thus a new, stable political order for Europe, ostensibly achieved at an institutional level with the double enlargements, was actually further away than it had been a decade earlier, because of rising tensions at its very center. In the face of these problems, the new Bush administration was set upon a political confrontation with the western European states. This confrontational strategy has been a central element in its international policy both before and after September 11.

## IV. Western Europe Faces the U.S. Drive to Restore Primacy in the 1990s

Since the start of the 1990s, the core decisions in European international politics have remained governed by national strategies on the part of the main western European powers. The main powers, especially the French and the British, have refused to subordinate their international operations to the discipline of any EU common foreign and security policy. They have viewed the European Union, along with its various external policy instruments, as an adjunct and potentially useful support mechanism for their national strategies. The national strategies of the main western European powers have been marked both by elements of cooperation and by conflicts. In this situation it is therefore wrong to view western Europe as some kind of collective actor on the international stage.

Yet this is not the whole story, for simultaneously there has been a substantial enhancement of EU activity in the international political field; in areas where the European Union has become involved in international political issues, there has been a greatly enhanced effort at policy coordination among all the EU states, mainly organized through the strengthened machinery of the European Council. Furthermore, the actual experience of attempting to work with the United States in the post–Cold War situation, particularly the experience in the western Balkans, has tended to push the main western European powers toward attempts to strengthen their political cooperation.

The state that has most consistently favored strong foreign policy cooperation through the European Union is Germany. It has continued to try to process the bulk of its foreign policy efforts through various multilateral organizations. French elites have been divided on how to respond to this German effort. No group in France favored a strategy of polarizing Europe against the new Germany. The divide came between two other options: making France the military-political leader of Europe—in other words a European regionalist France—or making France a small world power, maneuvering freely on the global level, using its seat on the UNSC, its bomb, its African neocolonial sphere, and its capacity for military power projection. The first strategy, embraced by Mitterrand, implied a close Franco-German axis and difficult issues as to how far France would champion EU institution-building in the external field; the second option implied France would *not* prioritize its relationship with Germany. Instead France would have a more Machiavellian and nationalist policy of maneuvering with and between the

Americans, the British, and the Germans (as well as the Russians and others). This latter option was the one to which Chirac inclined.

Thus after Chirac became president in 1995, he downgraded a joint Franco-German approach and made it clear to the Clinton administration that for France to rejoin the NATO military command, two conditions had to be satisfied: western Europe had to have a greater collective voice inside NATO, and European naval forces in the Mediterranean had to have a European command structure under a European admiral. The Clinton administration trashed the French offer, claiming that Chirac wanted to have command of the U.S. Sixth Fleet. Washington's idea was that France would enter the military command in order to subvert NATO unity later, and that it was strategically better to split Germany away from France rather than France from Germany. Of course, the United States wanted total control in the Mediterranean.

After that rebuff, Chirac explored the possibilities of Anglo-French military-political cooperation as joint leaders of western Europe's power projection. After the traumatic experience of having its interests in the Bosnian conflict ignored by Washington, London was much more sympathetic to the idea of greater autonomy for western European military-political initiatives. It was also fearful of losing influence in the approaching Eurozone. So the Blair government switched directions to back the idea of constructing an autonomous western European military capacity and attaching that capacity to the European Union. The resulting St. Malo declaration of Blair and Chirac in December 1998 was swiftly followed by the NATO war against Yugoslavia, and this only strengthened the resolve in London as well as other western European capitals to develop an EU-linked ESDP. This agenda was pursued feverishly in western Europe during the NATO war, and the policy was announced as the war ended.

This switch of orientation in London was not, in fact, a dramatic break in British national strategy. London remained determined to try to be the most influential western European state with Washington, and it continued to see itself as dependent on Washington for its nuclear missiles and thus its nuclear status, its intelligence links and, indeed, its seat on the UNSC. London continued with its joint military action with Washington against Iraq throughout the 1990s. But it also knew that Washington viewed Britain as a European power and valued it primarily insofar as London had real influence in western Europe. The St. Malo declaration and British support for the ESDP were designed to enhance this British influence in Europe despite the fact that Britain would not use the euro. The British program for Europe remained more or less identical to that of Washington: to enlarge the European Union rapidly to the point of political incoherence as an independent political force and to drive through Anglo-American socioeconomic "reform" of EU member states, dismantling the European social dimension and commitment to social liberalism. These goals were as strongly backed by the Labor government as they had been by the Major government before it.

Yet the 1990s also saw a qualitatively larger role for the European Union in questions of international political as well as economic policy. One side of this development can be explained by the challenge of reshaping east central

Europe in the collective interests of western European capitalism. But another side of this development was the new pressures upon the western European states to enhance the political authority of the European Union more generally. A third element was the fact that during the Clinton administration, the European Union turned out to be a valuable collective political instrument for the western European states in a number of important policy areas. We will briefly touch on all these new developments.

## The Common EU Approach toward East Central and Eastern Europe and the South

The collapse of communism in east central Europe presented an entirely new and very large challenge to the western European states. They were determined to develop a common EU policy to try to turn east central Europe into a series of support economies for western European capitalism at whatever the cost to the eastern societies. But this would require a strong collective EU *politics* toward the East and new EU foreign policy instruments. The key new policy instruments were what we can call the "democratization and human rights" diplomatic and aid instruments. The European Union cloaked its coercive reorganization of the social structures of the East to fit the interests of its capital under the auspices of "raising" the eastern European societies and states up to "European" standards of human rights, democracy, good governance, and the rule of law. At the same time, the European Union developed an ingenious "aid" program that both garnered support among east central European intellectuals and officials (who often gained small earnings from the programs) while simultaneously providing substantial funding for western European businesses interested in extending their operations eastward. East central Europe's economic development was "theorized" as western European foreign direct investment—let western European companies and banks buy whatever they wanted in the East, fitting their bargain purchases into their existing operations in western Europe.

The human rights, democracy, and good governance diplomacy (HRDGG), although shot through with hypocrisy and implicit double standards, proved immensely successful not only in legitimating EU operations toward the East but also in enthusing the liberal intelligentsia of western Europe.[1]

## The Desire to Enhance EU Domestic Authority and Legitimacy through Its Perceived External Role

The absence of democratic will within the European Union is both its great strength (as an instrument for capitalist restructuring) and its Achilles heel. Thus the elite owners of the EU machinery have constantly sought ways of strengthening the political authority and energy of the European Union *without* taking the fatal step of democratizing it as a federation. These efforts may be viewed as akin to marketing. As in any effective marketing operation, one looks for "product differentiation" and "unique selling points" (USP).

Up until the Maastricht Treaty, Europe's USP was, of course, its social dimension and welfare state approach. But after Maastricht, a new USP obviously had to be found, since Maastricht was all about liquidating the principles of social liberalism. In fact during the 1990s, the European Union developed a new USP: that of being a champion of liberal cosmopolitan law.

This new EU political identity emerged gradually. The first key step was the launching of the European Union's HRDGG diplomacy in east central Europe. Begun in 1989 with the European Union's democracy conditional on normalizing trade relations with east central Europe, it was strengthened at the Cologne Council in 1993, with the new human rights condition leveled at the region.

The HRDGG diplomacy was then turned into an EU world policy. It was not simply a propaganda device. Although the United States could reshape the domestic political economies of the South by offering regimes their security protection, the western European states on the whole could not. But by combining in the European Union and using the HRDGG diplomacy, they could seek to ensure property rights for their capital in the South by threatening to shut target states out of the EU market on HRDGG grounds if they failed to respect the property rights of EU capital in their jurisdiction (or indeed, if they failed to open their jurisdictions to EU capital in the first place).

This transformation of the European Union into a campaigning organization for HRDGG did indeed greatly enhance its domestic authority among liberal and left-liberal constituencies within the European Union. The technique could be applied in many other areas of policy. That technique was to engage in interregional, multilateral, or bilateral diplomacy with a view toward gaining a legally binding agreement with the other party or parties. It could be in the HRDGG field or on environmentalism or a whole host of other issues from arms control to almost the entire range of economic issues. In all such cases, multilateral conference diplomacy, the field where the European Union excelled, could be used to enshrine policy in binding treaty forms, with strong subsequent invigilation of compliance. The European Union was essentially using the legal technique that had been deployed internally since 1985 on an international scale. The WTO idea, promoted by the European Union and accepted by the United States, was a breakthrough in the economic field for this method of what could be called promoting "cosmopolitan law," which did not just deal with interstate issues but went "across the border" and governed the state's internal institutional arrangements.

During the 1990s, this cosmopolitan law concept became the European Union's big political idea, generating considerable enthusiasm within the European Union and indeed beyond it and offering at the same time a global strategy for what one could call a "soft imperial" world order. The advanced capitalist countries would subordinate themselves to supranational regimes in all the sectors where they had leading positions. They would then ask the rest of the world to subordinate itself to the same legal rules. If other states did not, they could be excluded from market access. If they did, their political economies and political cultures would be penetrated by Atlantic Alliance products, services, capitals, and cultures. The days of "Westphalian" sovereignty would be declared over. Sovereignty was to be a conditional license granted by the "international community" to states with adequate HRDGG standards, judged by the same international community—essentially the G-7 states.

In line with this new strategy, all the European Union member states sought to harmonize their policies in a wide range of discrete international policy areas in order to present a common front in the conference diplomacy that blossomed in the 1990s both in UN frameworks and in other forums. Such policy coordination did not prevent the main European states from maneuvering in a purely national way in the field of power politics. But it did mark a significant new dimension of cooperative policy making for western Europe. It has real ideological significance, giving the European Union a distinct authority both internally and externally.

## Cramping the Style of the United States

The European Union's big idea was in tune with the Clinton administration's *rhetoric* on globalization, the "enlargement of market democracy" (in the phrase of Anthony Lake), and on cooperative security. But it did not chime at all well with U.S. methods of expansionism. The United States has no tradition whatsoever of subordinating itself to any international law regimes, even in the trade field: the U.S. Senate never ratified GATT, and its supposed ratification of the WTO was actually a decision for *conditional adhesion*. U.S. expansionism operates through projecting its military power, offering states and regimes protection, and in return getting the necessary doors opened to U.S. organizations. Thus, the European Union's new identity was a challenge to the whole way in which the U.S. foreign policy was configured.

It was also an ideological challenge to the United States because it suggested that the world's problems could largely be solved by multilateral legally binding agreements rather than by the exercise of U.S. military power. There cannot be the slightest doubt that the EU states quite consciously used their big idea for this purpose: to constrain the exercise of U.S. hard power.

This was most clearly and, from a U.S. perspective, most dangerously evident in the EU states' strong support for the role of the United Nations and the authority of the UNSC, albeit with an effort, which Kofi Annan backed, to modify the UN Charter's strong principle of state sovereignty. Thus although during the Cold War, Washington could expect to strong-arm its allies through NATO structures, the western Europeans started insisting that NATO should be under the discipline of the UNSC. The Clinton administration was determined to defeat this line and succeeded in doing so with the NATO attack on Yugoslavia. But what was for Washington a new beginning was viewed by the

German government and others in western Europe as something that should never be repeated. The British position on this issue of the United Nations was ambivalent and unprincipled. The British did not want to adopt U.S. agnosticism on the United Nations, but did not want to lock itself into the western European position on the UNSC either.

## The Impasse at the End of the Clinton Administration

Thus during the 1990s, in conditions in which the old U.S. primacy order in western Europe had crumbled, the western European states went some way toward attempting to renegotiate the power relations of the Atlantic Alliance. They did so with a view to constructing a new imperial partnership for the joint expansion of Atlantic capital and for the joint Atlantic government of the affairs of the capitalist world. At the same time, the social changes they created in western Europe were very favorable ones, on the whole, for the expansion of U.S. capital there. But there were two features of the European effort that were decisive for Washington. The first was that, with the possible exception of the British, the western European states were trying to subvert any attempt to re-build U.S. primacy in Europe: they were after a more collegial system. The second decisive feature for Washington was the fact that the main western European states had failed to get their act together as a cohesive force. The European rejection of primacy made vigorous U.S. action necessary. The lack of cohesion amongst the main western European states made vigorous action by the United States possible, to split the western Europeans and bring them to heel.

## The Iraq Split and the Open Euro-Atlantic Crisis

The victory of Bush in the 2000 election immediately produced a feverish struggle between the EU states and the new administration over missile defense, Kyoto, the International Criminal Court (ICC), South Korea's sunshine policy, and many other issues, not least in the arms control field. The western European states knew very well that a confrontation was in the cards, and from day one of the new administration, the fight was on. Following September 11, the Bush administration articulated its response with a view to splitting western Europe.

The Clinton administration had been building client relations with a number of east central European states, and with the European Union's decision to go for rapid enlargement after the NATO attack on Kosovo, Washington knew that it had the capacity to use these clients to paralyze the European Union, if necessary. Washington also knew that it could drag the British behind it on any major military thrust against Iraq, and it could gain support from President Aznar of Spain, with whom it had been working closely in Latin America in the 1990s, and who was eager to make Spain a member of the G-8. Berlusconi in Italy was also a product of the corrupt U.S. Cold War system and could be relied upon as a pawn.

Under such conditions, the U.S. National Security Strategy document of September 2002 presented the western European states with a stark choice: if they supported the U.S. drive for an attack on Iraq they would be accepting a line that undermined the entire normative basis of EU external policy in the 1990s; but if they rejected the attack on Iraq, the United States could split the European Union. The French and German governments along with some others opted for resistance. The United States easily lined up Britain, Spain, Italy, Poland, and other regimes in east central Europe to split the European Union. The result is that the European Union has become a terrain of geopolitical rivalry between the United States and its client states on one side and a Franco-German informal alliance on the other side. At the same time, the NATO alliance is also in crisis, with the United States using the organization to try to block the emergence of a European political center with its own military instruments.

The difficulties of the Anglo-American occupation powers in Iraq after the overthrow of the Ba'athist regime there have not ended the Euro-Atlantic conflict; they have intensified it. Thus the long interregnum since the Soviet Bloc collapse is approaching its denouement. The Bush administration seems set upon blocking the emergence of a cohesive European center within the European Union and can probably use its British client along with the Spanish and Polish states to disrupt the European construction. At the same time, it seems likely that NATO's future would also be called into question in such a crisis. France and Germany have sought to concentrate upon building a Eurozone within the European Union in which the states involved would give each other security guarantees and coordinate their policies in both the security and monetary fields. This is evidently unacceptable to Washington.

## Conclusion

The trans-Atlantic conflict of the last decade and a half is counterintuitive for just about everybody. There are immensely powerful reasons for the two sides of the Atlantic to cooperate for mutual gain and power in the world economy and in world politics. Economic integration between the two centers is great: they share similar political economy regimes, they have had a broadly overlapping approach to how to shape regulatory regimes for the world economy, and they share common concerns about maintaining Atlantic ascendancy over both the South and East Asia.

The commitment of the American governing class to rebuilding its European primacy is very strong, but the efforts of a continental coalition to resist this and to use the European Union to renegotiate the trans-Atlantic relationship flies in the face of such primacy. Many commentators assume that the shared interests of the Atlantic business classes in a joint imperial expansion internationally that imposes a new neoliberal order within Europe will dissolve this political conflict. But such an assumption of the dominance of immediate economic interests of business organizations is one-sided and may prove false.

Capitalism is often viewed as an economic system in which the capitalist classes are preoccupied only with economics and the bottom line. If this were true, the current Atlantic crisis would not exist. Yet capitalism is, in reality, a social system whose functioning depends as much upon politics as economics. Liberal thought assumes quite falsely that capitalist economics works through some sort of autonomous, market-efficiency–driven logic. This is ideological. All capitalist economics is permeated with social power relations in which politics play a central, shaping role. This is true as much in international as in domestic economics. Handling class relations in the economic field requires authoritative politics; capitalist stability thus requires that the political and the economic must be aligned. Although enormous efforts are devoted to trying to convince populations that the current project for organizing capitalist economics is the natural and only way and that politics must conform to this supposed economic necessity, such notions are, in fact, false. How economics is organized depends upon politics in capitalism.

This is the basic truth behind the American governing class's commitment to primacy. It is, at bottom, a way of ensuring that U.S. projects for organizing international economics enjoy a political framework that ensures that U.S. capitalist economics becomes international economics as such. European political and economic restructuring during the 1980s and 1990s was in most respects an effort to bring western Europe into line with the American neoliberal project by means of a major reorganization of social relations and social power through the European Union. But this required a strong political authority in western Europe, and efforts to build it coincided with the Soviet Bloc collapse to generate the Atlantic interregnum of the 1990s and the attendant conflicts within the alliance. Neither side of the Atlantic has produced a new consensual concept for organizing the political center of international capitalism. The European concept of a collegial center using cosmopolitan law and placing U.S. military power under collective discipline is unacceptable to Washington. But its only answer is the old Achesonian idea of empire-through-primacy. It therefore seems likely that Atlantic harmony will be reestablished only through a struggle to victory for one side or the other. In this struggle, the institutional forms of the Atlantic world familiar for half a century— NATO and the European Commission/European Union—will no doubt be twisted this way and that and may buckle or indeed break up.

## Note

1. At the time when diplomacy was launched, the British government was using death squads in Northern Ireland, the Spanish government was engaged in similar activity in the Basque country, and no one could seriously argue that the Italian state, led in 1989 by Andreotti, had yet managed to implement minimal rule of law standards.

# References

Anderson, Perry. 1976. "The Antinomies of Antonio Gramsci." *New Left Review* 100 (November–January): 5–78.

Beloff, Max. 1976. *The United States and the Unity of Europe.* London: Greenwood.

Bobbitt, Philip. 2002. *The Shield of Achilles: War, Peace, and the Course of History.* New York: Knopf.

Brzezinski, Zbigniew. 1997. *The Grand Chess Board.* New York: Basic Books.

Calleo, David. 2001. *Rethinking Europe's Future.* Oxford: Princeton University Press.

Christopher, Warren. 1998. *In the Stream of History: Shaping Foreign Policy for a New Era.* Palo Alto, CA: Stanford University Press.

Cleveland, Harold van B. 1966. *The Atlantic Idea and Its European Rivals.* New York: McGraw Hill.

Cox, Robert. 1987. *Production, Power, and World Order.* New York: Columbia University Press.

Cumings, Bruce. 1993. "Revisionism, Postrevisionism, or the Poverty of Theory in Diplomatic History." *Diplomatic History* 20(4): 539–569.

Featherstone, Kevin, and Kenneth Dyson. 1999. *The Road to Maastricht: Negotiating Economic and Monetary Union.* Oxford, UK: Oxford University Press.

Garton Ash, Timothy. 1994. *In Europe's Name: Germany and the Divided Continent.* London: Jonathan Cape.

Gowan, Peter. 1999a. *The Global Gamble: Washington's Faustian Bid for World Dominance.* London: Verso.

———. 1999b. *The Twisted Road to Kosovo.* London: Labour Focus on Eastern Europe.

———. 1999c. "The NATO Powers and the Balkan Tragedy." *New Left Review* 234 (March–April): 83–105.

———. 2000. "Understanding the Kosovo War." *Socialist Register 2000.* London: Merlin Press.

———. 2001. "Globalisation: Process or Policy?" Paper presented at Colloquium, Center for Social Theory and Comparative History, UCLA, June 4.

———. 2002a. "The American Campaign for Global Sovereignty." In Leo Panitsch and Colin Leys, eds., *Fighting Identities: Race, Religion, and Ethnonationalism.* London: Merlin.

———. 2002b. "11 septembre, grand jeu américain et politique internationale." *Recherches internationales* 66: 11–34.

Harper, John Lamberton. 1994. *American Visions of Europe: Franklin D. Roosevelt, George F. Kennan, and Dean Acheson.* Cambridge: Cambridge University Press.

Hoffman, Stanley. 1978. *Primacy or World Order: American Foreign Policy since the Cold War.* New York: McGraw Hill.

Huntington, Samuel P. 1973. "Transnational Organizations in World Politics." *World Politics* 25 (April): 333–368.

Huntington, Samuel. 1993. "Why Primacy Matters." *International Security* 17(4): 68–83.

Hutton, Will. 2002. *The World We're In.* London: Little and Brown.

Isaacson, Walter, and Evan Thomas. 1986. *The Wise Men: Six Friends and the World They Made.* New York: Simon and Schuster.

Jervis, Robert. 1993. "International Primacy: Is the Game Worth the Candle?" *International Security* 17(4): 52–67.

Kagan, Robert. 2002. *Of Paradise and Power: America and Europe in the New World Order.* New York: Knopf.

Kolko, Gabriel. 1976. *Main Currents in Modern American History.* New York: Harper and Row.

LaFeber, Walter. 1999. "The Tension between Democracy and Capitalism during the American Century." In Michael Hogan, ed., *Ambiguous Legacy: U.S. Foreign Relations in the "American Century."* Cambridge: Cambridge University Press.

Laird, Melvin. 1991. *The Europeanisation of the Alliance.* Boulder, CO: Westview Press.

Lake, Anthony. 1993. "From Containment to Enlargement." Speech at the School of Advanced International Studies, Johns Hopkins University, Washington DC, September 21.

———. 1996. "Laying the Foundation for a Post–Cold War World: National Security in the 21st Century." Speech to the Chicago Council on Foreign Relations, May 24.

Leffler, Melvyn P. 1992. *A Preponderance of Power.* Palo Alto, CA: Stanford University Press.

Lehmann, Nicholas. 2002. "The Next World Order." *New Yorker,* April 1: 42–48.

Lindblom, Charles. 1977. *Politics and Markets: The World's Political and Economic Systems.* New York: Basic Books.

McCormick, Thomas J. 1995. *America's Half Century: U.S. Foreign Policy in the Cold War and After.* Baltimore: Johns Hopkins University Press.

Milward, Alan. 1993. *The European Rescue of the Nation State.* London: MacMillan.

Moravcsik, Andrew. 2000. *The Choice for Europe.* London: UCL Press.

Pfaff, William. 2001. "The Question of Hegemony." *Foreign Affairs* 80(1).

Posen, Barry R., and Andrew L. Ross. 1997. "Competing Visions of U.S. Grand Strategy." *International Security* 21(3).

Rosenberg, Justin. 1994. *The Empire of Civil Society.* London: Verso.

Simonian, Haig. 1985. *The Privileged Partnership: Franco-German Relations in the European Community, 1969–1984.* Oxford: Clarendon Press.

Winand, Pascaline. 1993. *Eisenhower, Kennedy and the United States of Europe.* London: MacMillan.

Wolfers, Arnold, ed. 1959. *Alliance Policy in the Cold War.* Baltimore, MD: Johns Hopkins University Press.

Wolfowitz, Paul. 2000. "Remembering the Future." *National Interest* 59 (Spring).

Woodward, Bob. 2002. "We Will Rally the World." *Washington Post,* January 28, p. A1.

Woodward, Bob, and Dan Balz. 2002. "A Day of Anger and Grief." *Washington Post,* January 30, p. A1.

# 6

# JAPAN: SIGNS OF EMPIRE, EMPIRE OF SIGNS?

### Ravi Arvind Palat

> More than 80 percent of total Asian foreign exchange reserves amounting to U.S. $600 billion are invested largely in North America and Europe. ... It can be argued therefore that Asia is financing much of the budget deficit of developed countries, particularly the United States, but has to try hard to attract money back into the region through foreign instruments. And the volatility of foreign portfolio investments has been a major cause of disruptions to the monetary and financial systems of the Asian economies. Some have even gone so far as to say that the Asian economies are providing the funding to hedge funds in non-Asian countries to play havoc with their currencies and financial markets.
> —Joseph Yam, September 1997 (quoted in Nordhaug 2002, 25)

These observations by the chief executive of the Hong Kong Monetary Authority, in the midst of an economic crisis enveloping several East and Southeast Asian economies in 1997–1998, mark a fundamental break in relations between these economies and the United States. Since the end of World War II, a U.S. presence had been central to the economic prosperity enjoyed by economies along Asia's Pacific coasts: first as a source of aid for postwar reconstruction, and always as a high-income market for East and Southeast Asian manufacturers. Additionally, in the late 1970s, as transfers of production overseas to offset high production costs had led to an accumulation of investment funds in

Japan, the U.S. Federal Reserve's decision to raise domestic interest rates above the world average in 1979 provided Japanese corporations a lucrative opportunity to channel their surplus investment funds to the United States. If the high U.S. dollar compelled a realignment of exchange rates between the yen and the dollar in the latter half of the 1980s, these realignments provided the platform for the massive expansion of manufacturing along the Pacific coasts of Asia.

Nevertheless, as we shall see, this shift came at the expense of undermining the Japanese financial and banking structure, the weaknesses of which were fully exposed by the financial crisis of 1997–1998. As Japan sought to contain the crisis through the creation of a multilateral regional financing facility, the United States moved to block this initiative since it would imperil the U.S. ability to draw on savings from other economies. It was the U.S. success in thwarting a regional resolution to the financial crisis in the short run, along with widespread perceptions that U.S. actions had intensified the magnitude and intensity of the financial meltdown of 1997–1998,[1] which fundamentally changed geostrategic equations.

States in the region had welcomed the inclusion of the United States in regional economic and security arrangements due to their apprehensions regarding Japanese plans for regional "hegemony" and lingering tensions from unresolved post–World War II conflicts—notably in the Korean peninsula and across the Taiwan Straits. High U.S. interest rates and soaring equity prices had also been a magnet for regional economies to invest their trade surpluses in the United States. Yet, when the United States was perceived as exploiting, through its control over the International Monetary Fund (IMF), their temporary difficulties in 1997–1998 to fundamentally restructure their social and economic structures and cannibalize their corporate crown jewels, governing and business elites in the region began to rethink their reluctance to institute a formal framework for regional economic integration.

An analysis of U.S. opposition to a regional solution to the economic crisis engulfing economies in East and Southeast Asia must be located within a broader context of currency realignments, interest rate changes, and industrial restructurings on both sides of the Pacific since the U.S. government entered the market for "footloose" capital in 1979. Accordingly, the first section traces changes in competitive conditions caused by shifts in exchange and interest rates, the transborder expansion of corporate networks in East and Southeast Asia, and the concomitant decline of the developmental state in the 1980s and 1990s. It argues that although a rapid increase in overseas lending helped Japanese banks cover up their massive exposure to bad loans after the Japanese equities and real estate bubble burst in 1990, the flood of cheap credit led to an unprecedented expansion of production in East and Southeast Asia without a proportionate increase in demand. Although a regional financing facility could have stemmed the collapse from spreading, when the United States needed capital inflows to the tune of $1.5 billion every day to finance its current account deficit (Clairmont 2003), such a facility would have hampered the ability of the United States to draw upon the trade surpluses generated by Japan, China, and the "dragon" economies.

The second section then suggests that the evolution of closer trade and financial relations among East and Southeast Asian states has diminished political tensions in the region, and the emergence of China as a regional counter-weight to Japan has led to a greater willingness among states to enter into bilateral and plurilateral trade agreements. Whereas regional economic integration had hitherto been forged by the transborder expansion of corporate pro-curement and production networks, intergovernmental agreements indicate the creation of an institutional framework for economic integration along the Pacific shores of Asia. These new regional arrangements suggest the possibility of a reversal of the repatriation of trade surpluses earned by East and Southeast Asian states to the United States to fund U.S. federal deficits and to maintain its high levels of consumption. If East and Southeast Asian states reinvest their trade surpluses in the region, it could serve as an autonomous engine of growth and free them from their reliance on the United States as a market of last resort (Rajan 2003, 2639).

The United States, however, is in increasing need of capital inflow to compensate for its low rates of domestic savings and high rates of investment. President George W. Bush successfully pushed for an additional $48 billion for defense, and the U.S. military budget for 2002–2003 equaled the combined defense outlays of the next 15 biggest military powers (Achcar 2002: 75–76), along with a prior $1.4 trillion tax cut; these expenses transformed a projected cumulative $5.6 trillion federal budget surplus over 10 years when he took office to expectations in March 2002 of a $1.8 trillion deficit over the same period (Maddrick 2003). Higher federal deficits, unless counterbalanced by large capital inflows, would lead to higher interest rates and further dampen economic activity, especially when the euro and possibly the yen could emerge as alternatives to the U.S. dollar as international reserve currencies. In this context, a reorientation of capital flows across the Pacific as East and Southeast Asian states reinvest their trade surpluses in the region would undermine the fragile foundations of U.S. dominance.

## Unraveling the U.S.-Japanese Alliance

After World War II, economic reconstruction in East and Southeast Asia hinged upon a U.S.-Japanese alliance. If states in the region initially resisted U.S. plans to reconstitute them as suppliers of raw materials to, and markets for, Japanese industry, the limits imposed on import-substituting industrialization strategies by their narrow domestic markets, along with increasing labor costs in Japan and imposition of export restrictions by core states on Japan led to the emergence of a regional integration of production by the late 1960s. Since small- and medium-sized companies faced the greatest cost pressures, they spearheaded the transborder expansion of Japanese production networks. Cognizant of resentments against the Japanese for their wartime atrocities, they entered into joint-venture projects with local partners in neighboring states rather than set up wholly owned operations. Since the *sôgo shôsha,* or general trading companies, provided infrastructural support for these joint ventures and coordinated subcontracting operations for firms, Japanese enterprises could exercise control over the production processes without equity control over factories overseas. Combined with a fall in global demand, the progressive transfer of manufacturing operations overseas, including heavy and chemical industries in the early to mid-1970s, led to a sharp decline in the demand for investment funds in Japan (Gao 2001, 162–164; Hatch and Yamamura 1996, 68).

In this context, the decision by the Federal Reserve in 1979 to raise real interest rates above the world average to combat its domestic inflation was welcomed by Japanese business and government elites. Higher interest rates in the United States and the growing U.S. federal deficit accelerated the outflow of capital from Japan, and the country became the biggest international creditor by the mid-1980s. Japanese investments overseas in long-term funds (most of them in U.S. dollar-denominated assets) increased from $11 billion in 1980 to $23 billion in 1981 and had reached $130 billion by 1986—over half the $220 billion U.S. federal deficit that year (Murphy 1996, 147). Thus, one "witnessed the extraordinary spectacle of Japanese financiers providing the credit required by the U.S. government to finance its budget deficits in order to subsidize the continuing growth of Japanese exports" (Brenner 2002, 54).

As investors in Japan sought higher returns abroad, a steep rise in demand for foreign currencies depressed the value of the yen in foreign exchange markets—it fell by 23.6 percent against the greenback between the end of 1980 and the end of 1984 (Itoh 1994, 38)—and conferred an additional competitive advantage on Japanese businesses. Conversely, although the sharp hike in interest rates in the United States rolled back inflation and bolstered the dollar as world currency, it also delivered a devastating blow to U.S. manufacturing: output fell by 10 percent and investment by 8 percent between 1979 and 1982. This was followed by an additional 15 percent fall in 1983, and a 13 percent decrease in employment in manufacturing (Brenner 2002, 50–56).

Hence, however effective the strategy of high interest rates may have been in combating domestic inflation, the evisceration of the U.S. industrial sector that followed eventually compelled the Reagan administration to negotiate a realignment of exchange rates at a G-7 meeting in New York's Plaza Hotel in 1985. The revaluation of the yen under the Plaza Accord—rising from ¥238 to the U.S. dollar in September 1985 to ¥170 to the dollar in April 1986 and to ¥120 by early 1988—stimulated a fresh wave of Japanese overseas investments. In comparative terms, the Japanese share of world foreign direct investment (FDI) increased from 6 percent in 1970 to 20 percent by the late 1980s; of equities outflows from 2 percent in 1970 to 25; of bond outflows from 15 percent to 55; and of short-term bank loans from 12 to 50 percent (Pempel 1999, 67–68).

However, while the Plaza Accord shifted competitive pressures onto Japanese capital, lower U.S. interest rates also led to a diversion of capital flows away from the United States (Brenner 2002, 84). Instead, the Asian region once again became a favored destination for Japanese investments. Although higher land and labor costs meant that investment volumes in North America were larger, Japanese manufacturing investments in Asia between 1986 and 1989 "exceeded the *cumulative* total for the whole of the 1951–1985 period" (Bernard and Ravenhill 1995, 181, emphasis in the original; Pempel 1999, 67; Rodan 1989, 199–200).

The contradictions of the Plaza Accord—a low dollar and low interest rates causing inflows of capital to the United States to drop precipitously, even flowing out of the United States on a net basis during much of 1987—threatened to undermine the global financial structure. To reduce these pressures, the West German and especially the Japanese governments agreed at a G-7 summit at the Louvre in 1987 to lower their rates of interest, and financial authorities of both governments agreed to cooperate with U.S. financial authorities in stabilizing the dollar within a certain band (Brenner 2002, 84–85; Gilpin 2000, 231). Far from lowering Japanese trade surpluses, however, a reduction of interest rates at home fueled a surge in speculative activity as Japanese corporations launched a massive investment-led boom in which capital goods substituted for consumption goods and speculation in stocks and real estate substituted for export markets.

When speculation and cutbacks in industrial employment threatened to unravel the coalitions that had kept the Liberal Democratic Party continuously in power since 1955, the Bank of Japan hiked interest rates to dampen speculation. However, this caused so precipitous a drop in land and stock values—between June and December 1990, land values in Tokyo declined by 50 percent and the Nikkei index by 40 percent—as well as of the yen in currency markets, that Japanese banks were exposed to potentially devastating losses. In a bid to recoup these losses, Japanese banks increased their lending to corporations and financial institutions in East and Southeast Asia. Since Japan accounted for fully one-third of world savings—in the mid-1990s, about 60 percent of liquid household assets were in banks in Japan in contrast to about 25 percent in the United States (Passell 1997)—bankers from overseas could borrow yen at less than 1 percent interest and then lend it to banks in economies along Asia's Pacific Rim and elsewhere at 2.5 to 3 percent interest. In turn, East and Southeast Asian banks charged their domestic borrowers 8 to 10 percent interest, and thus earned themselves a tidy profit. Alternatively, investors from the region could bypass their domestic bankers and borrow directly from banks in Japan, the United States, or western Europe—although interest rates on the U.S. dollar were not as low as on the yen, at approximately 5 percent, it was still cheaper than loans in other East and Southeast Asian currencies. U.S. investors even borrowed yen at low rates of interest, converted it into dollars, and then lent the dollars across the world. "In fact," Ron Bevacqua (1998, 415) notes,

"U.S. investors borrowed, converted, and re-lent so much yen that the USA, though the world's largest debtor, became a net lender of long-term capital in the mid-1990s."

The Asian rim accounted for a disproportionate share of these capital inflows. Credit grew rapidly between 1990 and 1996: by 24 percent per annum in Thailand, by 16 percent in Malaysia, by 14 percent in Indonesia, and by 10 percent in South Korea (Fuerbringer 1997; Jayanth 1998; Uchitelle 1997a, 1997b). These states were able to tap into this cheap money from Japan, and world financial markets more generally, by offering off-the-book guarantees for loans incurred by their domestic industrial enterprises and financial institutions, pegging their currencies to the U.S. dollar, deregulating cross-border flows of capital, and liberalizing their financial sectors. This was tantamount to the wholesale liquidation of the apparatus of the developmental state as the liberalization of capital flows conferred greater priority on inflation control rather than on strategic economic planning while currency pegs constrained governments' options in macroeconomic management. Nevertheless, unlike the case of low- and middle-income economies elsewhere in the world, where highly indebted governments were steamrolled into liberalizing their financial sectors by pressure from international financial institutions and core states, deregulation in East and Southeast Asia had the support of large domestic constituencies (Moran 1991, 111).

Meanwhile, after the high dollar had led to the shedding of inefficient and unproductive plants in the U.S. manufacturing sector in the early 1980s, low domestic interest rates and a low dollar prompted new investments after 1987. From languishing at an annual average rate of just 1.3 percent between 1982 and 1990, U.S. manufacturing investment rose steeply to an average annual rate of 9.5 percent between 1993 and 1997. This spurt of new investments and the reorganization of production processes also led to an annual average increase of 4.4 percent in labor productivity between 1993 and 1997 (Brenner 2002, 76–77). This paved the way for a surge in U.S. industry precisely when a recession led to a liquidation of Japanese assets in the early 1990s and further depressed the dollar.

The continuing recession in Japan and the corresponding repatriation of dollar-denominated Japanese assets further increased the relative value of the yen and simultaneously increased upward pressures on U.S. interest rates. Since a higher yen eroded Japanese trade surpluses and made it more difficult for Japanese investors to finance U.S. budget and current account deficits, the United States government joined German and Japanese authorities in depreciating the yen in the so-called reverse Plaza Accord of 1995, and the Japanese lowered their domestic interest rates—from 1.75 percent to 1 percent in April 1995 and even lower to 0.5 percent in September—to depreciate the yen (Brenner 2002, 130–132; Murphy 2000, 41–42).

The 60 percent depreciation of the Japanese yen against the dollar between April 1995 and April 1997 once again transformed competitive conditions along Asia's Pacific coasts, and investments that had once seemed prudent now appeared "excessive" (Johnson 1998, 658; Wade 1998b, 698). The rate of growth of exports from the East and Southeast Asian economies whose currencies were pegged to the dollar declined from 20 percent in 1994 and 1995 to a mere 5 percent in 1996.[2] Although U.S. manufacturers were able to hold wages down, the rise in labor productivity did not compensate for a 6 percent average annual rise in the value of the dollar following the reverse Plaza Accord. Consequently, as export prices declined by an average of 2.6 percent in both 1996 and 1997 to flatten profit rates in the manufacturing sector, there was increased speculation in equities. Simultaneously, to maintain a high dollar, the Japanese government as well as investors from all over the world poured money into U.S. government securities. Between 1995 and 1997, investors from overseas bought $0.7 trillion in U.S. government securities—a figure that not only exceeded the total new debt issued by the U.S. Treasury during this period but also $266.2 billion of U.S. government debt previously held by U.S. residents. This torrent of cash inflows pushed down interest rates on 30-year Treasury bonds and led to a stratospheric growth in stock prices: the New York Stock Exchange index rose by 80 percent between 1994 and 1997 and the Standard and Poor index more than doubled. Indeed, by the spring of 1997, the value of U.S. stocks was greater than the value of the U.S. GDP of about $8 trillion (Brenner 2002, 135–148; Gowan 1999, 119).

Precisely when several East and Southeast Asian states were faced with increasing competitive pressures as they had pegged their currencies to the U.S. dollar, a substantial devaluation of the Chinese renminbi in 1994 aggravated the situation immensely. In this new "scissors crisis," East and Southeast Asian economies were trapped in a pincer movement: the depreciation of the yen made it impossible for them to compete in upstream products embodying high-level technology as they could not match the labor cost advantages of China, Vietnam, and other low-income economies. However, rather than scaling down their investments in manufacturing when export markets contracted, investors continued to increase their productive capacity through a further bout of debt-led industrialization.

As prices collapsed due to overproduction, and currency appreciation constrained the growth of exports, firms used to a regimen of easy credit increasingly resorted to short-term borrowing to cover their debt payments (Palat 1999). This merely compounded the problem of growing mountains of debt denominated largely in unhedged foreign currencies for highly leveraged firms, especially since rates of domestic liquidity and inflation in the Asian "miracles" was far in excess of those countries to which their currencies were pegged: by 1997, banks in Indonesia, Malaysia, the Philippines, Thailand, and Singapore had collectively run up debts of $73 billion, or about 13 percent of their joint domestic output (Brenner 1997). Eventually, when the Thai government was unable to defend the baht in July 1997, investors stampeded to liquidate their assets, overseas banks declined to rollover short-term loans, and the crisis spread across the region.

As the scope of the crisis was becoming evident, the creation of an Asian Monetary Fund (AMF) was floated at a meeting of the Association of Southeast Asian States (ASEAN) in August 1997 and strongly endorsed by the governments of Taiwan and Japan. The Japanese government proposed the creation of a regional multilateral financing facility with an initial capitalization of $100 billion at the annual meeting of the G-7 finance ministers in Hong Kong in 1997. Although there was little doubt that the creation of such a firewall would have prevented the contagion from spreading throughout the region, it was aborted due to strong opposition by the United States, other western governments, and China. The U.S. government opposed the creation of a regional financial institution not only because it would decrease U.S. influence over the liberalization of trade and finance but also because of fears that if regional central banks had financed the operations of an AMF through the sale of U.S. Treasury instruments, it would precipitously raise long-term U.S. interest rates (Johnson 1998, 658; Nordhaug 2002, 526).

From this perspective, U.S. opposition to any attempt to roll back financial liberalization in the crisis-hit Asian economies rose from the need to draw on savings in other economies to compensate for its very low domestic savings rates, and to maintain its high rates of consumption and investment (Wade and Veneroso 1998, 35–38).[3] The greater the degree of world financial integration, the greater the ability of Wall Street firms to use the dollar's role as the international reserve currency to their advantage. Since U.S. Treasury bonds offer a means to borrow money cheaply from world markets, the intermediated funds could be recycled as FDI outflows, portfolio investments, and loans at much higher rates of interest. Thus, support for the IMF packages, which used bailout funds to sustain exchange rates at unsustainable levels, allowed investors in East and Southeast Asia to convert their money into dollars and whisk it away to safe havens in the United States rather than to stem the currency hemorrhage as it was intended to do (Stiglitz 2002, 95–96).

Indeed, rising equity prices, especially of technology stocks, meant that overseas investors continued to pump money into U.S. stocks, and the stock market boom helped turn the federal deficit into a small surplus by 1998. This "irrational exuberance" of the stock market, as Alan Greenspan, chairman of the U.S. Federal Reserve, famously characterized it, magnetically attracted foreign investments, especially after the meltdown in East Asia—and the ensuing flights of capital from Latin America and Russia in 1998.[4] From accounting for just 4 percent of the total net purchases of U.S. corporate equities in 1995, private investors from overseas accounted for 25.5 percent by 1999 and for 52 percent by the first half of 2000; their share of total corporate bond purchases rose from 17 percent to 44 percent during the same period. By the first half of 2000, holdings of gross U.S. assets by overseas investors amounted to $6.7 trillion or 78 percent of U.S. GDP, and since these assets could be liquidated relatively easily, the U.S. economy was more vulnerable to capital flows than ever before (Brenner 2002, 208–209).

By inflating the value of household assets, soaring equity prices triggered a parallel expansion in consumer expenditures; on durable manufactured goods, they surged from an average annual rate of 6.5 percent between 1992 and 1997 to 12 percent between 1997 and the first half of 2000. High consumer demand and easy access to capital, due to the powerful attraction posed by equity prices in the United States, led to a sustained growth in manufacturing investments—by an annual average of 12.3 percent between 1993 and 1999, with investments disproportionately concentrated in information technology (Brenner 2002, 202–205).[5]

However, the rise of the dollar since 1995, and especially after East and Southeast Asian currencies plunged in value since 1997, provided a devastating blow to manufacturing profits in the United States. Increased capacity had been exerting a steady downward pressure on profits. In dollar terms, manufacturing prices in the world market fell by an annual average rate of 4 percent between 1995 and 2000 as a result both of rampant overproduction and of East and Southeast Asian producers selling at distress prices. The coincidence of the rise of consumer expenditures in the United States and the appreciation of the dollar also facilitated a rapid expansion of imports—and the U.S. manufacturing trade deficit increased by two and a half times between the onset in 1997 of the crisis on the Asian rim and 2000. Correspondingly, the U.S. corporate manufacturing rate fell by 20 percent during this three-year period (Brenner 2002, 204–205, 209, 214–215, 237).

Yet, propelled by continued infusions of capital by overseas investors, equity prices continued to rise in 1999 and 2000—inflows of nonresidential investments rose by 11 percent in 1999 and by an annualized rate of 14 percent in the first half of 2000—as the NASDAQ index of high-technology stocks more than doubled. Driven by returns on venture capital that reached 165 percent in 1999, net purchases of U.S. stocks by overseas investors reached a new high of $172.9 billion the following year. Although the scale and velocity of such asset-price inflation stimulated further investments, it exacerbated the problem of overproduction, and by April 2001, the utilization capacity of telecommunications networks languished at a mere 2.5 percent, leading to massive declines in stock prices of industry giants like AT&T, Sprint, and Worldcom. These declines ricocheted onto makers of telecommunications equipment— switching routers, fiber-optic cables, and so forth—as computer makers announced substantial layoffs. Nontechnology sectors had of course been plagued by overcapacity for much longer—according to Federal Reserve estimates, manufacturing plants in the United States were operating at only 73 percent of capacity in December 2001.[6] The economic slowdown, by early 2001, began to deflate the stock market bubble and the value of household-owned equities fell by 31 percent between the first quarter of 2000 and the first quarter of 2001. This steep decline was almost immediately telegraphed by a significant dampening of consumer expenditures on durable goods, which further depressed stock prices in a vicious cycle (Bello 2001; Brenner 2002, 225–226, 244–245, 249, 251–252, 256–259; Therborn 2001, 97).

If the implementation of IMF conditions had served to divert capital flows to the United States, the financial meltdown of several "high-performing" East and Southeast Asian economies revealed the full extent of problems in the Japanese banking sector and prompted the government to promote a thorough-going reform. Although Japanese banks had been able to cover up the extent of domestic nonperforming loans by lending overseas, with Japanese banks hold-ing some 37 percent of private external liabilities of the "newly industrializing economies" in Asia,[7] the collapse of East and Southeast Asian economies high-lighted their lending practices. Intense pressure from international financial organizations, western governments, and investors compelled the Japanese gov-ernment to admit that potentially bad loans held by Japanese banks was ap-proximately ¥76.7 trillion or $583 billion in January 1998—more than twice the previous estimate. By March 2001, a government report estimated that some $150 billion of this amount was fully unrecoverable (Palat 2004).

Put differently, whereas Japan alone accounted for 45 percent of the glo-bal aggregate stock of market capitalization at the end of 1987 and the United States for 30 percent, by 1999 Japan's share had shrunk to 11 percent and the U.S. share had increased to 52 percent (Clairmont 2001; Tabb 1999, 77–78). The closest contemporary parallel to the Japanese asset deflation, which the OECD estimates reduced the nation's assets by $8 trillion in the 1990s, is the parallel annihilation of Soviet assets. Japanese business debt is hovering at close to 97 percent of GDP, and even after bad debts of ¥60 trillion were written off, Japanese banks are still saddled with unrecoverable debts estimated to be worth ¥35 trillion. Despite the government launching 13 major spending packages worth a total of ¥135 trillion (Clairmont 2001; McCormack 2001, xiii), there has been no sign of an economic revival.

If Japanese governing and business elites had no incentive to continue their alliance with the United States, the Chinese leadership too realized that it had been ill-advised to block the creation of an AMF. Its opposition had been based on its apprehension of a "yen hegemony," but also because it was seeking to play by the rules of the reigning international financial order to ease China's membership into the World Trade Organization (Bowles 2002, 241). However, when no such con-cessions were made in this regard despite China maintaining its exchange rate and not succumbing to pressures to devalue the renminbi (RMB), and despite injecting a measure of stability by launching a massive infrastructural development program, Chinese leaders felt slighted. Relations between Beijing and Washington worsened when U.S. airplanes bombed the Chinese Embassy in Belgrade during the NATO assault on Yugoslavia, and they refused to accept the "wrong map" explanation proffered by the Clinton administration. The Chinese leadership was further en-raged when the U.S. House of Representatives' Cox Report in 1999 accused China of stealing U.S. nuclear weapons technology and of penetrating U.S. nuclear weap-ons laboratories. The continued "demonization" of China, Paul Bowles (2002, 242–243) plausibly suggests, convinced its leadership to look more favorably to-ward emerging forms of regional integration that excluded the United States.

If smaller economies in the region were disappointed by China's opposition to the creation of an AMF, the Chinese leadership's refusal to devalue the RMB and its willingness to accept the adverse impact on the competitiveness of Chinese exports when regional currencies were plummeting won back China much political goodwill (Wang 2000, 154–156).[8] Japanese proposals to stabilize regional currencies by creating a regional financing facility, and the perception that the IMF had acted as a "creditor cartel, not an institution sensitive to its members' needs" also tempered deep-seated suspicions of Japanese motives among smaller economies in the region (Dieter and Higgot 2000). In short, if the U.S. Federal Reserve's decision to curb inflation at home by borrowing from world currency markets had set in motion processes that led to greater regional economic integration in East and Southeast Asia, the continuing U.S. addiction to capital inflows from the region have begun to erode trans-Pacific relations.

## Emerging Forms of Regionalism

Abiding animosities against the Japanese for their colonial occupation of Korea and Taiwan and for the atrocities their forces committed against China and most of Southeast Asia during World War II, along with more than a quarter-century of U.S. aggression in the Korean peninsula and Indochina, fundamentally conditioned processes of regional integration along the Pacific coasts of Asia. By the early 1960s as postwar reconstruction proceeded apace, Japanese governing elites sought recognition as an emerging regional power. They proposed the creation of an Asian Development Bank (ADB) to promote subsidized loans to low-income states. Unlike similar institutions in other world areas—the Inter-American Development Bank or the African Development Bank, for instance—where membership was restricted to states in the region, Tokyo's proposals for the ADB included the United States sharing an equal equity position with Japan (Lincoln 2002, 206–207). This was to blunt enduring resentments in the region against Japanese aggression. After all, Japan had concluded a peace treaty with South Korea only in 1965. Japanese government and business elites launched several initiatives to institute formal mechanisms for greater regional integration and, although none of them led to an institutional form, they were important for socializing regional policy elites (Ravenhill 2002a, 229–231), and the ADB itself was too large to promote regional integration.[9] Economic integration along Asia's Pacific perimeters was achieved primarily by the transborder expansion of corporate networks and did not acquire an institutional framework. When a major initiative launched in Canberra in November 1989, the Asia-Pacific Economic Cooperation (APEC), it even eschewed a noun to describe its institutional form. Stretching from the eastern borders of Poland to the Atlantic coasts of New England, APEC was of course more of a transregional forum, and conceptions of "open regionalism" associated with it meant little more than unilateral liberalism rather than a government-directed process to construct a free trade region (Ravenhill 2002a).

The absence of an institutional mechanism to promote regional integration has meant that the Japanese found themselves at a disadvantage in negotiations over multilateral trade agreements since they had no experience in negotiating regional trade agreements, unlike the United States and the European Union, who could draw on "reams of legal text" (Bowles 2002, 247). Precisely because regional economic integration along Asia's Pacific coasts had been initiated and largely sustained by the transborder expansion of Japanese corporate networks, no regionally accepted accounting standards or protocols for the legal treatment of financial activity had evolved, and Japanese governing elites complained that international standards were nothing but American ones that would wreck Japan's unique systems of regulation.[10] In particular, unlike the case in other states, Japanese *keiretsu,* or corporate clusters, had close relationships with their "main banks," and these banks were expected to support corporate activities regardless of profitability. Credit, then, was allocated to *keiretsu* through their claims on their main banks rather than through market processes (Murphy 2000, 36).

If regional integration had been stymied by animosities against Japan and intraregional tensions stemming from the Soviet-American rivalry and the imbrication of the United States in regional security and economic arrangements, the financial crisis of 1997–1998 sharply changed perceptions concerning closer regional integration among governing elites. Responses to the financial crisis of 1997–1998 by the United States, European states, and international financial institutions prompted all states along Asia's Pacific coasts to seek a stronger institutional framework for regional economic integration. Even though its AMF initiative had been thwarted, the Japanese government announced a new initiative offering $30 billion in aid denominated in yen to the five economies most adversely affected by the financial crisis—Thailand, Indonesia, the Philippines, South Korea, and Malaysia—without the stringent conditions attached to typical IMF bailouts. In addition, the New Miyazawa initiative, as this proposal has come to be known, also pledged an additional $20 billion to Vietnam to support economic reforms (Amyx 2000, 148–149; Nordhaug 2002, 529). The Japanese Ministry of Finance also stationed officials in Thailand and Vietnam to provide assistance in the use of yen loans and overseas debt management (Bowles 2002, 240).

These beginnings suggest a significant turn away from the hitherto accepted practice in East and Southeast Asia—with the exception of the Association of South-East Asian Nations (ASEAN),[11] which remained the only free-trade agreement in the region—to pursue unilateral liberalization measures rather than discriminatory bilateral trade agreements. Japanese business and governing elites, in particular, were apprehensive that because of their extremely diverse range of export markets, negotiating bilateral or plurilateral trade agreements might make Japan vulnerable to discriminatory regional trade agreements. However, in a 1999 white paper, the Ministry of International Trade and Industry (MITI) explicitly endorsed the creation of a free trade agreement in Northeast Asia, noting that such agreements had led to an expansion of trade and investment flows in other cases such as that of the EU and NAFTA; that the reduction of tariff and commercial barriers helped prepare participating economies to become more competitive in a global economy; and that regional agreements were the building blocks of multilateral trade agreements (Ravenhill 2002b, 179–180).

Finally, at their inaugural meeting on 13 May 2000, East Asian finance ministers representing the 10 ASEAN member-states as well as China, Japan, and South Korea agreed to create a network of currency swaps. By agreeing to work toward the creation of a regional liquidity fund, they envisaged a system whereby member-states can cushion the impact of currency fluctuations by having access to some of their partners' foreign exchange reserves. By the end of 2002, central banks of ASEAN member-states, plus China, Japan, and South Korea were estimated to hold some $1.5 trillion in foreign exchange reserves out of a global total of $2.5 trillion (Beattie 2003). Even if only a fraction of this were to be available, it could easily overcome liquidity crises without having to resort to the IMF or to U.S. or European banks. Chinese membership in the currency swap network also provided a counterbalance to Japanese influence, and the Chinese central bank was also insulated against volatile exchange rate fluctuations by comprehensive controls over capital flows. Moreover, as monetary arrangements are not discriminatory toward other states, they do not attract sanctions from the WTO. China has also committed itself to creating a free trade region with ASEAN by 2010 (Eckholm and Kahn 2002). Crucially, whereas corporate networks were the main mechanisms for regional integration before the crisis of 1997–1998, intragovernmental negotiations are proving to be the driving force for the new phase of regional integration in East and Southeast Asia.

Accompanying government-directed efforts toward regional integration was a recovery of intra-Asian trade after it had collapsed in 1998. Between 1990 and 2000, intra-Asian merchandise exports grew at an annual rate of 10 percent, even after accounting for a 17 percent drop in 1998, and accounted for 48.9 percent of merchandise exports of Asian economies. North America, in contrast, accounted for only 25.6 percent of merchandise exports from Asia (World Trade Organization 2001, table III.72). Central to the growth of this intra-Asian trade was the reemergence of China as the "workshop of the world." Low wages, a virtually limitless supply of docile labor, and political stability led to a relentless inflow of FDI to China, which emerged in 2002 as the largest recipient of FDI, overtaking the United States. In comparative terms, whereas Chinese exports have doubled in just the last five years, it took ten years for Germany to double its exports in the 1960s, and seven years for Japan in the 1970s (Roberts and Kynge 2003).[12]

Although large inflows of foreign investment to China led to a loss of jobs in East and Southeast Asia in some sectors,[13] the impact of China's transformation into the workshop of the world has generally been positive for the region. For one thing, Chinese firms—mainly state-owned enterprises—have also begun expanding overseas. According to the *World Investment Report, 2002,* the top 12 Chinese transnational corporations (TNCs) controlled more than $30 billion in foreign assets and employed more than 20,000 employees in their overseas operations, which generated $30 billion in sales (Iyengar 2003). For another, there is some evidence to suggest that at least 25 percent of "foreign" cash inflows to China represent investments by its domestic firms recycled through tax havens in Hong Kong and the Caribbean back to China (Buckman 2003). This suggests that the surge in FDI inflows to China does not necessarily imply that it has come at the cost of falling inflows to other economies, even though inflows of FDI to South Korea did fall from $15.2 billion in 2000 to $9.1 billion in 2002 and Indonesia suffered an annual decline of 35 percent in 2002 (Roberts and Kynge 2003; Ward 2003). Finally, the expanded scale of manufacturing in China also led to a massive expansion of Chinese imports of raw materials and sophisticated components and capital goods. The Deutsche Bank estimates that in 2002, China imported 21 percent of the alumina traded in the world, 24 percent of zinc, 28 percent of iron ore, 17 percent of copper, and 23 percent of stainless steel (Kynge 2003).

Since 1991, bilateral trade between Southeast Asia and China has been growing at an annual rate of 20 percent, rising from $7.9 billion in 1991 to $39.5 billion in 2002 (Rajan 2003, 2639). If China's transformation into a low-cost manufacturing exporter led it to register a trade surplus with the United States of $103 billion in 2002, surpassing Japan for the first time, China also posted a $68 billion deficit with the rest of Asia as it imported raw materials and high-technology components (*Financial Times* 2003b). Moreover, since the average wage in China is approximately 20 percent of the rates in Malaysia and Taiwan, and 10 percent of that in Singapore, many of these states ship many of their products to China for final processing and packing before they are shipped to the United States. China's role in the regional division of labor thus makes it the favorite villain for the loss of manufacturing jobs in the United States—even though China's main exports are goods that the United States has not produced for decades (Swann 2003).[14] As Jim Walker, chief economist for CLSA Emerging Markets notes, "People simplistically believe there will be a giant sucking sound as China absorbs Asian economies. The reality is that for every dollar of exports, China imports 92 cents" (quoted in Crampton 2003). Whereas Asia had been Japan's largest export market since 1991, Japanese exports to Asia in the first half of 2003—led by digital cameras, plasma TVs, automobiles, and audio equipment—rose to a record high of ¥11.88 trillion (Lewis 2003).

China has in fact become an engine of growth: it has overtaken the United States to become the largest export market for Japan, South Korea, and Hong Kong. Increasing economic integration within the region is not limited to merchandise trade: Singapore, Hong Kong, and even Thailand have been focusing on banking, education, healthcare, and tourism to compensate for the loss of low-wage manufacturing jobs to China. To counteract the flight of manufacturing to China, industrial restructuring in Japan has notably revolved around the introduction of cell-based manufacturing. Developed first by Sony, this system revolves around a group of workers ("cells") being responsible for the assembly of one product, or a range of related items, and is reputed to have increased productivity by 30 percent—by so much in fact that Sony brought its camcorder production back to Japan from China in the summer of 2002. By dismantling conveyor-belt assembly lines, the shift to a cell-based system is estimated to have made redundant some 20 km of space in Canon's 54 plants and led to the closure of 20 warehouses. Unburdened with fixed conveyor belt systems dedicated to a single product, companies that manufacture by small batches of workers can adopt more flexible production plans and change their product mix more nimbly. By putting together complex products following complex manuals, rather than performing the same monotonous task, employees are said to be "invigorated" (*Financial Times* 2003a; Nakamoto 2003). Recognizing the importance of reorienting the Japanese economy toward new growth sectors, the Ministry of Economy, Trade, and Industry—the new nomenclature for MITI after it was reorganized in 2001—also proposes to spend ¥24,000 billion over the next five years on information technology, environment, biotechnology, and nanotechnology. Similarly, unemployment in South Korea has held steady at 3.3 percent despite the increasing migration of manufacturing jobs to China, suggesting that the disappearing factory jobs were being replaced by other employment opportunities (Mallet 2003; Marshall 2003; Ward 2003). Nevertheless, although concerns that the surge in FDI to China have come at the expense of other East and Southeast Asian economies are exaggerated, greater inflows of manufacturing investments to China have had a disproportionately adverse impact on low-income economies in the region, especially Indonesia and the Philippines (Rajan 2003).

At the same time, the accumulation of large trade surpluses in China, Japan, and other East and Southeast Asian states has led them to routinely intervene in currency markets to prevent their currencies from appreciating too rapidly. When capital inflows to the United States from Europe decreased after the U.S. equities bubble burst in 2000, purchases of dollars by East and Southeast Asian states have provided a large part of the capital inflows required to finance the U.S. current account deficit—estimated at $500 billion in 2002 and growing at an annual rate of 10 percent (Clairmont 2003). Between December 2001 and the end of June 2003, the combined total of U.S. Treasury notes owned by China, Hong Kong, Japan, and South Korea rose from $512 billion to $696 billion (Wiggins 2003a).[15] By allowing U.S. interest rates to remain low, these cash infusions have led to more U.S. purchases of Asian goods.

Interventions by East Asian central banks to maintain a high dollar allow the United States to finance its current account deficits, but a high dollar leads to a further transfer of manufacturing operations overseas. Although this contradiction has led the United States to demand a realignment of exchange rates, unlike in the mid-1980s when it successfully negotiated the Plaza Accord, U.S. efforts to promote a similar resolution have been hamstrung by changed conditions of production. Most obviously, without currency inflows, U.S. interest rates would have to rise substantially to compensate for its low rate of domestic savings and to finance its current account deficit. Moreover, unlike the case of Japan in the 1980s, which was largely closed to foreign investments, large FDI inflows to China imply that a revaluation of the RMB would adversely affect many U.S. corporations that use cheap Chinese labor to make products that are exported to the United States and to other markets, since it would raise their labor costs.

Conversely, for East and Southeast Asian economies, the continued purchase of U.S. securities is a double-edged sword. Although it maintains a favorable exchange rate for them in terms of the U.S. dollar, since U.S. interest rates are extremely low, it is not a very lucrative proposition. If these economies reinvest their trade surpluses in the region, it would not only undermine the U.S. economy by raising interest rates but it would also free East and Southeast Asian markets from their addiction to U.S. markets. Indeed, since the U.S. equities bubble burst in 2000, there is some indication of a reorientation of capital flows from the United States. Inflows of foreign capital to the United States have steadily decreased—falling from $307.7 billion in 2000 to $130.8 billion in 2001 and to just $30.1 billion in 2002 (Organization for Economic Cooperation and Development 2003).

Meanwhile, rapid growth in manufacturing in China has seen urban incomes increase by an annual average of 17 percent since 1998 and rural incomes by 6 percent (Crampton 2003). This rise in incomes has created a lower middle-income class—defined as people with an annual average household income of $1,200. Thus the Chinese now buy more cell phones than consumers anywhere else, more film than the Japanese, and more vehicles than the Germans. As a result, foreign companies that once used China as an export base now sell most of their China-based production in the country itself (Kahn 2003).[16] In a related trend in South Korea, after the close relations between banks and politically connected enterprises were severed by the economic meltdown, the restructured banks have pursued consumer banking. The collapse of the U.S. asset bubble since mid-2000 shifted investment strategies and contributed to a greater density in intraregional capital flows. In 2001, the region's largest credit card issuer, Visa International, increased the numbers of cards issued by 25 percent to 310 million, and the volume of sales and cash withdrawals in Asia using Visa cards grew by 44 percent to $310 billion. Increased consumer expenditure in South Korea was reflected in a more than 11 percent increase in retail sales in 2001 as household lending overtook corporate lending for the first time. The following year, South Korea's 18 commercial banks posted profits of $5 billion, an 11.4 percent increase over 2001 (Kirk 2003; Thornhill 2002; Ward 2002). Similarly, the World Bank estimates that private consumption increased at an average annual rate of 8.8 percent in China between 1990 and 2000, and although the corresponding rate in Malaysia was only 3.8, in 2000 personal consumption grew at a galloping rate of 10.7 percent.

In short, the growth of intraregional trade and the emergence of China as a regional counterweight to Japan have begun to dispel earlier concerns about forging an institutional framework for economic integration in East and South-east Asia, as perceptions that U.S. actions aggravated the impact of the 1997–1998 crisis led governing and business elites to question their continued tendency to invest their trade surpluses in the United States, especially when U.S. interest rates were low. By maintaining their currency pegs by purchasing dollars and U.S. Treasury bonds, as Hong Kong's Joseph Yam noted, they were conceding "their sovereign right over monetary policy" (quoted in Hamilton-Hart 2003, 236) to the United States. In turn, this has led to greater reinvestments within the region and to the emergence of some intergovernmental mechanisms for regional economic integration.

Moreover, as governmental negotiations have begun to undergird regional economic integration, political tensions in the region have begun to thaw and this has led to South Korea and Japan distancing themselves from U.S. foreign policy positions in the region, notably with regard to North Korea. Elected on a proengagement platform, South Korean President Kim Dae-Jung made a historic trip to Pyongyang in June 2000. His "Sunshine Policy" offered a beleaguered North Korean regime desperately needed economic assistance, and a whole range of economic, cultural, and sporting exchanges were inaugurated. These included work toward reopening the Seoul-Pyongyang railway line, which connects South Korea to Europe through the trans-Siberian railway; construction of a Special Economic Zone north of the demilitarized zone by Hyundai; and a joint tourist development project at Mount Kumgang. Despite Washington castigating North Korean President Kim Jong Il as a charter member of an "axis of evil," between 60 and 70 percent of South Koreans do not see North Korea as a threat. Both Kim Dae-Jung and his successor, Roh Moo-Hyun, have rejected the Bush administration's confrontational approach toward Pyongyang. In September 2002, the Japanese Prime Minister Koizumi Junichiro also visited Pyongyang despite opposition from Washington. In 2001, North Korea adopted sweeping economic reforms—coining *kaegon* as the Korean equivalent of *perestroika,* and according to Chinese authorities, the North Korean leadership has determined that without security guarantees from the United States and access to economic assistance, the Democratic People's Republic of Korea will face economic collapse and social chaos. It is precisely the fear that such a collapse will trigger a flood of refugees south and pose an unbearable strain on its fragile economy that has led Seoul to publicly distance itself from Washington's increasingly belligerent posture toward Pyongyang. Rather than escalating tensions, O Wonchol, the architect of South Korea's industrial transformation under President Park Chung-Hee, has proposed a peninsula-wide division of labor and resources to more optimally utilize North Korea's relative abundance of mineral resources and reserves of high-quality low-wage labor (McCormack 2002).

On another axis of regional tension, in November 2002, China reached agreement with ASEAN to prevent clashes in the South China Sea concerning the Spratly Islands and other territorial disputes (Eckholm and Kahn 2002). Finally, if the election of an opposition candidate, Chen Shui-bian, for the first time in the history of Taiwan has led to calls for a formal declaration of independence and raised tensions with China, the rapid growth of Taiwanese investments in China has also prompted leading business owners to urge Taipei to rescind the ban on their joining the National People's Congress—China's parliament—and the Chinese People's Political Consultative Conference for them to have a formal voice in mainland politics (Lague 2001).

To recapitulate, raising the U.S. domestic rate of interest above the world average in 1979 rapidly transformed the United States from the world's largest creditor nation to the world's largest debtor nation. Given the dollar's role as the international reserve currency, investors from overseas tended to keep their foreign currency reserves in dollars and dollar-denominated government securities. By thus repatriating its trade deficits and drawing on the savings of other countries, the United States could maintain its high rates of consumption, and when large inflows of foreign capital lowered domestic interest rates, it spurred a speculative surge in equity prices, which again attracted a further influx of foreign capital. Central to these capital flows were the high rates of domestic savings and high current account surpluses in Japan and subsequently in other East and Southeast Asian economies.

Although this arrangement nicely suited Japanese government and business elites initially, as indicated by their enthusiasm for *kokusaika* ("internationalization") in the early 1980s, measures to moderate the contradictions of the Plaza Accord—the large inflows of capital to the United States would lower interest rates and reverse capital flows—increasingly eroded the foundations of Japanese banking and financial structures. Pressures to liberalize trade and capital flow and accept international accounting protocols that could not accommodate the peculiarities of Japanese corporate and financial relationships, indicated by growing apprehensions about *gurobaruka* ("globalization"), compounded difficulties facing Japanese elites. Finally, when the United States blocked efforts to provide a Japanese-led regional solution to the financial crisis in 1997–1998 and thereby worsened the situation so that the United States could continue to siphon domestic savings and trade surpluses from East and Southeast Asia, Japanese government and business elites began to seek alternate regional arrangements. At the same time, the Chinese leadership had become increasingly disillusioned with their relationship with the United States, was more receptive to multilateral arrangements within East and Southeast Asia, and moved to ease economic and security tensions with Southeast Asian states. Smaller East and Southeast Asian states, feeling betrayed by the harsh conditions imposed by international financial institutions, have also welcomed the move toward greater regional integration, especially since China and Japan act as counterweights to each other. For the first time since the end of World War II, regional elites in key East and Southeast Asian states have begun to distance themselves from the United States in favor of closer intraregional ties. Channeling trade surpluses within the region rather than repatriating them to the United States implies that the United States can no longer expect to harness large inflows of foreign capital to maintain its high levels of consumption and ballooning federal deficits while continuing to enjoy low interest rates.

## Notes

1. Echoing a widespread sentiment in the region, Walden Bello (1998) observed that never before has the IMF's "connection to its principle 'stockholder' been displayed as prominently as it is today when the words of wisdom coming from U.S. Treasury Secretary Robert Rubin and IMF Managing Director Michael Camdessus have become virtually indistinguishable."

2. The impact of a rise in the value of the dollar varied by the manner in which currencies were pegged to the greenback. Thailand and Hong Kong, for instance, maintained very close pegs, while the Indonesian rupiah was allowed to trade within a 12 percent band (Strange 1998, 81).

3. In 1995, gross domestic savings in South Korea and Thailand amounted to 36 percent of their GDP, and the corresponding figure for China was 42 percent. Gross domestic savings in the United States had declined from 19 percent of GDP in 1980 to 15 percent in 1995 (Wade 1998a, 1540).

4. Between June and September 1998, funds were withdrawn from Latin American money markets at three times the rate of withdrawal from Asian and Pacific funds; Venezuela and Brazil went deeply into deficit and Argentina teetered on the verge of collapse (*Economist* 1999; Wade and Veneroso 1998, 15–18). Similarly, the Russian economy has been stricken with financial problems since August 1998.

5. Investments in computers and peripherals and software accounted for 28 percent and 15 percent respectively of the aggregate nonresidential investments between 1990 and 1999 (Brenner 2002, 234).

6. Even when factories are operating at full capacity, appearances may be deceptive. Contracts between the United Auto Workers and the U.S. automobile companies—valid until September 2003—require the automakers to pay their employees full salaries whether they are working or not. Hence, it was more economical for GM, Ford, and Chrysler to produce and sell cars at a small loss rather than to shut plants down completely. When the contracts expire, however, current estimates suggest that some 15,000 workers will be laid off—and as each job lost at a final assembly plant could lead to the loss of four jobs for part suppliers, the effects would be magnified (Pearlstein 2002).

7. Asian economies accounted for 19 percent of Japanese banks' overseas lending in 1991 and 26 percent in 1994. Additionally, Japanese banks provided about 75 percent of China's bilateral borrowings by the early 1990s (Pempel 1999, 68).

8. China was largely insulated from the financial crisis of 1997–1998 because its currency was not convertible for capital account transactions and because its economic growth was propelled by FDI inflows rather than by debt financing. However, as exports had accounted for almost 30 percent of the Chinese GDP in the 1990s, the fall in export orders from the ailing East and Southeast Asian economies caused only a 0.58 percent growth in Chinese exports in 1998 compared to a 21 percent growth the previous year. In this context, China's refusal to devalue the RMB meant that its footwear, textiles, and electronics sectors suffered substantial losses. It should be noted that Chinese currency controls were not especially effective, and in 1997 its balance of payments data indicated

$22.7 billion in "errors and omissions"; in the following year, despite a trade surplus of $30 billion and an FDI inflow of $31.4 billion, its foreign exchange reserves remained unchanged (Wang 2000, 153–154).

9. At its formation, it was composed of 34 members, including South Asian states, and it has expanded its membership in recent years to include the former Soviet Central Asian republics. Although its member-states have increased to 58 today, the parity in voting shares between Japan and the United States—13 percent each—has remained unchanged (Lincoln 2002, 207–208).

10. A former Japanese vice-minister for finance, Sakakibara Eisuke, charged that global standards are nothing but "American standards," and Kaneko Masaru argued that "by politely acceding to international accounting standards in order to make it easy for American financial industry to invest in Japanese stocks, [Japan is] working hard for the destruction of its own system" (quoted in Grimes 2000, 59).

11. Brunei, Cambodia, Indonesia, Laos, Malaysia, the Philippines, Singapore, Thailand, and Vietnam.

12. By another estimate, China's gross industrial output grew from 2.4 percent of global industrial production in 1993 to 4.7 percent in 2002. Chinese purchases of industrial products, however, also rose to 4.6 percent of world industrial production in 2002. This implies that the net increase in China's manufacturing exports amounted to only a 0.18 percent of world manufacturing production. Broken down by sectors, Chinese exports of textiles and light consumer goods recorded massive increases, and its imports of machinery and capital equipment also recorded substantial increases (Andersen 2003).

13. In 2001 alone, Malaysia's industrial center in Penang lost some 16,000 high-paying electronics jobs to China (Eckholm and Kahn 2002). The U.S. Department of Labor estimates that as a result of cheaper imports, especially from China, prices of television sets have dropped by 9 percent each year since 1998, and the price of sports equipment by 3 percent each year. Drops of this magnitude have reduced the competitiveness of U.S. manufacturers and contributed to the growth in U.S. unemployment (Legget 2002).

14. Uncharacteristically, John Taylor, undersecretary of the Treasury for International Affairs in the Bush administration, said "The share of jobs in manufacturing has been going down for 50 years, so that particular development cannot be attributed to any one country or event" (Goodman 2003).

15. At the end of June 2003, Japan owned some $442 billion worth of U.S. Treasury securities and was the largest holder, followed by the UK with $123 billion and China with $122 billion. According to Lehman Brothers, Asian economies accounted for 39 percent of global purchases of U.S. bonds, and European economies for a shade less than 43 percent (Wiggins 2003b).

16. As far as automobiles are concerned, this may reflect the fact that despite low wages, costs of production in China are among the highest in the world—as much as 20–30 percent higher than in the United States—due to a high degree of fragmentation of the supply chain, steep distribution costs, and the need to import technologically sophisticated components (Mackintosh and McGregor 2003).

# References

Achcar, Gilbert. 2002. *The Clash of Barbarians: September 11 and the Making of the New World Disorder*. New York: Monthly Review Press.

Amyx, Jennifer A. 2000. "Political Impediments to Far-Reaching Banking Reforms in Japan: Implications for Asia." In G. M. Noble and J. Ravenhill, eds., *The Asian Financial Crisis and the Architecture of Global Finance.* Cambridge: Cambridge University Press, pp. 132–151.

Andersen, Jonathan. 2003. "China Is a Force to Reckon With but Not to Fear." *Financial Times,* February 25.

Beattie, Alan. 2003. "Storing Up Trouble: Asia's Policy of Accumulating Reserves Becomes a Source of Friction with an Indebted U.S." *Financial Times,* September 24.

Bello, Walden. 1998. "What Is the IMF's Agenda for Asia?" *Focus on Trade* 22, January 27.

———. 2001. "Genoa and the Multiple Crises of Globalisation." Amsterdam: Transnational Institute.

Bernard, Mitchell, and John Ravenhill. 1995. "Beyond Product Cycles and Flying Geese: Regionalization, Hierarchy, and the Industrialization of East Asia." *World Politics* XLVII (2): 171–209.

Bevacqua, Ron. 1998. "Whither the Japanese Model? The Asian Economic Crisis and the Continuation of Cold War Politics in the Pacific Rim." *Review of International Political Economy* 1: 410–423.

Bowles, Paul. 2002. "Asia's Post-Crisis Regionalism: Bringing the State Back In, Keeping the (United) States Out." *Review of International Political Economy* 9(2): 230–256.

Bremner, Brian. 1997. "Rescuing Asia." *Business Week,* November 17.

Brenner, Robert. 2002. *The Boom and the Bubble: The U.S. in the World Economy.* London: Verso.

Buckman, Rebecca. 2003. "Exaggerating the China Threat." *Far Eastern Economic Review,* May 15.

Clairmont, Frederic F. 2001. "Implosion of Japanese Capitalism." *Economic and Political Weekly,* April 28.

———. 2003. "United States: The Debt Mountain." *Economic and Political Weekly,* February 1.

Crampton, Thomas. 2003. "A Strong China May Give Boost to Its Neighbors." *International Herald Tribune,* January 23.

Dieter, Herbert, and Richard Higgot. 2000. "East Asia Looks to Its Own Resources." *Financial Times,* May 16.

Eckholm, Eric, and Joseph Kahn. 2002. "Asia Worries about Growth of China's Economic Power." *New York Times,* November 24.

*Economist.* 1999. "Emerging Market Indicators." January 30.

*Financial Times.* 2003a. "Cell Assembly Takes the Production Line Back to the Future." September 24.

———. 2003b. "U.S. Is Main Beneficiary of China's Fixed Currency Policy, Says American Chamber of Commerce." September 26.

Fuerbringer, Jonathan. 1997. "How Asian Currencies Tumbled So Quickly." *New York Times,* December 10.

Gao, Bai. 2001. *Japan's Economic Dilemma: The Institutional Origins of Prosperity and Stagnation.* Cambridge: Cambridge University Press.

Gilpin, Robert. 2000. *The Challenge of Global Capitalism: The World Economy in the 21st Century.* Princeton, NJ: Princeton University Press.

Goodman, Peter S. 2003. "China Resists U.S. Pressure to Relax Rate for Currency." *Washington Post,* September 1.

Gowan, Peter. 1999. *The Global Gamble: Washington's Faustian Bid for World Dominance.* New York: Verso.

Grimes, William W. 2000. "Japan and Globalization: From Opportunity to Restraint." In S. S. Kim, ed., *East Asia and Globalization*. Lanham, MD: Rowman and Littlefield, pp. 55–79.

Hamilton-Hart, Natasha. 2003. "Asia's New Regionalism: Government Capacity and Cooperation in the Western Pacific." *Review of International Political Economy* 10(2): 222–245.

Hatch, Walter, and Kozo Yamamura. 1996. *Asia in Japan's Embrace: Building a Regional Production Alliance*. Cambridge: Cambridge University Press.

Itoh, Makoto. 1994. "Is the Japanese Economy in Crisis?" *Review of International Political Economy* 1(1): 29–51.

Iyengar, Jayanthi. 2003. "Wrong Turn Seen in China's Economic Roadmap." *Asia Times*, April 1.

Jayanth, V. 1998. "Currency Turmoil, a Creation of the Private Sector." *Hindu*, January 26.

Johnson, Chalmers. 1998. "Economic Crisis in East Asia: The Clash of Capitalisms." *Cambridge Journal of Economics* 22: 653–661.

Kahn, Joseph. 2003. "Made in China, Bought in China: Multinationals Succeed, Two Decades Later." *New York Times*, January 5.

Kirk, Don. 2003. "Large Banks in South Korea Report a Big Jump in Profits." *New York Times*, January 23.

Kynge, James. 2003. "Chronic Overinvestment, Excess Supply, and Endemic Corruption: Can China Keep Its Booming Economy on Track?" *Financial Times*, September 23.

Lague, David. 2001. "Money Speaks." *Far Eastern Economic Review*, CLXIV (33): 24.

Legget, Karby. 2002. "The World's Factory Floor." *Wall Street Journal*, November 10.

Lewis, Leo. 2003. "Chinese Prosperity Holds Key to Return of the Good Times in Land of the Rising Sun." *Financial Times*, August 23.

Lincoln, Edward J. 2002. "The Asian Development Bank: Time to Wind It Up?" In M. Beeson, ed., *Reconfiguring East Asia: Regional Institutions and Organizations after the Crisis*. London: Routledge/Curzon, pp. 205–225.

Mackintosh, James, and Richard McGregor. 2003. "A Leap over the Cliff: Are the Big Profits to Be Made in China Blinding Foreign Carmakers to the Risks Ahead?" *Financial Times*, August 25.

Madrick, Jeff. 2003. "A Deficit, Any Way It Is Sliced." *New York Times*, April 17.

Mallet, Victor. 2003. "'You See More Chinese Goods in India, Indians Working in Tokyo or Kuala Lumpur—Flows of People and Ideas.'" *Financial Times*, September 25.

Marshall, Tyler. 2003. "Asia Benefits from China's Shopping Spree." *Los Angeles Times*, September 1.

McCormack, Gavan. 2001. *The Emptiness of Japanese Affluence*. Armonk, NY: M. E. Sharpe.

———. 2002. "North Korea in the Vice." *New Left Review* 2/18 (Nov.–Dec.): 5–27.

Moran, Michael. 1991. *The Politics of the Financial Services Revolution: The USA, UK, and Japan*. London: Macmillan.

Murphy, R. Taggart. 1996. *The Weight of the Yen: How Denial Imperils America's Future and Ruins an Alliance*. New York: W. W. Norton.

———. 2000. "Japan's Economic Crisis." *New Left Review* 2/1 (Jan.–Feb.): 25–52.

Nakamoto, Michiyo. 2003. "A Speedier Route from Order to Camcorder." *Financial Times*, February 12.

Nordhaug, Kristen. 2002. "The Political Economy of the Dollar and the Yen in East Asia." *Journal of Contemporary Asia* 32(3): 517–535.

Organization for Economic Cooperation and Development. 2003. *Trends and Recent Developments in Foreign Direct Investment*. Paris: OECD.

Palat, Ravi Arvind. 1999. "Miracles of the Day Before? The Great Asian Meltdown and the Changing World-Economy." *Development and Society* 28(1): 1–47.
———. 2004. *Capitalist Restructuring and the Pacific Rim.* New York: Routledge.
Passell, Peter. 1997. "Asian Tigers May Falter, but Japan Lion Is the Worry." *New York Times,* November 13.
Pearlstein, Steven. 2002. "Too Much Supply, Too Little Demand: Businesses Have Few Incentives to Expand or Hire, Economists Say," *Washington Post,* August 25.
Pempel, T. J. 1999. "Regional Ups, Regional Downs." In T. J. Pempel, ed. *The Politics of the Asian Economic Crisis.* Ithaca, NY: Cornell University Press, pp. 62–78.
Rajan, Ramkishen. 2003. "Emergence of China as an Economic Power: What Does It Imply for South-East Asia?" *Economic and Political Weekly,* June 28: 2639–2643.
Ravenhill, John. 2002a. "Institutional Evolution at the Trans-Regional Level: APEC and the Promotion of Liberalisation." In M. Beeson, ed., *Reconfiguring East Asia: Regional Institutions and Organizations after the Crisis.* London: Routledge/Curzon, pp. 227–246.
———. 2002b. "A Three Bloc World? The New East Asian Regionalism." *International Relations of the Asia-Pacific* 2(2): 167–195.
Roberts, Dan, and James Kynge. 2003. "The New Workshop of the World." *Financial Times,* February 3.
Rodan, Garry. 1989. *The Political Economy of Singapore's Industrialization: National State and International Capital.* Kuala Lumpur: Forum.
Stiglitz, Joseph E. 2002. *Globalization and Its Discontents.* New York: W. W. Norton.
Strange, Susan. 1998. *Mad Money: When Markets Outgrow Governments.* Ann Arbor: University of Michigan Press.
Swann, Christopher. 2003. "Weak Renminbi Is Both Boon and Bane for the U.S. Foreign Exchange." *Financial Times,* July 26.
Tabb, William K. 1999. "The End of the Japanese Postwar System." *Monthly Review* LI (3): 71–80.
Therborn, Goran. 2001. "Into the 21st Century: The New Parameters of Global Politics." *New Left Review* 2/10 (July–Aug.): 87–110.
Thornhill, John. 2002. "Asia Awakes." *Financial Times,* April 1.
Uchitelle, Louis. 1997a. "Borrowing Asia's Trouble." *New York Times,* December 28.
———. 1997b. "Global Good Times, Meet the Global Glut." *New York Times,* November 16.
Wade, Robert. 1998a. "The Asian Debt-and-Development Crisis of 1997–?: Causes and Consequences." *World Development* 26(8): 1535–1553.
———. 1998b. "From 'Miracle' to 'Cronyism': Explaining the Great Asian Slump." *Cambridge Journal of Economics* 22(6): 693–706.
Wade, Robert, and Frank Veneroso. 1998. "The Gathering World Slump and the Battle over Capital Controls." *New Left Review* 231 (September–October): 13–42.
Wang, Hongying. 2000. "Dangers and Opportunities: The Implications of the Asian Financial Crisis." In G. M. Noble and J. Ravenhill, eds., *The Asian Financial Crisis and the Architecture of Global Finance.* Cambridge: Cambridge University Press, pp. 152–169.
Ward, Andrew. 2002. "Shoppers Turn South Korea's Economy Around." *Financial Times,* August 9.
———. 2003. "South Korea Feels the Chill in China's Growing Shadow." *Financial Times,* September 25.
Wiggins, Jenny. 2003a. "Asian Debt Withdrawal Threat to U.S. Deficit." *Financial Times,* September 7.

————. 2003b. "U.S. Bonds Face Gloomier Future as Selling Continues to Increase." *Financial Times,* September 7.

World Trade Organization. 2001. *International Trade Statistics, 2001.* Geneva: World Trade Organization.

# 7

# RISING INTRA-CORE RIVALRY AND THE U.S. TURN TOWARD EAST ASIA

## John Gulick

Since the demise of the Soviet Union more than a decade ago, the world-systemic primacy of the United States has rested on two pillars—the exceptional status of the dollar in global monetary arrangements, credit markets, and trade transactions (Calleo 2001, 217–218; Hudson 2003, 1–35; Liu 2002), and the absolute supremacy of the U.S. military (Dapice 2003; Lieven 2003).[1] At first blush, there appears to be a lack of historical parallelism in such a claim. On the one hand, the *de facto* dollar standard predates the Soviet collapse by roughly 20 years. On the other hand, the total superiority of the U.S. military did not come to pass until the Soviet collapse itself, of which it was basically an automatic outcome. However, the demise of the Soviet Union not only re-sulted, by default, in the radically unmatched ability of the United States to exercise military force across the globe. It also enabled the United States to push ahead more intensively with reconfiguring the world-economy in a man-ner that allows it to extract disproportionate advantages from its seigniorage privileges ("financial globalization"), a process that initially gained momentum at least a decade before the Soviet collapse (Gowan 1999). Between the late 1970s and late 1980s, the Federal Reserve and Treasury Department had begun to perfect the craft of alternatively swinging the dollar up and down to cover the U.S. annual balance of payment deficits and to extort U.S.- and market-friendly concessions from the South, and to a lesser degree, the North. When the Soviet Union met its end in the early 1990s, additional room was cleared for the United States to reshape global finance in the dual interest of monetizing the considerable debt it owes to other regions of the core and opening overseas markets to the penetration of U.S.-based capital, and few states had the wherewithal to resist this sea-change.

In this chapter I advance two interlinked propositions, both of which concern emergent contours of intra-core rivalry and alliance in the world-system. The first proposition is that the leading powers of the European Union (EU) pose the most salient immediate threat to the sustenance of U.S. hegemony. The basis for this assertion is that the rise of the euro presents a clear and imminent danger to the aforementioned *de facto* dollar standard. The second proposition is that the United States, fearing that it cannot sufficiently polarize the constituent members of the European Union to subvert the challenge the euro poses to the dollar's dominance, does and will continue to pressure the leading centers of East Asian liquidity and growth, Japan and China, to restructure their economies in a fashion subtly tailored to the prolongation of U.S. hegemony. Durable historic antagonisms between and the consequent inability of Japan and China to form a genuinely autonomous partnership regarding regional trade, investment, and security matters make this strategy attractive to Washington, and its appeal should become more evident over time. I conclude by briefly speculating about the effects of China's increasing integration into global circuits of trade, investment, and finance. To the extent that the United States attempts to prolong its world-systemic primacy by steering to its advantage China's deepening reintegration, the fate of its hegemonic status largely hinges on Beijing's capacity to transcend myriad ecological, social, and political shocks resulting from this same involvement. In the medium to long run, environmental degradation and natural resource bottlenecks, rising peasant and worker unrest, and loss of central government legitimacy and control will appear as insuperable contradictions of China's incorporation into the world-economy. These contradictions, rather than the strengthening of EU economic power and the eventual attainment of EU defense independence, will prove to be the greatest accelerator of U.S. hegemonic decline.

# I. The Two Pillars of U.S. Hegemony

Although over the course of the last decade and a half the two pillars of U.S. hegemony have girded one another, the nature of the symbiotic relationship between the two has shifted since the Bush administration took office in early 2001. During the 1990s, the dollar was the principal weapon the United States used to defend its hegemony, with its absolute military supremacy playing a secondary yet indispensable role. With the spectacular puncturing of first the NASDAQ and then the Dow Jones bubbles in 2000–2001, and the seizure of the so-called national security apparatus by the Bush administration hawks, the Pentagon came to displace the Treasury Department as the command center of a wounded and dangerous U.S. imperium. Despite the bellicose nature of the Bush administration's foreign policy, however, the reversal of relations between the dollar and the military as instruments of U.S. hegemonic defense did not represent a fundamental break with the dyadic equation of the preceding 10 years (Tabb 2003). Rather, the Wall Street meltdown necessitated that the United States depend more heavily on sheer force and intimidation in support of its imperiled hegemony, including support of the seigniorage privileges threatened by the very same Wall Street meltdown.

During the closing decades of the century, the United States, under the mystifying banner of "globalization," deployed dollar dominance to simultaneously appropriate the capital resources of its erstwhile junior partners in western Europe and East Asia and squeeze dry the peoples (and what was left of the bourgeoisies) of the South (Amin 2003, 19). This process was achieved through a combination of consensual and coercive domination, with a heavy accent on the former, especially when applied to putative allies of the United States in the core. For a host of interlocking reasons, the junior partners-cum-competitors essentially balked at challenging U.S. monetary-financial predation, continuing to convert their considerable balance of payment surfeits into dollar-denominated liquid assets (most notably U.S. government bonds), as a result of which they presided over feeble economic performance at home (Amin 2003; Hudson 2003; Liu 2002). Hence, subscription to the *de facto* dollar standard allowed them to make use of the resultant sluggish growth rate as a lever to wrench marginal reforms from partisans of the corporatist welfare state and employ market-friendly measures to revamp their allegedly outmoded economies (Calleo 2001, 169, 180; Gowan 2003, 41, 43). They also went along because they did not have the capacity, imagination, or conviction to forge an agreement between their business and labor constituencies to embark on regional reflation (Amin 2003). Last but not least, the would-be rivals capitulated to U.S. monetary-financial machinations in part because they were unable or unwilling to fully cut themselves loose from the antiquated Cold War security pacts to which they had been tethered since the late 1940s and early 1950s. Regardless of whether post-Soviet threats to their tranquility were real or imagined, as long as western Europe and East Asia remained wedded to military alliances dominated by U.S. decisionmakers, hardware, and troops, they could not boldly confront the dollar's preeminence as store of value, instrument of credit, and means of payment.

As the *de facto* dollar standard allowed the United States to run perennially massive current account deficits *vis-à-vis* its western European and East Asian partners without suffering through economic contractions, it also enabled New York, far more than other centers of world finance such as Frankfurt or Tokyo, to reap disproportionate gains from structural adjustment policies undertaken by (or imposed upon) most members of the former Soviet Bloc and the South

(Gowan 1999). The Treasury Department had virtually controlling authority over the IMF (and less so the World Bank), thus ensuring that the privatization of state-owned assets, the opening of new markets, the liberalization of financial sectors, the awarding of public works contracts, and so on would tendentiously favor American rather than western European or East Asian capitalist interests. Also, debt payments collected by the banks, multilateral and private, that followed in their wake were usually denominated in dollars: that is, the austerity-related hardships borne by the world's majority helped to prop up a specifically *U.S.* hegemony (Hudson 2003).

During the 1990s, very rarely did the U.S. military play or need to play a direct role in the plunder of the South. With very few and partial exceptions, all semiperipheral and peripheral states large enough or geostrategically important enough for the United States to care about gravitated toward rather than away from the Washington Consensus. The reasons for this are legion and differ by continent, region, and country. Most notably, the fall of the Soviet Union eliminated from the scene the foremost patron of regimes who attempted to resist participation in the world-system on corporate capital's terms. Equally if not more crucially, the ignominious collapse of the Eastern Bloc delegitimated developmental models of the postwar period. Furthermore, the fall of the Soviet Union put an end to U.S. tolerance of client regimes that were formerly allowed to flout the ground rules of the world-economy in exchange for their service as Cold War dependencies.

Whether by dint of economic compulsion, ideological conviction, or loss of geopolitical client status, in the 1990s almost all semiperipheral and peripheral states of consequence adopted or moved toward adopting policies pleasing to the IMF, the U.S. Treasury Department, and Wall Street. The ultimate fate of those very few that did contravene the Washington Consensus, whatever their respective political colorings, revealed the underlying symbiotic relationship between "globalization" and the U.S. diplomatic-military apparatus for what it truly was; it also revealed the tangible linkage between U.S. hostility toward renegade sovereigns in the South as well as its attempts to rein in, and remain the overlord of, potential rivals in the North. Consider the case of the United States placing sanctions not only on the "rogue states" of Cuba, Iran, and Libya but also on non–U.S. transnational corporations (TNCs) and overseas affiliates of U.S. TNCs that conducted business with these outlawed states (a policy that flagrantly violated bedrock principles of international law). This policy was simultaneously aimed at two targets: (1) those lingering states of geostrategic or political importance in the South—be they statist, Islamist, or Arab nationalist—that had refused to reshape their economies in the image preferred by the U.S.-dominated multilateral banks and Wall Street (Gindin 2003, 119); and (2) rivals in the North, especially EU member states, that were trying to strengthen themselves at the expense of the United States by initiating and deepening trade and investment ties with the aforementioned "rogue states" (Gowan 2003; Shalom 1999, 33–39). A second example, broadly if not precisely similar, would be the two U.S.-led military interventions in the highly geostrategic Balkan Peninsula. In dubiously and infamously asserting that U.S. firepower (especially long-range airpower) was "indispensable" to assuring civil and interstate peace, the United States also assured that a region not yet fully remade along market-friendly lines would so be remade, but not in a way unduly favorable to EU—although unfavorable to U.S.—capital.

Because it firmly laid the conceptual foundation for U.S.-led military intervention in the name of protecting the human rights of a politically oppressed people—identical to one premise the Bush administration supplied for invading and occupying Iraq—NATO's 1999 incursion into Kosovo and Serbia is an excellent jumping off point for quickly dissecting the tactical differences and strategic continuities between the foreign policies of the Clinton and Bush administrations. Compared to that of Clinton, the foreign policy of the Bush team undeniably puts a heavier stress on the use of military force and more flagrantly disregards the preferences of its erstwhile allies in the core (Tabb 2003). But the changes in foreign policy adopted by the Bush administration reflect the exigencies imposed by the shrinkage of the securities and dollar bubbles, and the possibilities opened up by the attacks of September 11, rather than a realignment of the U.S. security state's overarching objectives and guiding strategies (Calleo 2001, 375; Gowan 2003, 48).

Both before and during the present administration's term in office, one of the means the United States has employed in pursuit of this end is a specific type of military intervention conducted in selective locales outside the capitalist core but ultimately aimed at nominal allies and potential rivals of the United States within it. Both NATO's aerial assault on Serbia and the Anglo-American invasion and occupation of Iraq involved the United States marshalling a threadbare coalition subordinated to U.S. military planning and execution. Both missions targeted a region or state sharing two characteristics: global geostrategic significance in intra-core rivalry. They were designed to yield results that would circumscribe western Europe and East Asia's room for maneuver in world politics and would bolster the instruments of U.S. hegemony. By preempting truly consultative and cooperative intra-core solutions to reputed human rights abuses and security problems in geostrategically significant "trouble zones" outside the North, the United States tried to deny its potential rivals independent political influence over pivotal areas outside the core and thus reinforce their dependence upon U.S. power.

In sum, what most distinguishes Bush's foreign policy from that of Clinton is the world-historic conjuncture in which it has been enacted rather than the programmatic vision upon which it is founded. During Clinton's second term, the European Union, seeking to forge a distinctive identity in the realm of global governance, had emerged as a strong champion of international law, in muted opposition toward the U.S. tendency toward "creeping unilateralism" (Calleo 2001, 375–376; Gowan 2003, 45). This latent rift between the United States and the European Union did not evolve into naked polarization until

Bush took the seat of the White House, but again, this naked polarization owed more to the rapidly changing world-historic context than anything else. The pivotal events in this changing context were the popping of the U.S. stock market bubble in 2000–2001, and the events of September 11, 2001. By compelling non-European states to at least consider shifting some of their central bank currency reserves from dollars to euros, the former event jeopardized U.S. seigniorage privileges. By awarding the Bush administration *carte blanche* to administer military strikes in broad swathes of the South—especially West and Central Asia—the latter event created the opportunity for the United States to defend its slipping seigniorage privileges by means of unilateral aggression.

In and of itself, the rise of the euro does not threaten U.S. hegemony, because U.S.–based companies can take advantage of the dollar-euro adjustment to increase their sales in Europe and elsewhere, as they have periodically done since the Bretton Woods monetary arrangements were effectively abandoned in the early 1970s. What disturbs Washington are the medium- and long-range political consequences of dollar devaluation and euro revaluation. The cascading expectation of lower relative returns on dollar-denominated assets might prompt central banks the world over to cease investing their reserves in dollar-denominated assets, setting off an uncontrollable, self-reinforcing cycle of reserve currency repositioning and dollar devaluation (Henderson 2003; Sommers 2003). Fearing loss of export markets and subsequent stagnation, the European Union might also respond to the secular elevation of the euro by scrapping the fiscal strictures of the Stability and Growth Pact. Furthermore, insofar as the elevation of the euro generates increasing momentum toward an EU-centered growth strategy, it also generates increasing momentum toward the development of stronger federal institutions and political unity in the European Union (Calleo 2001, 205–206, 330).

In other words, compounding worries about the medium- and long-range political consequences of dollar-euro adjustment spurred the United States to make good on one long-standing plank of its post–Cold War foreign policy: to stem a regional challenge to its world-systemic primacy by wielding military force, if necessary. Reacting to the bursting of the Wall Street bubble and capitalizing upon the events of September 11, the United States brushed off most of its nominal allies and potential rivals, and invaded and occupied Iraq, in part to strangle in its cradle the euro threat to the *de facto* dollar standard, and more importantly the empowering of an economically and politically autonomous European Union that would conceivably follow from it (Mayer 2003). The United States hoped that the installation of a pliable client regime in post-Ba'athist Iraq would neutralize the euro threat and prop up the *de facto* dollar standard in myriad ways. Two (and only two) mechanisms by which this might plausibly be accomplished include (1) using influence over the output and pricing of Iraqi oil to discipline OPEC members and ensure that they continue accepting only dollars as means of payment and continue depositing receipts in dollar-denominated accounts (Ferguson and Johnson 2002; Gowan 2003, 40; Judis 2003); and (2) using fortified control over the Middle East in general and over Persian Gulf oil in particular as a strategic lever against East Asian oil-importing states that have toyed with diversifying their currency reserves as well as against oil-importing members of the European Union itself (Escobar 2002; Parenti 2003). In the sections that follow, I will elaborate on my argument as to how and why the European Union constitutes the most immediate and significant threat to the world-systemic primacy of the United States; explore how the United States might counter the EU challenge by turning to East Asia, irrespective of how its imperial exploits in the Middle East pan out; and speculate about why U.S. attempts to harness East Asian, especially Chinese, development to the prolongation of its hegemony might be doomed to failure.

## II. The EU Challenge to U.S. World-Systemic Primacy

An article of faith among critical scholars of international relations is that the tearing down of the Berlin Wall and the fall of the Soviet Union presented a massive dilemma for Washington. Absent the Soviet threat, by what rationales and means could the United States now keep its junior partners in Europe on a short leash and ensure that the consolidation of the European Union would not lead to an eventual challenge to U.S. hegemony? The hawks who rule the roost in the Pentagon today had formulated an answer as early as 1992, an answer that became public when a draft of the Defense Planning Guidance document was leaked: to continue to tether the economic heartland of the European Union to U.S.-dominated security arrangements, most obviously NATO (Gibbs 2001). Washington was preoccupied with blunting Franco-German moves toward establishing EU defense independence not so much because it feared that the gaping difference between American and European military strength would eventually be closed. Rather, it was more concerned that a European heartland not locked into a U.S.-dominated security structure would be afforded more free play in matters pertaining to North-North and North-South relations. That the euro might rival the dollar as "world money," putting an end to considerable U.S. seigniorage privileges, was a matter of cardinal import to policymakers in Washington throughout the early 1990s as they crafted plans to stave off EU defense independence (Calleo 2001, 380; Gibbs 2001). However, in the early 1990s, the euro threat was more imagined than real. During the first half of the decade, the adoption of the euro was several years away and its career uncertain (given the budgetary lack of discipline of several EU member states). Also, there was relative improvement in U.S. economic performance. During the second half of the decade, the United States became such a giant magnet for transnational portfolio investment flows, and the euro performed pitifully at its debut. So the issue of the euro remained at a low boil. The issue that did headline trans-Atlantic relations during the 1990s was the construction of a revived and expanded NATO—the instrument by which the United States would constrain

EU defense independence and thus putatively limit the emergence of a competing pole of financial accumulation.

In short, the United States has won the battle to limit EU defense independence but it may yet lose the war. The first victory for the United States was getting the Franco-German hub of the European Union to temper its enthusiasm for a European Security and Defense Identity (ESDI), principally by rallying Britain and smaller, weaker European states against the Franco-German scheme (Gibbs 2001). The second victory, by far and away the grander triumph for the United States, was incorporating former Warsaw Pact signatories into NATO and rebranding NATO as a vehicle for protecting Europe against recrudescent Russia and for policing ethno-racial strife on Europe's Balkan frontier (Calleo 2001, 183; Gibbs 2001; Gowan 2001, 46–47). For the United States, this second victory was doubly advantageous: it diluted the Franco-German presence in NATO and created a new function for NATO that western European "cruise missile socialists" could buy into, including proponents of "humanitarian intervention" in France and Germany (Gibbs 2001). Even more significantly, by enlisting East European states into NATO before they entered the European Union, the United States effectively assured that these states would exhibit more fealty to it than to its Franco-German alternative (Gibbs 2001; Steele 2003; Wallerstein 2002b). What is more, an unalloyed belt of virtual U.S. military vassals now physically cuts off western Europe from Russia, and a deepening geoeconomic as well as military-diplomatic liaison between western Europe and Russia is precisely what is required to make a hypothetical European assault on American hegemony real (Gowan 2003, 47; Wallerstein 2002b).

However, due to the Bush administration's reckless campaign to delay imperial decline by staging endless wars in defiance of its erstwhile junior partners, the United States may yet snatch defeat from the jaws of its successive victories. The Pentagon's proposal to retool NATO yet again—this time into a "rapid reaction force" that obligingly serves U.S. geostrategic prerogatives far away from Europe itself—might extinguish whatever dying commitments France and Germany have towards NATO's mere existence (Calleo 2001, 319–320; Kupchan 2002). The ultimate refusal of the Bush administration to call upon NATO for the destruction of Afghanistan, and the inability of the Bush administration to cajole and bully NATO into invading Iraq, vividly indicates that the organization does not accord with the latest set of functions the United States has vaingloriously imposed on it, and that it courts irrelevance (Kupchan 2002; Wallerstein 2002b). Furthermore, in the prelude to the invasion of Iraq, the absolute contempt shown by the Bush administration toward even the pretense of weighing the input of its junior partners in Europe must have convinced France and Germany (and Russia, for that matter) that they have little choice but to forge ahead, step-by-step, with a common defense policy fully outside the aegis of the United States. Even though this troika was unable to derail the administration from occupying Iraq and laying its hands on its ample petroleum reserves, and even though for the moment this troika has humbly prostrated itself before

U.S. power (Ali 2003), it beggars disbelief that this humiliating sequence of events will not generate momentum toward the resuscitation of the ESDI in some form. The reigning significance of such a move toward genuine European defense independence is not that it will create a check on the global projection of U.S. military power. Rather, Europe's enhanced self-protection capabilities will diminish whatever leverage the United States has over EU financial, investment, monetary, and trade policies (Gibbs 2001)—including especially the European Union's mounting campaign to encourage its trading partners and borrowers of credit to convert their central bank currency reserves from dollars to euros, the secret weapon in the EU arsenal against a U.S. hegemony propped up by dollar dominance.

An essential underpinning of U.S. hegemony is the dollar's stature as the nearly exclusive form of "world money," both as central bank reserve currency and as means of payment for key commodities such as oil. By the late 1990s, the dollar accounted for more than two-thirds of official currency reserves in the world's central banks, and roughly half of all world exports were invoiced in dollars (Yarjani 2002). Global demand for the dollar, of course, magically levitates the value of dollar-denominated assets well above the level "market fundamentals" would otherwise necessitate. The artificial overvaluation of these assets enables the United States to offset its merchandise trade deficit (and now, to underwrite resurgent federal and state government budget deficits) simply by luring overseas investors to purchase Wall Street securities and U.S. Treasury bonds, among other dollar-denominated assets. To grotesquely oversimplify, dollar dominance allows American firms, households, and government to "live far beyond their means"—i.e., to maintain high levels of consumption even though the competitiveness and size of its industrial base continues to wither, and even though its businesses, wealthy families, and individuals carry an increasingly light tax burden. By enabling U.S. households to buy cheap imported consumer goods as its manufacturing base shrinks, and by enabling the U.S. federal government to spend a great deal more than it garners in revenue, dollar dominance girds two critical pillars of U.S. hegemony: popular support for ruling elites and profligate overseas military spending.

Although share prices did not fall as far as weak U.S. corporate profitability reports warranted (another byproduct of U.S. seigniorage privileges), when large amounts of air leaked from the Wall Street bubble in 2000–2001, the ability of the United States to service its growing balance of payments deficit without suffering through harsh, contractionary adjustments was called into question. In the wake of this development, Washington came under severe pressure to suppress all challenges to dollar dominance. For the rise of euro as a reserve currency and an instrument of exchange alternative to the dollar was elevated from a distant and minor irritant to an immediate and grave danger (Henderson 2003; Sommers 2003). One may convincingly conceptualize subsequent rifts between the United States and the European Union as being driven by covert and overt U.S. attempts to bolster dollar dominance by subverting the euro challenge and by the European Union countering these attempts. Simmering trade and investment tensions between the United States and the European Union exploded because the threat to dollar dominance posed by the euro alternative cast these tensions in a new and more profound light. Each trade and investment dispute provoked a strong counterattack because the stakes were now so much higher. The EU ban on imports of genetically modified organisms now signified not lost export revenue for U.S. companies but a lost chance for ameliorating the U.S. merchandise trade balance. The WTO's ruling in favor of the European Union that the U.S. government could no longer extend tax breaks to foreign sales affiliates of U.S.-based corporations signified not lost export earnings for these corporations but a snowballing trade deficit. Finally, two reasons why the United States was so determined to invade and occupy Iraq "with or without" UN Security Council consent, against the strenuous objections of the core members of the Eurozone, were (1) it wanted to punish a country that had opted to denominate its oil exports in euros (Iraq had taken this measure in November 2000 to cultivate EU support for the lifting of economic sanctions) (Recknagel 2000) and thereby send a message to all small and weak states that breaking away from dollar dominance would be met with harsh reprisals; and (2) it wanted to ensure that oil exports derived from the world's second-largest supply of proven reserves would be priced in dollars and that these petroleum receipts would be held in dollar accounts (in the Iraqi Central Bank, in U.S. private banks, or elsewhere).

## III. The U.S. Turn toward East Asia

Endowing itself with the right to unilaterally conduct warfare and impose client regimes in geostrategically sensitive zones of the South—especially West and Central Asia—are facets of a long-range scheme adapted by the United States to fend off the looming challenge the European Union poses to dollar dominance and its world-systemic primacy. Because it appears to be such a sea-change from the foreign policy of its predecessor (on the surface, at least), and because it is currently being tested in Iraq, the preemptive strategy outlined by the Bush administration appears to be the be-all and end-all of the U.S. strategy to defend its embattled hegemony. Yet, U.S. efforts to prolong its hegemony cannot and will not rest merely on a single-note program to cow and subvert its emergent EU rivals. A latent facet of present U.S. strategy that promises to become more pronounced over time involves cajoling and coercing a reluctant Japan, along with an eager China, to press ahead with their respective reforms in a manner that will temporally extend U.S. hegemony (Reifer 2002).

The increasing appeal of this strategy for Washington rests in the continuing schism between the two economic and military giants of East Asia, China and Japan. Unlike the mainstays of the European Union, France and Germany, China and Japan are currently, and for the foreseeable future will remain, incapable of anchoring anything resembling a coherent East Asian trade, investment, and monetary bloc, much less a regional security apparatus independent of U.S. tutelage. In essence, the still rocky bilateral relationship between China and Japan—that is, their inability to institutionalize joint cooperation in the twin realms of capital accumulation and defense policy—undermines the possibility of an East Asian multilateralism inimical to U.S. regional and global designs (Wallerstein 2002a). What is more, the poor horizontal relationship between China and Japan enables the United States to exact concessions from each of them separately, most notably in the arena of restructuring their economies in accordance with the perquisites of U.S. corporate capital. Indeed, seizing upon this ongoing rift between China and Japan is a conscious element of U.S. strategy to buttress its hegemony. Reflecting Washington's fear that someday China and Japan might, in unison, lead East Asia on a development and security path decoupled from *pax Americana,* the strategy of playing "divide and rule" in East Asia is explicitly mapped out in a 2001 report published by the Pentagon-friendly RAND Corporation. Suggestions contained in this report are clearly mirrored in the formulation of the Bush administration's "new" national security doctrine, which forcefully affirms the U.S. resolve to stave off the emergence of an autonomous rival power anywhere in the world, including a China-Japan liaison in East Asia (Khalilzad 2001).

To paint in broad strokes, U.S. overall strategy in East Asia involves taking advantage of existing antagonisms between China and Japan as well as creating new ones. Perhaps the biggest stumbling block in the way of a full and final rapprochement between China and Japan is the ghost of Japanese colonial rule. Recent political developments in Japan have rekindled the sense of distrust and even hatred that most Chinese have toward Japan, thus making it almost impossible for the Chinese Communist Party (CCP) to pursue some form of serious partnership with Japan, were it so inclined. In the trough of the economic stagnation that has paralyzed Japan for more than a decade, the ultranationalist right wing has become a resurgent social force. Adjusting themselves to this evolving reality, elected officials in Japan's ruling Liberal Democratic Party (LDP) have demonstrated a growing willingness to placate the nationalist wing with symbolic gestures that wound Chinese sensibilities and rouse suspicions about recrudescent Japanese militarism. To mention only two of many examples, on repeated occasions Japanese Prime Minister Koizumi has visited the shrines of World War II veterans in the face of protestations from Beijing, and the government has steadfastly refused to revise school textbooks that do not realistically depict war crimes committed against the Chinese during the period of Japanese imperial expansion (Conachy 2002).

The United States also proactively sows seeds of distrust between China and Japan. The principal tool for so doing, of course, is the U.S.-Japan security alliance, long the fulcrum of American presence in East Asia and formally renewed in 1999 (Feffer 2000, 45–62; Foster 2001). The redrawn agreement throws several kindred barriers in the way of systematic cooperation between the giants of Asia. On the one hand, it more or less perpetuates the subordination of Japanese defense policy and security to U.S. global and regional aspirations (Johnson 1999, 46). Because a keystone of U.S. global and regional geostrategy is the neutralization of a powerful and independent China, this plainly inhibits Japan from forging a more harmonious bilateral relationship with it. Moreover, to the degree that Japan is actually fastened to U.S. aims around the world and in East Asia, this is bound to generate Chinese acrimony toward Japan. The U.S. offer to share theater missile defense (TMD) technology with Japan represents the extension of this logic, whereby Japan is guaranteed shielding from a hypothetically hostile China that is in fact hostile only to the United States striving to establish first strike capability so that it may persist with its meddling in East Asian affairs (Johnson 1999, 46; Suryanarayana 2003).

On the other hand, in partial deference to burgeoning Japanese neonationalism, the guidelines of the refashioned U.S.-Japan pact also permit Japan's so-called "self-defense forces" to roam and conduct missions beyond Japanese shores, thus raising Chinese hackles about Japanese offensive rearmament (Feffer 2000, 51). For example, the United States is now openly letting Japan launch its own spy satellites, and Japanese defense officials are reputedly working on plans to convert warships into aircraft carriers (Suryanarayana 2003). A particularly telltale example of how the redrawn agreement simultaneously preserves Japanese conformity to U.S. goals and draws more substantially on Japanese assets in so doing is what its guidelines allow and encourage in the event China responds to an outright declaration of Taiwanese independence with an armed attack on the island. Should such an incident come to pass, the guidelines recommend that Japan supplement U.S. military operations with intelligence-gathering, surveillance, and minesweeping activities, among other actions (Johnson 1999, 51). The very recent Japanese decision to deploy "peace-keeping" troops to assist in the "reconstruction" of post-Saddam Iraq, despite the questionable constitutionality of it so doing, further illustrates how the reinvigorated U.S.-Japan security alliance at one and the same time reinforces Japan's satrap-like relationship with the United States and fuels Chinese worries about Japanese military build-up (French 2003; Suryanarayana 2003).

The way in which the United States has both provoked and stage-managed the latest installment of the never-ending North Korean "crisis" furnishes another example of how Washington manipulates the East Asian security environment in order to splinter China and Japan. The Bush administration could reasonably expect that when it declared its nonsupport for South Korea's "sunshine policy" toward the North, and then explicitly put Kim Jong Il's regime in its gunsights by including it among the "axis of evil," North Korea would publicly resume its nuclear weapons program unless the United States promised never to attack (Shorrock 2003). The United States also likely anticipated that inducing North Korean brinkmanship would encourage Japan to more enthusiastically embrace TMD cooperation with the United States, and certain Japanese political figures to publicly mull over Japan acquiring a nuclear deterrent of its own—which indeed they did (Erikson 2003). The predictable reaction of China to such pronouncements coming from Tokyo, of course, has been a growing nervousness that Japan is sincerely serious about offensive rearmament, which undermines the long-run possibility of China and Japan creating a lasting structure for addressing and resolving regional security problems that omits the United States. Additionally, the manner in which the United States has tried to keep the lid on the North Korean "crisis" it stirred up is suggestive of a viable grand strategy to prevent bilateral Chinese-Japanese cooperation from maturing. The United States, knowing full well that a continuously low-boiling North Korea "crisis" suits its divide-and-rule approach in East Asia but a wholesale conflagration would not, has deputized China, North Korea's primary food and fuel supplier, to talk Kim Jong Il down from the most extreme forms of brinkmanship (Lobe 2003). Not only does delegating such a role to China prevent the North Korean "crisis" from spilling beyond bounds useful to the United States, but it also lessens the chances that China and Japan will bilaterally work a feasible solution to the "crisis" on their own, since China's privileged position derives from U.S. mediation (Berkofsky 2003).

Ever-deepening investment and trade linkages between Japan and China would at least seem to suggest that in coming years U.S. attempts to thwart various forms of cooperation between the two, especially security and financial-monetary cooperation, will succumb to the realities of intensifying regional economic interdependence. Indeed, Japanese TNCs are continually stepping up their level of direct investment in China, and consumer goods produced on Chinese soil absorb greater and greater amounts of intermediate goods (especially steel), parts, components, and industrial machinery from Japan with each passing year (Holland 2002). However, ever since it discreetly allowed Japan to ease its embargo against China in the early 1960s, the United States has superintended a bundle of policies and institutions designed to assure that growing trade and investment ties between Japan and China do not lead to the formation of an East Asian accumulation regime over which it has no purchase (Cumings 1999, 205–206). In the early 1970s, when mounting frustration with nascent U.S. protectionism spurred the Japanese government and Japanese firms to pursue deeper trade and investment links with post–Cultural Revolution China, the United States undercut the trend by restoring diplomatic relations with China and inviting China to rejoin the capitalist world market under U.S. escort (Halliday and McCormack 1973, 131, 212–213; Schurmann 1974, 556–558). In the decade that followed the negotiation of the Plaza Accord (1985–1995), when the skyrocketing value of the yen relative to the dollar unleashed a tide of foreign direct investment in the semiperiphery and periphery of East Asia by Japanese TNCs, the pegging of Southeast Asian currencies to the plummeting dollar ensured that most of this burst of Japanese investment ended up in Southeast Asia, not mainland China (So and Chiu 1995, 223–233). Moreover, when U.S. hysteria about the Japanese economic threat reached its peak in the late 1980s and early 1990s, the United States exploited the tragedy of the

Tiananmen Square massacre to slow the flow of foreign direct investment in China (So and Chiu 1995, 272). By the time foreign direct investment began to gush back into China at an unprecedented rate, Japanese firms were coping with the unpleasant aftereffects of the collapse of the Japanese real estate bubble, itself a predictable outcome of the yen revaluation foisted on Japan nearly ten years before (Brenner 2002, 155).

The People's Bank of China also proved to be anything but beholden to Japanese accumulation imperatives in 1994, when it lowered the yuan's dollar peg so that mostly overseas Chinese investing in the mainland could better tap the U.S. export market (Marshall 1998). In tandem with the "reverse Plaza Accord" of 1995, this maneuver, of course, set into motion the East Asian financial and economic crisis of 1997–1998, which in one fell swoop devastated the economies of Japan's Southeast Asian hinterland, devalued the assets of Japanese TNCs heavily invested in that hinterland, and nearly thrust into receivership Japan's banking system, throwing the sputtering Japanese recovery into reverse (Brenner 2002, 155). China's successful admission to the WTO, a decision over which the U.S. Congress held pivotal leverage, is the latest U.S. ploy that militates against the formation of a new "East Asian coprosperity sphere," in which Japanese TNCs and the Chinese state would conceivably play a leading role. Per the rules and regulations of WTO membership, Japanese firms have to compete on an equal footing with others for access to Chinese product markets, investment opportunities, joint venture partners, subcontractors, and labor. By the same token, Chinese enterprises will not become unduly beholden to Japanese high-tech companies for technology transfer, at least not any more so than to their U.S.- and Europe-based competitors. Moreover, to the extent that China's accession to the WTO will pry open its once highly protected business and financial service markets to penetration by world capital, surely American firms are better poised than their Japanese counterparts to reap a disproportionate advantage. In short, China's deepening participation in the world market according to the multilateral standards of the WTO means that Japan, especially its small- and medium-sized manufacturers, will be savaged by low-cost Chinese imports, while Japanese TNCs will not be able to compensate by cutting preferential deals to set up supply chain networks in China.

The prospect that Japanese TNCs using China as a low-wage, medium-skill production site will lead to a closer pan-regional partnership between the two is further diminished by the fact that the two are competing, not cooperating, over deeper economic integration with the states of Southeast Asia (Blank 2002). Using privileged access to its vast and rapidly growing internal market as the carrot, and the threat of undercutting all Southeast Asian assemblers of labor-intensive consumer goods as the stick, China in 2002 began negotiating a framework for trade liberalization with the members of ASEAN, beating Japan to the punch (Aglionby 2002). Although its territorial interests in the South China Sea and its geostrategic interests in the Strait of Malacca may be the paramount causes of China unilaterally racing ahead with these negotiations, the objective effects of a trade liberalization scheme that more tightly binds Southeast Asia and China and excludes Japan in the process are clear enough. Two likely results are that Japanese TNCs will lose their grip over highly profitable capital goods markets and captive supply networks in Southeast Asia. Because China is a much larger and much more robust customer than Japan of Southeast Asian agricultural surpluses, the consolidation of an interstate regime of accumulation between Southeast Asia and China will generate the capital and investment funds necessary for the former to eventually upgrade its capital goods sector. This will reduce Southeast Asia's technological dependence on turnkey equipment transplanted by or purchased from Japanese TNCs, which in turn will allow the region's high-tech manufacturers to liberate themselves from the distribution channels dominated by the very same rent-collecting Japanese TNCs. Not only might intensive trade cooperation between ASEAN and China lower Southeast Asian demand for Japanese industrial machinery and weaken the control that Japanese TNCs exercise over the pricing and destination of Southeast Asian parts and components but also it could well divert the export of critical Southeast Asian natural resources from Japan to China.[2]

Because of the fissure between China and Japan—a fissure that Washington does its best to exploit and widen—the United States is able to engineer geoeconomic relations with the two giants of East Asia in a direction favorable to the prolongation of its hegemony. The preeminent concern of the United States is that China and Japan, whose respective central banks are the top two purchasers of U.S. Treasury bills and hence the top two underwriters of U.S. government debt and sponsors of U.S. global militarism, continue to hold the lion's share of their bottomless currency reserves in dollar-denominated liquid assets (Wolf 2003). A very strong inducement for them to continue to do so—and indeed, for them to urge the central banks of other states to continue to do so—is the sheer fact that a large-scale de-dollarization of the world's currency reserves would probably trigger such a wild devaluation of the greenback that the value of China and Japan's generous dollar-denominated holdings would immediately shrink, not to mention the fact that so too would the purchasing power of their top export customer (McDonald 2002). The structural power of this inducement was proven on the cusp of the U.S. invasion of Iraq, when the Japanese government called upon central bank authorities and financial ministers all over the globe to support the dollar in the event foreign exchange speculators responded negatively to the U.S. military incursion.

So long as China and Japan keep their end of the bargain and play along with the *de facto* dollar standard that exempts the United States from living by the precepts of austerity that it preaches, Washington tolerates Chinese and Japanese economic policies that at least partially appear to endanger its hegemonic imperatives but in fact do not. Many commentators suggest that China, aided and abetted by the stampede of U.S. TNCs that are relocating or subcontracting labor-intensive production to its territories is chipping away at the U.S. hegemony by keeping the dollar-yuan exchange rate artificially low, dumping mountains of low-cost consumer goods on the U.S. market, and boring out what remains of the U.S. industrial base (Hiebert 2003). However, although a few outmoded sectors of the U.S. industrial base may be harmed by the precipitous emergence of China as the "workshop of the world," if anything U.S. hegemony has been strengthened, not mitigated, by this recent development. First and foremost, this is because most of the revenues deriving from China's colossal merchandise trade surplus with the United States are plowed into dollar-denominated bonds (both public and corporate) and securities, thus reinforcing the *de facto* dollar standard. What is more, the artificially low dollar-yuan exchange rate allows U.S.-based TNCs to set up shop in China cheaply, buy inputs made therein cheaply, and provide their workers at home with imported cheap consumer goods so as to hold down the wage bill—all of which eases stress on the thin profit margins of U.S. productive capital (Restall 2003).

For reasons that are obvious enough, in China the overlapping state and private enterprises who court U.S. FDI and target U.S. markets favor the current dollar-yuan exchange rate protocol, but so too do the highest echelons of the CCP, not in the least because China faces an increasingly severe excess capacity problem and in effect is using what some have dubbed "exchange rate mercantilism" as an employment and social policy (Restall 2003; Wolf 2003). The CCP's acquiescence to this arrangement is virtually guaranteed by the fact that it has staked its legitimacy and sheer survival on plowing ahead with an economic model dependent upon continuity of FDI flows and parity access to U.S. markets. Having decisively tied its political future to an emergent class whose fortunes are embedded in the trans-Pacific commodity chain, the CCP all but confirmed this dependence at its Sixteenth National Congress held in November 2002 (Gittings 2002).

It naturally follows from the formula of U.S.-China geoeconomic integration outlined above that the United States expresses little or no consternation about the rising trend of Japanese TNCs relocating or subcontracting their labor-intensive production to China. Far from representing the construction of an autonomous East Asian accumulation bloc centered on Japan and China, Japanese FDI in China enlarges the pool of profits ultimately invested in dollar-denominated liquid assets. Whether the growing streams of semifinished and finished goods assembled in China under the auspices of Japanese TNCs are sent to Japan, the United States, or a third destination, a big portion of the greater mass of export revenues consequently accruing to China end up in dollar-denominated financial instruments and buttress U.S. seigniorage privileges. For that matter, Japanese FDI in China arguably shores up the *de facto* dollar standard in at least two other mutually interacting ways. By placing labor-intensive assembly operations offshore to China, importing artificially devalued semifinished goods from affiliates or subcontractors therein, and then re-exporting to the world markets from home territory, hard-pressed Japanese TNCs restore their global competitiveness and the government enhances its export revenues. Not only does the presence of intra- and extra-East Asian production and distribution chains imply the boosting of Japanese export revenues, a big portion of which end up in dollar-denominated liquid assets, it strengthens the bargaining power of the United States as it prods the Japanese government to implement Washington Consensus–style economic reforms, especially in the business service and financial market sectors.

Because the United States is, in the last instance, the guarantor of the dollar-yuan protocol that enables strapped Japanese TNCs to restore their world market competitiveness by utilizing China as a low-wage, medium-skill export platform, Tokyo is obligated to yield on at least some neoliberal economic reforms it is loath to adopt. For example, with Prime Minister Koizumi's blessing, Japan's top economic ministry has permitted titanic Wall Street investment houses to snap up shares in Japanese banks heavily bogged down with nonperforming loans (Ibison 2003). Among other things, this will augment the influence U.S. capital has over the restructuring of troubled and insolvent Japanese corporations—including their possible consolidation, sale, or closure as well as changes in their mode of governance. An increase in the inventory of debt-compromised economic resources that Wall Street has within its grasp certainly has positive ramifications for the *de facto* dollar standard as does the piecemeal remodeling of postwar Japanese capitalism to fit Washington Consensus standards more broadly. To bring the analysis full circle, what adds punch to the United States having so much sway over the "two steps forward, one step back" liberalization of the Japanese economy is Tokyo's continuing foreign policy slavishness toward and security dependence upon the United States, which reproduces China's suspicion toward Japan. Enmity between China and Japan effectively bars the two giants of East Asia from erecting the EU-style monetary architecture that would shelter Japanese banks specifically and Japanese capitalism more generally from the predation of U.S. financial institutions.

## IV. Conclusion: Contradictions of the U.S.-Chinese Geoeconomic Alliance

I have cursorily indicated that a major part of the U.S. strategy to prolong its hegemony is to leverage to its own advantage China's increasing openness to the forces and rhythms of global capitalism. To the extent that the United States continues to tether its hegemonic struggle to China's opening up, it may actually provoke the hastening rather than the stemming of its decline. This is so because those qualities of China's policies that make its deepening geoeconomic integration so appealing to U.S. ruling and corporate elites—especially Wall Street, cotton, grain, and soybean exporters, and TNCs with assembly plants and outsourcing networks in China—are precisely those aspects of "economic reform" that have the greatest potential to trip a series of environmental, fiscal, social, and political crises in China. A concatenation of these crises would wreck China's dynamism and stability, and along with it big U.S. rentier, producer, and mercantile groups whose fortunes will have become inextricably wedded to China's fortunes.

For example, the terms under which China was admitted to the WTO stipulate that by the year 2007 foreign-owned commercial banks can open branches in China and accept local currency deposits from ordinary Chinese citizens (Lague 2002). Much of the Chinese population is cognizant that the balance sheets of China's state-owned banks are marred by a thicket of bad loans that will never be serviced unless the central government continues to bail them out as well as their errant creditors with injections of cash, export credits, and other subsidies, methods which either are losing support from the CCP's top decisionmakers or are technically in violation of WTO rules and regulations. Because of this, the entry of foreign-owned financial institutions into China's commercial banking sector might precipitate a run on the state-owned commercial banks. This, in turn, would drastically weaken the state-owned commercial banks, and they would have little choice but to respond to a run on their vaults by cutting off "lifeline" loans to thousands of ailing, state-owned enterprises (SOEs) that are woefully inefficient by the standards of the world market (Forney 2002). In 2002, a flurry of protests initiated by furloughed and sacked SOE workers revealed the degree to which plant closures can spark a maelstrom of social unrest and even political instability (*Economist* 2003); most experts believe that financial sector reform incumbent upon China per its WTO entry will only quicken the heady pace at which SOEs are being shut down and their workers laid off.

The phased-in deregulation of China's agricultural commodity markets so that prices conform more closely to those set by capital-intensive agribusiness operating in the United States and elsewhere in the North provides another example of how China's integration into the world market may bring short-term gain for politically powerful segments of U.S. capital but in the medium and long term reap a whirlwind of social unrest in China that will speed the downfall of U.S. hegemony. Under the provisions of China's WTO entry, by 2004 agricultural tariffs will be cut from an overall average of 31 to 14 percent, and state procurement and other price support programs for staple grains will be slashed radically (Collier 2000; Fang 2000). Forced to raise per-acre yields to match or beat the price of low-cost cotton, grain, soybean, and other crop imports from abroad, Chinese peasants will not be able to survive by resorting to increased use of fertilizers or pesticides, because arable land has already been doused with petroleum-derived synthetics to the limits of its natural capacity. The leading solution to raising agricultural productivity is a machinery-intensive and labor-displacing one. Credible estimates suggest that in the coming decade in excess of 100 million peasants will be uprooted from the land (Collier 2000; Forney 2002). Early signs of peasant revolt driven by the steep reduction in agricultural commodity tariffs and the curbing of domestic price supports are starting to appear. In late 2002, 30,000 sugarcane-growing tenants in Guanxi province demonstrated against dropping sugar prices by taking over a local government building, and 10,000 tobacco farmers in Yunnan converged on the provincial capital to protest against falling purchase prices paid by the tobacco bureau (Arms 2002).

If indeed the grim projection that at least 100 million peasants will be ousted from the land by the market rationalization of agricultural production holds true, they will compete with redundant SOE workers and new labor market entrants for jobs in the private sector, which, although growing fast, will not be growing fast enough to soak up the bulging reserve army of labor (Chan 2001; Watts 2003). Even though China recently became the world-economy's largest magnet of FDI, much of this investment takes the form of highly capital-intensive plants and equipment and does little to generate net employment growth. Despite the fact that in 2002 China's economy officially registered 8 percent growth, the official unemployment rate failed to decline (Lague 2003). What really enabled China's central government to keep joblessness from rising further than it did and triggering more social unrest than indeed did occur was massive spending on large-scale public works projects. However, China's accession to the WTO has diminished one of its primary sources of state revenue, customs collection (Chandrasekhar 2002). Now that Beijing's budget deficit has exceeded 3 percent of GDP—the magic threshold for all states in the global system who wish to avoid a downgrading of their credit rating, save the seigneurial United States—its ability to offset the ongoing economic and social dislocation resulting from the acceleration of its "economic reform" and "opening up" policies with generous outlays of public spending has been severely compromised (Lague 2003).

In sum, to rescue itself from headlong decline, the United States is counting on the CCP to continue its regimentation of the current developmental model. The means the United States has at its disposal are the tools to exert pressure on China and make certain that the specific form of world market integration pursued by the CCP does not undermine U.S. hegemony, including the renewed U.S.-Japan security alliance, arms transfers to Taiwan, domination of the oceanic conduits of oil transport, the research and development of nuclear missile defense, the post–September 11 military encirclement of China in Central and Southeast Asia, and the threat of presenting dumping charges against it before the WTO (Bezlova 2003; Murray 2002). Yet the very mode of China's reintegration into the world-economy, a hybrid based largely on the willful preferences of its political leadership but also on the reality of the structural power enjoyed by the United States in the world-system, contains at its heart various contradictions—environmental, fiscal, social, and political—that will eventually pose severe strains on the pace of economic expansion in China. And because the United States will have staked the destiny of its hegemony on China's future, the aforementioned strains and a resultant slowdown of growth therein will accelerate its very demise. In other words, the unsustainable nature of China's economic success, not the strengthening of EU economic clout and defense independence per se, will prove to be the ultimate gravedigger of U.S. power.

# Notes

1. Hudson (2003) keenly points out that contrary to conventional wisdom, the linchpin of dollar dominance is the fact that the world monetary system obligates West European and East Asian central banks to hold their currency reserves almost exclusively in the form of low-yielding U.S. Treasury bills, which among other things allows U.S. investors (mutual funds, pension funds, insurance companies, and the like) to concentrate their holdings in much more liquid and generally higher-yielding corporate security and bond markets.

2. Parenthetically, by no means is Southeast Asia the only geographical arena where China is attempting to outmaneuver Japan in a contest to secure reliable supplies of critical natural resources. For example, China and Japan are both courting Russia to build a long-distance pipeline that would deliver millions of tons of West Siberian oil to either (but not both) of their respective jurisdictions (Bremmer and Clark 2003).

# References

Aglionby, John. 2002. "The Red Dragon Roars." *Guardian,* November 7.

Ali, Tariq. 2003. "Re-Colonizing Iraq." *New Left Review* 2/21 (May–June): 5–19.

Amin, Samir. 2003. "Confronting the Empire." *Monthly Review* 55(3): 15–22.

Arms, Katherine. 2002. "China Workers Protest amid Leadership Move." United Press International Wire Service, November 5.

Arrighi, Giovanni, and Beverly Silver. 1999. *Chaos and Governance in the Modern World-System.* Minneapolis: University of Minnesota Press.

Berkofsky, Axel. 2003. "Japan: Missing Partner in U.S.–North Korea Talks." *Asia Times,* April 22.

Bezlova, Antoaneta. 2003. "Why China Doesn't Mind the War in Iraq." *Asia Times,* March 26.

Blank, Stephen. 2002. "The Ominous Subtext to U.S.-China Relations." *Asia Times,* November 21.

Bremmer, Ian, and Bruce Clark. 2003. "The Other Great Game." *Moscow Times,* May 12.

Brenner, Robert. 2002. *The Boom and the Bubble: The U.S. in the World Economy.* New York: Verso Press.

Calleo, David P. 2001. *Rethinking Europe's Future.* Princeton, NJ: Princeton University Press.

Chan, Kam Wing. 2001. "Recent Migration in China: Patterns, Trends, and Policies." *Asian Perspective* 25(4): 127–156.

Chandrasekhar, C. P. 2002. "A Challenge in China." *Frontline* 19(7).

Collier, Robert. 2000. "China Bets on the Future." *San Francisco Chronicle,* May 16.

Conachy, James. 2002. "Asylum Incident Fuels Anti-China Rhetoric in Japan." *World Socialist* Website, May 27, available at http://www.wsws.org/articles/2002/may2002/japan27_prn.shtml.

Cumings, Bruce. 1999. *Parallax Visions: Making Sense of American–East Asian Relations at the End of the Century.* Durham, NC: Duke University Press.

Dapice, David. 2003. "Does the 'Hyper-Power' Have Feet of Clay?" *YaleGlobal,* March 3: http://yaleglobal.yale.edu/display.article?id=1103.

*Economist.* 2003. "Containing Unrest." January 18.

Elliot, Larry. 2003. "Bubble Blowers Run Out of Puff." *Guardian,* March 10.

Erikson, Marc. 2003. "Japan Could 'Go Nuclear' in Months," *Asia Times,* January 14.

Escobar, Pepe. 2002. "China, Russia, and the Iraqi Oil Game." *Asia Times,* October 31.

Fang, Bay. 2000. "Growing Troubles Down on the Farm." *U.S. News and World Report* 128 (21): 40.

Farag, Fatemah. 2002. "Empire of Chaos Challenged: An Interview with Samir Amin." *Al-Ahram Weekly Online,* available at http://weekly.ahram.org.eg/2002/609/intrvw.htm.

Feffer, John. 2000. "Gunboat Globalization: The Intersection of Economics and Security in East Asia." *Social Justice* 27(4):45–62.

Ferguson, Thomas, and Robert A. Johnson. 2002. "Oil Economics Lubricates Push for War." *Los Angeles Times,* October 13, p. M3.

French, Howard. 2003. "Japan Faces Burden: Its Own Defense" *New York Times,* July 22, p. A1.

Forney, Matt. 2002. "Workers' Wasteland." *Time Asia,* November 1.

Foster, John Bellamy. 2001. "Imperialism and 'Empire.'" *Monthly Review* 53(7): 1–10.

Gibbs, David. 2001. "Washington's New Interventionism: U.S. Hegemony and Inter-Imperialist Rivalries." *Monthly Review* 53(4): 15–37.

Gindin, Sam. 2003. "Prospects for Anti-Imperialism." *Monthly Review* 55(3): 117–124.

Gittings, John. 2002. "China Turns Its Back on Communism to Join Long March of the Capitalists." *Guardian,* November 9.

Gowan, Peter. 1999. *The Global Gamble: Washington's Faustian Bid for World Dominance.* New York: Verso.

———. 2003. "U.S. Hegemony Today." *Monthly Review* 55(3): 30–50.

Grandin, Greg. 2003. "What's a Neo-Liberal to Do?" *Nation* 276 (9).

Henderson, Hazel. 2003. "Iraq, the Dollar, and the Euro." Available at: http://www.hazelhenderson.com/Iraq,%20the%20Dollar%20and%20the%20Euro.htm.

Hiebert, Murray. 2003. "Fighting China on U.S. Soil." *Far Eastern Economic Review* 166 (33).

Hoffman, Thomas. 2003. "Gartner: One in 20 End-User IT Jobs to Move Offshore by Late 2004." *ComputerWorld,* July 30.

Holland, Tom. 2002. "External Risks, Internal Rewards." *Far Eastern Economic Review* 165(34).

Halliday, Jon, and Gavan McCormack. 1973. *Japanese Imperialism Today.* New York: Monthly Review Press.

Hudson, Michael. 2003. *Super Imperialism.* Sterling, VA: Pluto Press.

Ibison, David. 2003. "As the Nikkei Slides and Nationalization Looms, Wall Street Buys into Japan's Banks." *Financial Times,* March 13, p. 19.

Johnson, Chalmers. 1999. "In Search of a New Cold War." *Bulletin of the Atomic Scientists,* 55 (5): 44–51.

Judis, John. 2003. "Over a Barrel: Who Will Control Iraq's Oil?" *New Republic Online,* January 20.

Khalilzad, Zalmay, Jonathan D. Pollack, and David T. Orletsky. 2001. *The United States and Asia: Toward a New U.S. Strategy and Force Posture.* Santa Monica, CA: Rand.

Klare, Michael. 2003. "The New Geopolitics." *Monthly Review* 55(3): 51–56.

Kupchan, Charles. 2002. "The Last Days of the Atlantic Alliance." *Financial Times,* November 18, p. 23.

Lague, David. 2002. "On the Road to Ruin." *Far Eastern Economic Review,* November 14: 32–35.

148    *John Gulick*

————. 2003. "Public Spending Explodes." *Far Eastern Economic Review,* January 30.

Lieven, Anatol. 2003. "A Trap of Their Own Making." *London Review of Books* 25(9).

Liu, Henry C. K. 2002. "U.S. Dollar Hegemony Has Got to Go." *Asia Times,* April 11.

Lobe, Jim. 2003. "Korea Crisis Fuels Isolationism." *Asia Times,* January 16.

Marshall, Jonathan. 1988. "China Struggling against Full-Blown Price Deflation." *San Francisco Chronicle,* February 23, p. B1.

Mayer, Arno. 2003. "Beyond the Drumbeat: Iraq, Preventive War, 'Old Europe.'" *Monthly Review* 54(10): 17–21.

McDonald, Scott B. 2002. "China Not Immune to U.S. Woes." *Asia Times,* July 27.

Murray, David. 2002. "Challenge in the East." *Guardian,* January 30.

Parenti, Christian. 2003. "Why Iraq? Mapping Planet America." *Brooklyn Rail,* April.

Recknagel, Charles. 2000. "Iraq: Baghdad Moves to Euro." *Radio Free Europe,* November 1.

Reifer, Thomas. 2002. "Geopolitics, Globalization, and Alternative Regionalisms." Paper presented at the ASEM4 People conference in Copenhagen, Denmark, September 19–23.

Restall, Hugh. 2003. "Why China Is a Paper Tiger." *Wall Street Journal,* July 31.

Schurmann, Franz. 1974. *The Logic of World Power.* New York: Pantheon Press.

Shalom, Stephen. 1999. "The Continuity of U.S. Imperialism." *New Politics* 7(2): 33–39.

Shorrock, Tim. 2003. "A Dangerous Game in Korea." *Nation* 276(3): 18–20.

So, Alvin, and Stephen Chiu. 1995. *East Asia and the World Economy.* Thousand Oaks, CA: Sage Publications.

Sommers, Jeffrey. 2003. "Dollar Crisis and American Empire." *Znet,* June 20. Available at: http://www.zmag.org/content/showarticle.cfm?SectionID=10&ItemID=3803.

Steele, Jonathan. 2003. "The New Vassals." *Guardian,* February 7.

Suryanarayana, P. S. 2003. "East Asia and the Superpower." *Frontline,* available at http://www.frontlineonnet.com/fl2017/stories/20030829000706000.htm.

Tabb, William. 2003. "The Two Wings of the Eagle." *Monthly Review* 55(3): 76–82.

Thornton, Philip. 2003. "Reform of Stability and Growth Pact Moves Closer." *Independent,* July 18.

Thottham, Jyoti. 2003. "Where the Good Jobs Are Going." *Time,* July 28.

Wallerstein, Immanuel. 2002a. "Japan and the Modern World-System." Commentary No. 94, August 1. Available at: http://fbc.binghamton.edu/94en.htm.

————. 2002b. "Why NATO?" Commentary No. 84, March 1. Available at: http://fbc.binghamton.edu/84en.htm.

Watts, Jonathan. 2003. "Snow Opens Fire against China's Cheap Exports." *Guardian,* September 2.

Wolf, Martin. 2003. "Asia Is Footing the Bill for American Guns and Butter." *Financial Times,* February 18, p. 17.

Yarjani, Javad. 2002. "The Choice of Currency for the Denomination of the Oil Bill." Speech given by the Head of OPEC's Petroleum Market Analysis Department and invited by Spanish Minister of Economic Affairs, April 14, Oviedo, Spain: http://www.opec.org/NewsInfo/Speeches/sp2002/spAraqueSpainApr14.htm.

# 8

# EUROPE AS ALTERNATIVE EMPIRE: A VIEW FROM THE PERIPHERY

*Çağlar Keyder*

## I.

Long beleaguered as the battlefield where the East/West dilemma is played out, Turkey today finds itself in the center of the intensifying conflict between Europe and the United States. The tensions of this conflict are reflected in the struggle between rival social forces within Turkey, as these articulate with external demands and opportunities. Until the present conjuncture, Turkey's elite had been under no pressure to choose between the two incarnations of the western ideal; only now when U.S. unilateralist empire-building is so clearly at odds with EU multilateralism, and "the West" is clearly not a single entity, does the issue become a predicament.

Turkey's candidacy to the European Union has been suspect in some European circles because, among other things, the United States has so actively supported it. Several reasonable arguments exist as to why Turkey would find it difficult to relinquish its status as client to the hegemon. Foremost perhaps is the indisputable fact that Turkey's military continues to dominate the country not only politically but also ideologically and culturally, and the generals are tied to their American patrons in overt and covert ways, ranging from hardware dependence to shared war college and battlefield experience. The Turkish military has been cool to the prospect of the European Union, mostly because institutional and judicial change required by membership would not allow them to continue to exercise their unchallenged tutelage over civilian politics. Even the active involvement of the United States in pushing for Turkey's membership does not assuage their anxiety. In fact, the military and their extensions in civilian government continue to be uneasy about the prospect of EU membership. This has become overt now that the prospect is palpable. Prime Minister Ecevit's grim face on the night of the Helsinki summit in December 1999, when Turkey was admitted to candidacy, reminded TV viewers more of a victim on the way to the gallows than a politician whose country had just achieved a long-sought goal. He, along with more strident voices in the conservative judiciary and some of the less restrained members of the high command who belligerently voiced their opposition, appeared, more than anything, to fear the changes that might weaken what had always been a remarkably resilient state elite. As of this writing, top generals in the military have been more vocal and unrestrained in voicing their misgivings.

The self-serving political calculations of the military and the entrenched state elite certainly constitute the primary factor in Turkey's ambivalent relationship with the European Union. There is, however, another deeper and more cultural factor, perhaps more difficult to overcome, that also favored American patronage. U.S. hegemony was remarkably successful in winning hearts and minds: it was, after all "developmentalism" and its optimism that really liberated Turkish peasants after World War II from their centuries-old stagnation. For many Turks, their first real encounter with the outside world was in the Korean War, fighting alongside American G.I.s. The first shiny objects of desire on which they learned to tinker and pretended to understand the new language of technology were the Detroit dream machines. Under the exhortation of their leaders and in the images of Hollywood, the middle classes learned to consume and the more ambitious aspired to become millionaires. By contrast the face of Europe was stern. Not only was the memory of World War I and its aftermath, War of Liberation with the Greeks, fresh, but nationalist and Kemalist discourse made sure that everyone understood how Turkey's independence was won in a struggle against the great powers of Europe. Schoolchildren and citizens alike were never allowed to forget the intrepid hostility of the West as it tried to expand its own colonial empires by dismantling Turkey's.

During the time of U.S.-engineered development, contact with Europe only validated the official discourse and aggravated existing suspicions. Turkey was, after all, the designated "other" in the definition of Europe's historical uniqueness, and orientalist condescension was hardly disguised in most European attitudes. This gave way to more overt distrust when *gastarbeiter*s (guest workers) from Anatolian villages were received with a lack of civility verging on disdain in Germany and elsewhere. The United States, by contrast, was imagined as the true land of diversity: Americans harbored no prejudice against Turks, and Turks, in turn, felt that they did not have to prove their credentials before they could interact with them. It was not until the 1980s, with the gradual assimilation of the Turkish population in Europe, greater contact of the populations especially through tourism and football, and links generated through candidacy to the European Union, that the rift was gradually repaired.

The dialogue between Turkey and the European Union always hid more tension than the parties openly admitted. First, some Europeans suspected Turkey was a potential U.S. fifth column, but could not say so for fear of offending both the United States and Turkey. Secondly, the European Union was entrapped in its own rhetoric of being a "union of the willing": ostensibly everyone could join upon fulfilling the Copenhagen criteria,[1] but behind closed doors most agreed that Turkey should not become a member state because it just was not "European" enough, or was too Islamic, culturally speaking. A few daring politicians did voice these suspicions and accused others of hypocrisy, but officially the negotiations had to proceed along the accepted platform of national programs and reforms, and annual progress reports prepared by the European Commission in Brussels. Thirdly, and perhaps more telling, was that the Turks themselves, at least initially, were ambivalent about the prospect of membership. This calculus changed, however, in the 1990s.

## II.

Of all peripheral societies committed to projects of modernization through nation-state construction, the Turkish example was unique in its unequivocal equation of modernization with westernization. The nationalist and nationalizing elite assumed responsibility for modernization of the society, in all its dimensions (cf. Brubaker 1996). They also identified modernity with their understanding of the European experience. The legitimizing identity espoused by the republicans was an amalgam of statist nationalism and militant efforts to relegate religion as well as all particularisms (defined as cultures distinct from the state-approved) to the private sphere. Needless to say, this strategy looked with suspicion on autonomous dynamics originating in the society. Economic and political liberalism as well as expressions of allegiance to alternative identities were regarded as threats to the fundamental project of westernization. The project became problematic after the end of the Cold War. With the new wave of democracy and human rights, and the consecration of economic liberalism as the required policy dictated by various supranational commitments, the state could no longer defend its tutelary position vis-à-vis the society: there had to be concessions. Turkey's project of "Europeanization" acquired particular saliency at this juncture; and the application for membership to the European Union became a test of the sincerity of the state elite.

Surprisingly, given the nature of the Ottoman Empire, the official construct of legitimating identity in Turkey, ethnic nationalism was not frontally challenged for most of the duration of the republic. The ambivalent relationship with the imperial past had required Kemalists to reach for an ethnicity that was far in the distant and mythical past. This official nationalism, astonishing in its bold deliberateness, and validated solely by the intentionality of the state, served as the recipe of national identity and was rewarded with considerable success. Generations of schoolchildren became Turks through its devices. To achieve such levels of success, however, the state had to be vigilant and unforgiving, and had to retain all powers of management over the society. In addition, the state had to deliver: modernization represented its side of the bargain.

The repressive and ideological apparatus of the state combined with the various populist bargains of the developmentalist era sustained the illusion that the state's version of Turkish identity had gained a more than adequate foothold. Serious challenges only surfaced during the 1980s, notably in the form of political Islam and Kurdish nationalism. Coinciding with the global rise of religious and ethnic movements, these groups gained strength through the growing inability of the state to sustain its developmentalist mission. The state's increasing powerlessness to monopolize the media, especially before it was re-regulated through the market in the early 1990s, added to the strength of the challenge.

It may have been justifiable during the 1980s to see Turkey as following the path taken by other southern European countries: strengthening of social forces in favor of democratization, legal and political reform, and market liberalism. This was a period when the state was relaxing its stronghold over the economy, and the end of the military regime in 1983 was greeted with an exuberant flourishing of civil society. There were new political parties declaring commitment to economic and political liberalism; the media exploded after decades of confinement to state monopoly; and civil society organizations of various interests and persuasions were reclaiming public debate. In 1987, President Özal, in an act of valiant bravado, made a formal application for membership to the European Community. This was a bid to be included in the first wave of expansion of Europe, which incorporated the formerly authoritarian countries of Spain, Portugal, and Greece. Had Brussels at this time considered Turkey as recuperable as southern Europe was seen to be in the late 1970s, or as eastern Europe has been since the collapse of the socialist bloc, the course of recent Turkish history would have been very different.

Once again, however, the real tensions remained hidden. Even when Özal forwarded the application for membership, his own party members felt the need to float a story that this was just a ruse to show once and for all that Turkey was not wanted in Europe, and an outright refusal would provide an opportunity to turn to the Islamic world. In fact, at this time both the Islamic and the nationalist political forces were staunchly against a closer association with Europe, and what remained of the left had not yet totally outgrown its fascination with third-worldism (Keyder 1993). Despite the relaxation of statist control over the economy, Turkey's bourgeoisie was yet far from charting an independent course, fearing the loss of cozy profits of a protected market and state subsidies. Unlike southern Europe in the 1970s, Turkish society of the 1980s had not yet generated social forces of sufficient scale to regard Europe and its liberal model as the preferable alternative to the political, economic, or cultural dominance of the state model. In southern Europe, these social forces had been structured into a bloc by a bourgeoisie that had weaned itself from the dominance of statist and authoritarian tendencies, and had instead turned to liberalism and northern markets (Poulantzas 1975).

Toward the end of the 1980s, however, a challenge to state-imposed identity was growing. The society entered a course of increasing self-reliance and autonomy, not to mention cultural self-confidence, particularly among the youth; globalization and a self-generated sense of belonging in the modern world were reflected in middle-class lifestyles, especially in Istanbul, as the media became both a conduit and mirror of these changes. Identities were defined and redefined in a volatile fashion, rejecting state-imposed strictures at every turn. Along with these frontal attacks there also came an estrangement between the state and the intelligentsia. Until then, the dissent within the intelligentsia had not questioned the basic premises of statist developmentalism and official constructions of identity; the debate had been confined to the choice of instruments along a left-right continuum. Now, however, liberalism became a major contender among the ranks of those who had been presumed to be the principal carriers of the official message.

The political stage during the entire decade of the 1990s was occupied by two movements that had always been represented as mortal threats to the survival of the Turkish republic: political Islam and Kurdish nationalism. The apparent vitality and appeal of these movements demonstrated the fragility of the official discourse of legitimizing identity that all inhabitants of the country were secular Turks. These movements set the stage for the emergence of a full map of religious and ethnic diversity, of identities remembered and longing to be vindicated. Balkan, Aegean, trans-Caucasian and Arab lineages were rediscovered; Alevis became fully visible. The richness of ethnic backgrounds reflecting the heady Ottoman brew came to be celebrated. In an evolution similar to the Islamic movement, the Kurdish movement also became less monolithic, and left separatist nationalism behind in favor of democracy, cultural rights, and pluralism. As a result of these developments, it became apparent that a strong democratic front was forming to challenge the state's authoritarian control over the society. In response, the state became more insistent on national unity; instead of a measured *glasnost,* the barrage of nationalist rhetoric was redoubled, the Kemalist mantra was repeated with vigilance.

Against this backdrop of contest between a coercive state apparatus attempting to quash all expression other than its narrow definition of Turkish identity and a civil society in efflorescence, the issue of membership in the European Union and the protracted negotiations on Turkey's candidacy acquired new immediacy. Opposition groups, now aware that they had neither the resources nor the ability to mobilize social forces to defeat the state, came to see the candidacy process as the only way of winning support for greater democracy, rule of law, and an expanded pluralism. By the late 1990s, the Islamic and the Kurdish movements, human rights activists, and more generally those groups working toward the strengthening of civil society were advocating rapid fulfillment of the conditions required for full candidacy. In addition to this change of heart among the two most visible and organized movements, the leftist intelligentsia (still commanding an important place in forming public opinion) had transformed itself into a more liberal, European-style social democracy, and had become fervently pro-European in the process.

Finally, the more established grand bourgeoisie, the industrialists of Istanbul as represented by the powerful industrialists' association TÜSIAD, started to lobby for the political reforms required for membership in the European Union. Their growing global links and their frustration with Ankara led them to take an independent stance on matters ranging from the Kurdish situation and human rights to the excesses of official historiography in textbooks. For this coalition of interests, brought together in their wish to tame the state, advocating a rapid fulfillment of the conditions for EU candidacy was a safer option than direct confrontation with the formidable powers of the governing elite. Public opinion polls now indicated that a solid majority (exceeding two-thirds of the population) supported EU membership. Although this support probably did not reflect a clear understanding of what membership would actually entail, it represented a strategic choice for reforming the Turkish state by anchoring the process to the momentum and the prestige of the European project.

In contrast to all these ideals invested in Europe, the United States was seen, especially by those on the Turkish left, very much through a Latin American lens as the cynical power pulling the military strings behind the scenes. It was generally regarded as pragmatic, self-serving, and opportunistic in its human rights rhetoric. Americans did not get involved with the struggle going on within Turkey. By contrast, the European road map was clear: EU officials could obviously exert much-needed pressure on the Turkish state, and for political and civil rights activists, it was relatively easy to coordinate the platform of national struggle with the European Union's agenda (Müftüler-Bac 1997; Ugur 2000). For the military, however, the U.S. connection was crucial. The war against Kurdish nationalism had sapped vital resources, and one of the ways the military could continue to have access to an inflated budget and modernized weapons was through the special relationship with its counterpart in the Pentagon. In the neat division characterizing the debate during these years it was assumed that the United States was on the side of the state against the alliance between the European Union and the society.

## III.

What made these complex negotiations possible and extended crucial support to the social forces for democratization was that the state elite and the politicians, despite what their concrete practice betrayed, continued to profess a commitment to the European ideal. Withdrawal of the application for candidacy was never entertained as an option. Rather, the state elite and the politicians seemed satisfied with the stand-off whereby Turkey would be seen as a perpetual supplicant for membership and the European Union as a fickle and ultimately disinterested object of desire. This stalemate, partially engineered by the Turkish state itself, gave it the opportunity to validate that part of the nationalist discourse that cast Europe as carrying an essentially Christian culturalist attitude against a Turkey that would never be accepted no matter what it achieved. It was also the case, however, that because of the state elite's declared commitment to the European project, appeal to "European" norms invoking the requirements of EU candidacy remained a legitimate—in fact the only—form of critique available to that segment of civil society advocating greater democracy, rule of law, and human rights.

The unexpected development at this juncture was the European Union's initial willingness to accommodate Turkey. The change occurred at the level of the European Council and the European Commission; at the popular level, polls showed that support for Turkey's candidacy remained well below majority, although higher in the South than in the North. In fact, by the mid-1990s the European Union had acquired a major presence in Turkey. Euro-parliamentarians regularly visited areas of conflict, inspected prisons, and gave overt support to human rights organizations. The EU office in Ankara funded projects with the objective of strengthening civil society; contacts were established through nongovernmental organization (NGO) activities ranging from working with homeless children to sponsoring environmental activists. Official visits served to remind the public that this special relationship continued on course. Judgments of the European Court of Human Rights were debated and became accepted as part of Turkish jurisprudence. Perhaps inadvertently, the European Union had become a player in Turkish politics and public opinion. In other words, Turkey's heretofore insular political scene had been penetrated with the reach of new Europe-centered networks into which civil society, political parties, and state agencies found themselves drawn. These networks rapidly gained momentum toward constructing a common public sphere, as a result of which they became a factor in the decisionmaking process. It is possible to explain the commission's late 1999 decision to accept Turkey as a candidate as a preference for reinforcing these networks so as to regulate Turkey's political development from within. With such networks in place, the accounting began to favor inclusion; the cost of excluding Turkey became higher than the cost of including it (Öniş 2003).

The European Union's change of heart was not occasioned by a shift in public opinion. It should, however, be seen within the context of the second wave of expansion toward the ex-Soviet bloc countries of eastern Europe. This post–Cold War acceptance of enlargement contributed to the formation of a welcoming stance toward Turkey, in that the European Union was forced to admit that it was an expanding entity—not a deepening super state but something closer to a differentiated empire. Long discussed formulae such as variable geometry and two or three speeds in harmonization now had more concrete meaning. On the other hand, the end of the Cold War also drew a new line of demarcation— including those lands that belonged within European culture, defined as the Christian lands that the Ottoman Empire had not conquered, or had "temporarily" subjugated, but excluding Turkey. Cold War divisions were now obsolete, and Europe ended at the Greek and Bulgarian borders. These two competing evaluations, stemming out of the second wave of expansion, the imperial versus the culturalist, have defined the parameters of the EU ambivalence regarding Turkey's candidacy.

The European Union's decision to extend candidacy status to Turkey caught the state elite in Ankara and the politicians fully by surprise. In their understanding, conceding sovereignty to the European Union so overtly would be equivalent to admitting that the era of national liberation and nation-building from above had finished, that the state was no longer needed in its unchallenged status as social engineer. Having counted on perpetual postponement by Brussels, the state elite now found themselves subscribed to a project that threatened their very existence. Reforms toward EU membership required the dismantling of an entire statist system in the economy as well as in the political culture; the state could no longer be seen as the sole defining authority of the common good. The ideal of "nation as community" would have to yield to rule of law; enforcement of civil and political rights would strengthen the civil society, weaken the entrenched political class, and eradicate arbitrary rule, which had customarily been justified in the name of stability and national security (Keyder 1997; Kasaba and Bozdoğan 2000). The collective rights of the Kurdish minority would have to be recognized, and secularism would have to be redefined to allow freedoms of religious organization and expression. Perhaps most controversial, the military would have to abdicate its regency over the state.

It is important to realize that despite its perennial boast of being the only Islamic country that is democratic, Turkey is also distinguished by its history of military interventions. The latest of these was in 1980 when the military reinstituted civilian government in three years, but only after they had written a constitution that practically kept the military in a continuing unchallenged position vis-à-vis civilian government. One new organ of governance was particularly important: the National Security Council (NSC). NSC was meant to serve as the real government of the country since the military felt that the affairs of the state were too important to leave to elected politicians. By means of this council's permanent secretariat, military planners dictated to the civilian government surprisingly detailed programs ranging from security policy to educational practice. Nonetheless, this expected tutelage would have eroded with elections and civilian rule, except that during the entire decade of the 1990s, the country was involved in a war in its eastern regions against Kurdish separatist guerillas. The war was conducted by the military, which had initially made the decision that armed confrontation rather than dialogue and negotiation was the preferred strategy and cultural rights could not be entertained until the guerrillas were soundly defeated. The military was thus able to perpetuate its status and did not have to face any criticism until after it felt that the war had been won. Since the capture of the Kurdish leader in 1999 and the cessation of hostilities, however, the military has been reluctant to give up its status. It is this conjuncture, within which civilianization has come to be associated with greater integration with the European Union, through which Turkey is now living (cf. Jung and Piccoli 2001).

## IV.

Given their structural and conjunctural reluctance to give up political power, the state elite had driven themselves into an impasse with regard to the European Union, and it was a sudden awareness of this that mobilized them to reflect on the extent of Turkey's commitment to the European project (Sofos 2000). There was no longer room for hypocrisy or self-delusion, and the calculations based on perpetuating indecision were no longer relevant. Accordingly, opposition, especially from the military but also from within the ranks of the bureaucracy and the judiciary was openly voiced for the first time. As it became clear that the Copenhagen criteria were not negotiable, various explanations were advanced as to why the Turkish state could not possibly apply them. It was suddenly discovered that membership in the European Union would entail a loss of sovereignty. Top generals opined that the European Union, using the pretext of cultural rights, wanted to divide Turkey along ethnic lines, and the ultra right was mobilized to defend the unitary national structure against European demands, religious fundamentalists, and separatists.

It was clear that the state elite would not easily give up their prerogatives, and would make use of the entire gamut of arguments stemming from "national security" concerns in order to stave off the threat of accession. This was not particularly difficult given the political structure and the composition of the government in 1999. This motley coalition under Ecevit's premiership remained in power until the elections in November 2002. All the major parties, and in particular the three that formed the government, were squarely within the statist camp. Ecevit's Democratic Left Party, remnants of a third-worldist and nationalist left, was hardly distinguishable from the nationalist right that formed the second largest wing of the coalition. The third party, Motherland, was too mired in a history of corruption to enjoy any credibility. Against this backdrop of a reluctant state elite bolstered by a spineless political class, the EU option receded as a state policy, kept alive only through the bureaucratic momentum launched after the Helsinki summit.

This new alignment represented an unexpected reversal. Since the beginning of the westernization adventure, the modernizing impulse had been integrally vested in the state elite, who regarded the masses with great suspicion. If EU membership criteria were realized, however, they would lose their position as modernizers in control. Now it was the masses—the Kurds, along with those voting for the religious parties who joined the liberals and the new left—who would be pushing for a speedier timetable. Each of these groups approached the implicit alliance with different goals and priorities, but their agendas intersected in the demand for the state to grant greater freedom to the society—in minority rights, in religious affairs, and in the public sphere.

This new alignment was reinforced when Turkey was struck by a massive economic crisis in 2001, made all the more dire because it had been postponed for so long through palliative measures. The seriousness of the crisis occasioned cathartic soul-searching among the populace. There was general agreement that the crisis was the result of corrupt statism, that Turkey was a relic of the old world, and that fundamental restructuring of the state-society relationship, which would render politicians and top bureaucrats accountable through legislative reform, was long overdue. The EU candidacy was invoked as a concrete objective that provided the country with a road map ranging over the entire contested terrain.

The pro-EU forces in Turkey were delivered an unexpected breakthrough in November 2002 when the "Islamic Democrat" Justice and Development Party won the elections. Not only had the party actually promised to work for membership, but it was the only political force not compromised by its relationship with the state elite. Instead, the party consisted of outsiders who could reasonably be expected to follow through with their promise. In fact, even before they had formed the government, the leader of the party, Erdogan, started making the rounds in European capitals in order to garner support for Turkey's accession negotiations to be scheduled during the upcoming summit in December. This was the first time in more than a decade that a government was formed by a single party, and thus a party leader could in fact with authority promise to implement a program of reforms, without fearing (or hiding behind) sabotage by coalition partners. It was also at this time that the culturalist opposition within the European Union engaged in a frontal and forthright attack against accommodating Turkey. Giscard d'Estaing, who had been named president of the convention, with the mandate to draft a constitution for the European Union, declared that Turkey should not be encouraged any further because it was not a European country and was, furthermore, mostly Muslim. Brussels officials were embarrassed; some socialist deputies asked for Giscard's resignation and once again calls were made for defining Europe's borders.

Arguably, this conjuncture, when the leaders of the Justice and Development Party were attempting to impose popular democracy and civilian control over the state elite, provided a unique opportunity to support and strengthen democratic reforms in Turkey. With Erdoğan's declaration, the ball was in the European Union's court. If in the Copenhagen Summit in December 2002 the EU heads of state could have decided that Turkey would be supported and given an unambiguous timetable for accession negotiations to start, there would be a different future for both Turkey and the European Union. At this crucial juncture and potential turning point, however, Brussels officials protested that they were not convinced that the new government could actually control the military and the judiciary. Together with encouraging words and pats on the back, the Turkish government was asked to prove in deeds what it had achieved on paper. Indeed, the government was successful in pushing through the parliament a succession of legislations, dubbed democratization packages. According to these packages, restrictions on freedom of speech are lifted, criminal procedure improved to protect against torture and maltreatment by the police, and language rights granted to the Kurdish minority. The practice so far, however, supports the skepticism of the commission in Brussels that civilians will never have enough power against the entrenched state elite, and especially against the military. Thus, the police continue to behave as they have always done, the judiciary is not convinced that the new freedoms are real, and the military appear unfazed by the new restrictions on their conduct. In other words, the effectiveness of legal activism has proven limited. The suspicion that perhaps there is something more than legislation to the changing of political and civic culture, and that transformation cannot be as swift as desired, has now hit the pro-European party. This suspicion indirectly validates the European culturalist position, to the chagrin of the Europeanizers, and, it is safe to say, to the delight of the state elite.

However, there is still a lot that rides on the European Union's attitude toward Turkey's candidacy. If, in fact, there is a project within the European Union to situate Europe as an alternative to U.S. unilateralism, then expansion toward a key region in the world makes eminent sense. In fact, there are some signs that there has been a still timid veering within the European Union toward this position. Turkey has been, without fanfare, but with the full support of the French and the Germans, included in the category of the later accession countries, along with Bulgaria and Romania, although there has been no official decision as to when a date will be given for the start of negotiations. In the best alternative, this date was determined in December 2004. This informal inclusion means that there is Turkish representation in the important summits, such as the Rome meeting to discuss the draft constitution in October 2003. This attitude may be interpreted again as the European Union is trying to regulate Turkish developments from within, but its import is now bigger because it is also transparently an attempt to woo Turkey away from the United States and the American sphere of "new" Europeans.

Had the Copenhagen Summit in early 2003 delivered a favorable message to Turkey's new governing party, the margin by which the Turkish Parliament voted against allowing the U.S. army to be stationed in Turkey prior to the occupation of Iraq would no doubt have been more decisive. Not only would the government have felt less anxious about being left alone in the world and more committed to "old Europe," but the deputies would have felt more unrestrained to reflect the overwhelming public opposition to the prospect of war. But the summit ended in the most disappointing manner for Turkey: the ten countries of the first wave were granted membership within the year, Bulgaria and Romania were given a definite timetable, and Turkey's bid was again postponed to be reconsidered at the end of 2004. Following this rebuff, there was a barrage of propaganda in the establishment press to the effect that Turkey had risked remaining alone in the coming turbulent times, and that after the rejection by the European Union, the only viable option was closer cooperation with the United States. The military seized the moment and gradually socialized the new government into their national security agenda. Within a month Erdogan was parroting the state elite's line regarding the necessity of caution in political reforms and the need to be intransigent concerning "our strategic interests in Cyprus."

After the division within the ranks of the European Union in the days leading to the Iraq war, the national security argument in Turkey acquired more salience. It was reported in Turkish papers that when the foreign minister went to the White House in February 2003 and feebly protested that Turkey had obligations toward Europe as well, the U.S. president retorted by saying, "Europe is no more, I have divided it." On the eve of the vote to decide on the stationing of U.S. troops in Turkish territory, it seemed fairly certain that under pressure from the party leadership, Parliament would ratify the sentiments of dejection and helplessness by joining the coalition of the willing. In the end, however, concerns about public opinion prevailed, albeit by a small margin, and the motion was defeated, blocking the U.S. plan to attack Iraq from the north. The state elite were astounded; the pro-American media were up in arms, predicting catastrophe. Hence, it was not surprising that later the same year the state elite would give the vote another try. By this time the neophyte government had been imbued with national security rhetoric and the Kurdish separatist threat card softened the public resistance to adventurism. If Turkey, in fact, sends troops to Iraq, the suspicion that it would serve as an American Trojan horse would have proven valid and the affair with the European Union will most likely be suspended for a long while; the military will have consolidated its ascendancy and the democratization packages will be forgotten in the ensuing chaos.

## V.

Turkey's candidacy was accompanied by much debate on the geographical and cultural bases of European identity. Cultural difference was frequently brought onto the agenda, mainly by out-of-office center-right politicians—notably Giscard d'Estaing and Helmut Kohl. What prevailed in the Helsinki Summit of December 1999, however, was not a culturalist understanding of European identity, but Europe as a new civilizational project bringing together a political community defined by allegiance to a common set of rules, with the Copenhagen criteria for candidacy articulating the minimum constitutional requirements. There have, of course, been different conceptions of the telos of European integration, ranging from the establishment of a customs union to the formation of a United States of Europe. The normative definition of the European

Union is not clearly spelled out, nor is it a fixed target. As the European Union evolves, its self-conception moves along the spectrum between the establishment of a super state in need of prior grounding based on shared identity, and a constitutionally guaranteed association signaling the inception of a new model political unit, distinct from a federation, yet different than the narrow association of a common market. Although the debate on the nature of the European Union has obvious implications for its attitude toward Turkey's membership, the discussion on Turkey's membership also becomes a proxy for the debate on the nature and the boundaries of the European Union (Sjursen 2000). Those who favor Turkey's accession would like to see the European Union's enlargement project extend beyond the boundaries of Europe's cultural sphere. Such an extension would not only provide a world-historical rebuke to the claim that the world is divided into "civilizations" based on the primacy of unchangeable cultures (cf. Huntington 1996), but would also establish the European Union as a viable alternative to the empire being aggressively promoted from the other side of the Atlantic. In effect, by embracing its historical other, the European Union will have redefined itself as a new form of empire, targeting an association on the basis of law and constitutional allegiance.

There is nothing in the European Union's charter that excludes the option of unbounded expansion; rather the constraint comes from inside. The convention, held supposedly to clarify the nature of the entity, has so far perpetuated the ambivalence. In fact, there were two real options: the European Union as federation based on the culturalist precepts of a homogenizing nation-state versus a European Union as civic and constitutional empire with differentiated subsidiaries (Delanty 1998). The first option would require greater unification and deepening around a core of shared heritage and history, with an implicit Christian consciousness. It is arguable that this option is no longer available after U.S. policy indeed divided the continent into old and new. This would have been a fortress Europe, trying to preserve its uniqueness, its social compact, and its privileges. However, this alternative would not offer much to any peoples left outside and would pose no challenge to the emerging U.S. empire, since a cultural Europe would already have achieved closure and would be occupied with deepening rather than expansion.[2]

The second option is that of empire constituted not through conquest but by the willing allegiance of member states to the law of the European Union. When law is the principal source of attraction and legitimation, schoolchildren do not have to learn about "our ancestors the Romans," or about "our unique cultural values as Europeans," or even "our Christian heritage"—an epithet that has, in any case, been preempted by the White House. Europe could be composed of a cool, dispassionate, carefully assessed membership, the result of deliberation and choice based on interest and calculation. It would institute governance based on constitution and juridification, with overlapping layers of autonomy and affiliation (cf. Tully 2002). Without coercive incorporation, imperial expansion would follow political competition, representation of alternatives, parliamentary decisions and referenda with some democratic legitimacy. In fact, an accession decided against culture and history that highlights the dispassionate element and emphasizes the overcoming of adverse predispositions would be all the more valuable. The European Union would then really become a universalist empire espousing a clearly spelled out alternative project for governing globalization.

An optimistic scenario for the near future is that all of the European Union states will gravitate around old Europe's implicit strategy to establish a counterweight to the United States—a scenario that would have to bring in those waiting outside the fortress, in the faux bourgs, if it is to attain inclusive credibility. The variable geometry of concentric circles that has been proposed for the European Union would seem to be compatible with such peripheral incorporation. A Christian "club" that would necessarily be protective and inward-looking has no chance of succeeding as an alternative. Indeed, from the geopolitical point of view, but more importantly because of the perspective of incorporating a substantially Muslim nation (Islam is the second religion within the European Union), Turkey would seem to be a necessary component of such a scenario, if only because it was the first to apply among other likely candidates. In fact, for the European Union to really become an alternative, it has to expand not only toward new countries to its east, but also toward the predominantly Muslim countries of North Africa, the most obvious near periphery. This, however, will require an unambiguous will to grow into a universalist empire on the part of Europe, and, in the candidate countries, an alignment of internal forces in the direction of the values exemplified by a constitutional entity.

## Notes

1. According to the Copenhagen criteria, "membership requires that the candidate country:
-has achieved stability of institutions guaranteeing democracy, the rule of law, human rights, and respect for and protection of minorities,
-the existence of a functioning market economy as well as the capacity to cope with competitive pressures and market forces within the Union, and
-[has] the ability to take on the obligations of membership, including adherence to the aims of political, economic and monetary union."

2. Whether this option is even available in the face of pressures of globalization is also debatable. See Castells (1998) and Habermas (1999).

# References

Brubaker, Rogers. 1996. *Nationalism Reframed.* Cambridge, UK: Cambridge University Press.

Castells, Manuel. 1998. *End of Millennium.* Oxford: Blackwell.

Delanty, R. 1998. "Social Theory and European Transformation: Is There a European Society?" *Sociological Research Online* 3(1), available at http://www.socresonline.org.uk/socresonline/3/1/1.html.

Habermas, Jürgen. 1999. "The European Nation-State and the Pressures of Globalization." *New Left Review* 235 (May–June): 46–59.

Huntington, Samuel. 1996. *The Clash of Civilizations and the Remaking of World Order.* New York: Simon and Schuster.

Jung, Dietrich, and Wolfango Piccoli. 2001. *Turkey at the Crossroads.* London: Zed Books.

Kasaba, Reşat, and Sibel Bozdoğan. 2000. "Turkey at a Crossroad." *Journal of International Affairs* 54(1): 1–20.

Keyder, Çağlar. 1993. "The Dilemma of Cultural Identity on the Margin of Europe." *Review: A Journal of the Fernand Braudel Center* 16(1): 19–33.

———. 1997. "Whither the Project of Modernity? Turkey in the 1990s." In S. Bozdogan and R. Kasaba, eds., *Rethinking the Project of Modernity in Turkey.* Seattle: University of Washington Press, pp. 37–51.

Müftüler-Bac, Meltem. 1997. *Turkey's Relations with a Changing Europe.* Manchester, UK: Manchester University Press.

Öniş, Ziya. 2003. "Domestic Politics, International Norms, and Challenges to the State: Turkey-EU Relations in the Post-Helsinki Era." In Ali Çarkoğlu and Barry Rubin, eds., *Turkey and the European Union: Domestic Politics, Economic Integration, and International Dynamics.* London: Frank Cass, pp. 9–34.

Poulantzas, Nicos. 1975. *The Crisis of the Dictatorships: Portugal, Greece, Spain.* London: New Left Books.

Sofos, Spyros A. 2000. "Reluctant Europeans? European Integration and the Transformation of Turkish Politics." *South European Society and Politics* 5(2): 243–260.

Sjursen, Helene. 2000. "Why Expand? The Question of Justification in the EU's Enlargement Policy." ARENA Working Papers, WP 01/6.

Tully, James. 2002. "The Kantian Idea of Europe: Critical and Cosmopolitan Perspectives." In Anthony Pagden, ed., *The Idea of Europe from Antiquity to the European Union.* Cambridge: Cambridge University Press, pp. 331–358.

Uğur, Mehmet. 2000. "The Anchor-Credibility Problem in EU-Turkey Relations." In Jackie Gower and John Redmond, eds., *Enlarging the European Union.* Aldershot, UK: Ashgate.

# 9

# HEGEMONIC RIVALRY AND THE PERIPHERY: THE CASE OF THE TRANS-ATLANTIC "BANANA WARS"

## Keith Nurse

The world-systems approach to hegemonic cycles argues that the movement from hegemonic supremacy to imperial rivalry is attended by the expansion of colonialism or the growing domination of the core regions over the periphery (Bergesen and Schoenberg 1980; Bousquet 1980; Chase-Dunn 1978). When power is dispersed among imperial rivals, vying powers tend to define spheres of influence to defend or expand their share of global value-added markets. This trend is expressed in the formation of regional blocs and a shift from multilateralism to bilateralism or unilateralism. The sharpening of core-periphery relations ultimately raises the resistance quotient and leads to demands for decolonization and alternative modes of governance.

The tendentious movement toward colonialism is reinforced by the economic crisis transmitted to the periphery on account of the cyclical downturn (e.g., the emergence of a new techno-economic paradigm and the rationalization of production) that coincides with the phase of rivalry. As a result, peripheral exports lose their market power (e.g., declining terms of trade). These trends spell weaker bargaining power in world markets and a substantial transfer of capital to the core through cheaper food, raw materials, manufacturing, and brain drain. Innovation in the core and the relocation of declining sectors calls for new material inputs and services from the periphery, thereby increasing its dependence on imported technology and management (Nurse 1998). Enhanced competition among peripheral states reduces export earnings from the traditional export sectors as well as new export-oriented investments, and consequently leads to adverse terms of trade, balance of payments problems, and debt crises. Debt administration emerges as a key mechanism for political governance of the periphery (Stewart 1993). Intensifying competition ultimately manifests itself in the periphery in increased unemployment and falling standards of living for its populations. These problems ultimately translate into increased vulnerability to internal instability and intervention from outside.

The "banana wars" is one of the trans-Atlantic trade disputes between the United States and the European Union, and one of the first cases to be handled within the new World Trade Organization (WTO) system (Francis 2000; Petersmann 1994). The other disputes between the two rivals have been over U.S. foreign sales corporations' hidden export promotion, the European Union's import ban on meat of hormone-treated animals, and the tariff protection of the U.S. steel industry (Badinger, Breuss, and Mahlberg 2002, 524). The banana wars, too, have to be placed in the context of the continuing conflicts between the United States and European Union over EU Common Agricultural Policy (CAP) and food export subsidies, which impact world agricultural trade and prices.

The so-called banana wars have accordingly been played out at the European Court of Justice (ECJ), the General Agreement on Trade and Tariffs (GATT), and the World Trade Organization (WTO). The source of the conflict stems from the creation, in tandem with the establishment of the Single European Market, of a Common Market Organization for Bananas (CMOB), which replaced the fragmented national market structure of the European Community (Nurse and Sandiford 1995).

The trade conflict over bananas is considered the most legally and politically complex dispute settlement case with which the WTO has dealt so far. It was also the first case in the WTO dispute-settlement system that allowed for retaliatory measures, a key feature of the new rule-based trade organization (Komuro 2000, 75–78). The banana wars attracted global media attention in 1999 when the United States imposed retaliatory measures—100 percent *ad valorem* duties—on imports of a variety of European products worth $191.4 million after the WTO found against the European Union in a dispute over trade restrictions on banana imports. The U.S. retaliatory measures targeted European exports ranging from Scottish cashmere to lead-acid storage batteries, handbags, and sweet biscuits. Ecuador also sought and was granted retaliatory measures by the WTO to the tune of $201.6 million. In 2001, the United States and Ecuador dropped retaliatory measures after the European Union agreed to implement a tariff-only regime by January 2006.

The trans-Atlantic banana wars hence are not just about contestation among core states. For they have had a direct impact on the economic and political fortunes of the world-economy's peripheral regions—and on their states, firms, and growers. Since bananas are grown in tropical—and peripheral—zones, they give an excellent insight into the evolving geopolitical context of the core-periphery relations. This chapter outlines the structure and operations of the world banana trade, and then examines the key features of the common market organization for bananas and the international legal challenges that have arisen. It then examines the changing global political economy of bananas and assesses the significance of the banana case for understanding the impact of the rising intracore rivalry on peripheral regions.

## The Political Economy of Banana Trade

The banana is the most important tropical fresh fruit in global trade, surpassing apples and citrus in importance. It is second only to coffee in terms of agricultural export earnings. The main markets for the banana are those of the United States, Europe, and Japan, which account, respectively, for 29.3, 27.8, and 8.5 percent of world imports. Europe is due to become the largest import market with European Union enlargement in 2004 and is at the moment the most profitable market with the highest per capita consumption, with retail prices 50 percent above those in the United States, although prices between the two regions have been converging in the last four years (FAO 2003). Crucially, banana traders are allowed to operate in the EU market as large vertically integrated firms, whereas no allowance is made for them in the U.S. market to handle the fruit beyond the port of entry (Litvak and Maule 1977). The EU market, therefore, allows the major banana traders to maximize on economies of scale and scope.

The characteristics and the logistics of the banana trade influence market operations and the organizational structure of the industry. For one, its trade is the most complex and industrialized in the category of fruit and vegetables. The fruit differs from other tropical products entering global trade (e.g., rubber, cocoa, sugar, and coffee), since it is a heavy, bulky, fragile, highly perishable commodity that cannot be stored. Rough handling easily erodes its value. Meeting these market demands requires a highly coordinated commodity chain: planting and harvesting, shipping, quality control, ripening, marketing, distribution, and retail. This calls for heavy investments in specialized refrigeration and ventilation equipment at all stages between production and consumption. These factors combine to create a strong barrier for new entrants into the banana industry. The organization, production, and distribution of the industry hence leads to an oligopolistic control, and generates relatively high returns for the upstream phases of the commodity chain as opposed to that of production (Ellis 1981; Litvak and Maule 1977). In fact, it is estimated that producers' share of the final retail price is no more than 10 percent, whereas that of distributors and retailers ranges from 40 to 50 percent (Nurse and Sandiford 1995). These characteristics explain its attraction to the transnational corporations

(TNCs) and their dominance in its production, handling, and distribution. A total of three TNCs—Chiquita, Dole, and Del Monte—account for 70 percent of world trade.

A top retail item for global distributors and supermarket chains like Wal-Mart, Tesco, Ahold, Carrefour, Metro, and Itoyokado, the banana has become an important item of consumption.[1] Cheap, filling, and nutritious, it has come to play in the twentieth century a role similar to that of sugar in the nineteenth (Jenkins 2000). Like sugar, its imports have been encouraged in the core zones to improve the popular diet. In the popular imagination, the banana often conjures up images of something-less-than-serious as exemplified in terms like "going bananas," "slipping on banana peels," and "banana republics." In juxta-position, the banana has also been viewed as a symbol of freedom, democracy, and modernity. Along with jeans and rock music, it was one of the key symbols associated with German unification. In 2001 when the European Union launched its currency, German Chancellor Gerhardt Schroeder chose to spend his very first euros on bananas.

In contrast, the image of bananas in the producing regions is such that "bananas represent hard work and the basis of the family income, and the people do not tell banana jokes or slip on banana peels" (Jenkins 2000, 154). The main exporters of bananas are the Latin American producers, who account for approxi-mately 75 percent of world trade and are the dominant suppliers to the North American and European markets. Ecuador alone, the largest exporter and residual supplier, accounts for 34 percent of the world market. The next largest producer region is the Far East (14 percent), with the Philippines as the main exporter supplying Japan and Asia. The other main banana exporters are, with 5 percent, the African, Caribbean, and Pacific (ACP) countries (i.e., Cameroon, Cote d'Ivoire, Jamaica, Suriname, Belize, and the Windward Islands). Among the banana export-ers are also the European Union's overseas countries and territories (OCT) such as the Canary Islands, Martinique, Guadeloupe, Madeira, and Crete, whose produce is consumed solely within the European Union (FAO 2003).

## The Trans-Atlantic Banana Wars

The establishment of the Single European Market (SEM) in 1993 has unleashed a series of conflicts between the European Union and the United States (and Japan) over the final shape of this market: the drawn-out dispute over banana trade has come to serve as a test-case as to how accessible this single market, the largest market for banana exports, would eventually be to non-European players. Prior to the establishment of the single market, rules governing the importation and marketing of bananas were set along national lines as enshrined in either the Treaty of Rome or in contractual commitments under the Lomé Convention (such as the Banana Protocol) as well as the political imperative of protecting EU producers from overseas competition. [2]

As the protected EU and ACP producers accounted for 21 and 19 percent of the Europe-bound banana trade respectively, Latin American producers supplied the remaining 60 percent. The EU and ACP producers marketed very little of their produce outside the European market. The French and Spanish markets absorbed over 90 percent of EU-produced bananas, and France and the United Kingdom together imported 85 percent of ACP bananas.

The establishment of the single market required that the segmented banana market be revamped accordingly, and the existing restrictions on the movement within the European Union of goods, labor, and capital be removed. As mentioned, the importation of bananas was not subject to a common policy except for the common tariff of 20 percent *ad valorem* that was instituted in 1963. The planned creation of a Common Market Organization for Bananas engendered heated debate within the European Council of Ministers and proved to be one of the most contentious issues in the lead-up to the creation of the single market. There was intense debate between member states, between those who espoused the removal of all restrictions on its trade (Germany, Belgium, Luxembourg, the Netherlands, and Denmark) and those that wanted some form of protectionism to be maintained (France, Spain, Portugal, and Greece). The former group called for no quotas, a tariff of 20 percent maximum, and temporary aid for EU and ACP producers; the latter for tariff-quotas and a licensing system.

The quantitative restrictions proposed by some members of the European Union within the framework of the proposed CMOB led five Latin American suppliers (Colombia, Costa Rica, Guatemala, Nicaragua, and Venezuela) to file a complaint at the GATT in February 1993 on account of the plan's discriminatory and "trade-distorting" measures—and of direct payments by the European Union to ACP producers as a means of aid. In support of its banana companies, Chiquita and Dole, and because of its ongoing conflict with Europe over agricultural subsidies, the United States exhibited a keen interest in the case and threw its political weight behind the Latin American states. The complainants argued that the dispute was not about the Lomé Convention but rather about whether non-ACP GATT members could enjoy their GATT rights of nondiscrimination and unfettered access to the EU market.

The quantitative restrictions set by France, Italy, Portugal, Spain, and the United Kingdom during the creation of the single market were found in 1993 by the GATT panel to be inconsistent with GATT Article XI.1. The panel also found that the European Union's preferential treatment of ACP suppliers under the Lomé convention violated Article I (most-favored-nation treatment [MFN]) and was discriminatory against non-ACP GATT members (*GATT Panel Report, DS32/R*). The report recommended that contracting parties request the European Union to bring the quantitative restrictions and the tariff preference into conformity with GATT, or that the European Union seek a waiver for its Lomé preferences for bananas under GATT Article XXV.[3] The EU and ACP countries were able to block the panel report because the GATT dispute settlement procedures allowed a losing party to exercise a veto over the adoption of a panel report under the "positive consensus" rule (Komuro 2000, 6).

On a different front, Germany, backed by Belgium and the Netherlands, initiated proceedings in June 1993 at the European Court of Justice (ECJ) to prevent the implementation of the common market organization of bananas. The German government argued that the CMOB was in breach of the Banana Protocol annexed to the 1957 Treaty of Rome, which permitted the German government to import bananas free of duty (Everling 1996). In October 1994, the advocate general of the ECJ rejected the alleged infringement on the grounds that "accepting the applicant's point of view would make the common organization of the market in bananas impossible" and that "the 'Banana Protocol' cannot have the effect of derogating from a basis provision of the Treaty on European Union" (ECJ 1994, 22).

In spite of the legal challenges at the GATT and the ECJ, the CMOB came into effect in July 1993. The CMOB permits the free movement of bananas within the European Union and thus allows for a competitive environment for third-country bananas. In effect, the CMOB (European Council Regulation No. 404/93) removed the unrestricted market access and reduced the margins that ACP banana exporters and marketers enjoyed under the previous regime, validated under Article 115 of the Treaty of Rome and the Banana Protocol of the Lomé Convention.[4] The CMOB aimed to reconcile the varied and competing interests in the banana trade. It had to harmonize the goals of the SEM (EU consumer and producer interests, budgetary restraints, efficiency aims, and competition policy) with extra-European obligations like the legal commitment to the ACP under the Banana Protocol of the Lomé Convention and the commitments in the GATT/WTO framework arising from the Uruguay Round of multilateral negotiations. The CMOB attempted to achieve these competing goals by constraining supply expansion and rent-seeking through a *tariff-rate quota* on third-country bananas (e.g., "dollar zone" bananas) and a licensing system that redistributes the tariff rents to EU and ACP fruit traders by allocating licenses for the import of non-EU and non-ACP bananas.[5] The licensing system operated as a cross subsidy for ACP and EU fruit traders, thereby enhancing their participation in the banana market. In fact, they were able to improve their competitiveness and profitability through the licensing mechanism, which granted them 30 percent of the third-country licenses.

The establishment of the CMOB triggered a second GATT panel by the same five Latin American banana exporters. In much the same vein as the first GATT panel, the second panel concluded that the CMOB was inconsistent with the GATT. The finding was that the tariff preference to ACP countries discriminated against third-country bananas and thus violated GATT Article I.1. The license allocation system was also found to be in violation of the nondiscrimination principle in terms of national treatment (Article III.4) and the MFN treatment (Article I.1) (GATT Panel Report, DS38/R).

In similar fashion, the European Union was able to block the panel report under the positive consensus rule. What differed in the second panel proceeding was the response of the European Union to the challenge. Whereas in the first proceeding, the old regime had already been superseded by the time the panel report came out, this time the European Union was anxious to avoid a GATT panel decision that would weaken its position on other trade negotiations at the Uruguay Round. In anticipation of a negative result from the GATT panel, the European Union negotiated a Banana Framework Agreement (BFA) with the Latin American complainants. The new framework required the complainants not to pursue the panel report and to refrain from initiating dispute settlement procedures until 2003. In return, the European Union, under pressure from Germany and Holland, offered to increase the banana quota from 2.0 million tons in 1993 to 2.1 in 1994 and to 2.2 in 1995 with an in-quota tariff rate of 75 ecus per ton. The EU also introduced a quota allocation system based on countries' average exports over the previous three years. Under this system Costa Rica's market share rose to 23.4 from 19 percent in 1992, and that of Colombia increased from 18 percent to 22. In contrast, Ecuador's market share dropped from 27.7 to 20.2 percent in part because it boosted its exports in anticipation of a liberalized single market. The BFA allowed the four GATT members to grant special export certificates for up to 70 percent of their quota, which had the effect of redistributing the quota rent and enhancing the bargaining power of the banana-producing countries, much to the annoyance of the banana TNCs.

Guatemala declined the offer but Costa Rica, Colombia, Venezuela, and Nicaragua signed the BFA and it was written into the text of the final act of the GATT Uruguay Round. The BFA stirred up much conflict among the concerned parties. Within the Latin American group, the European Union's offer resulted in a split in their united front. Ecuador, the largest banana exporter to the European Union, along with Guatemala and Panama, argued that the European Union's proposal, which involved a country-by-country allocation system, was detrimental to their interests.

The settlement of the GATT dispute through the BFA provoked a new challenge to the CMOB, this time from the United States at the behest of Chiquita and the Hawaii Banana Industry Association. These associations applied to the U.S. trade representative (USTR) for relief under Section 301 of the Trade Act of 1974 from the banana policies of the European Union and the BFA settlement. The policies and the practices implicit in the CMOB and the GATT BFA were viewed by Chiquita, the largest of the U.S. TNCs, as leading to an erosion of their market share in Europe and as being particularly "unreasonable," "discriminatory," and "burdensome and restrictive" of U.S. commerce. At first, the USTR initiated an investigation into the preferential treatment extended by the European Union to ACP banana exporters. In December 1994, the United States agreed to drop this challenge in response to a plea by the Caribbean Community (CARICOM) countries at the Summit of the Americas meeting held in Miami, but also because at a GATT meeting in Geneva, the waiver for Lomé preferences was reaffirmed by a two-thirds majority vote.

The United States subsequently focussed its objections to the GATT BFA between the European Union and the four Latin American countries. Based upon the Section 301 complaint lodged by Chiquita, the United States demanded (1) an enlargement of the EU quota for Latin American banana imports, (2) the abolition of the GATT BFA between the European Union and the Latin American countries of Costa Rica, Colombia, Nicaragua, and Venezuela, and (3) the abolition of the licensing system that allowed 30 percent of the third-country import licenses to be granted to the traders that handle ACP and EU bananas.

In February 1996, the USTR 301 action was carried over to a complaint in the WTO initiated by the United States and cosigned by Ecuador, Guatemala, Honduras, and Mexico. After unsuccessful consultations, the dispute settlement body acceded to the creation of a dispute panel. The case proved to be very complex in that the dispute involved 20 WTO members (five complainants and one respondent representing 15 EU member states) and a number of interested parties such as Japan and the ACP countries. The dispute also drew on a wide number of multilateral trade agreements such as the GATT, along with new WTO agreements like the Agreement on Agriculture, the Agreement on Import Licensing Procedures, the Agreement on Trade-Related Investment Measures (TRIMS), and the General Agreement on Trade in Services (GATS). In addition, the dispute had to take into consideration the legal instrument establishing the CMOB (EC Regulation 404/93 and its amendments), the BFA, and the GATT/WTO waiver (Komuro 2000).

EU officials argued that the United States did not provide specific details about the damage to U.S. companies arising from the CMOB. The EU view was premised on the fact that Chiquita does not produce any bananas in the United States and that the Hawaiian Banana Industry Association produces and sells exclusively within the United States. The EU position was that the trade in goods between the United States and the European Union was not affected and thus questioned the *locus standi* of the United States in pursuing this matter. News reports at the time indicated that Carl Lindner, the president of Chiquita, had actively lobbied the U.S. administration to intervene on this matter.[6]

The WTO panel of May 1997 ruled that the issue was not just about actual trade but also about competitive opportunities. The findings of the panel report were that the CMOB was inconsistent with the European Union's obligations under Articles I: 1, II: 4, X: 3, and XIII: 1 of the GATT, Article 1.3 of the Licensing Agreement, and Articles II and XVII of the GATS. In September 1997, the appellate body of the dispute settlement system upheld the panel decision of May 1997. In essence, the decision maintained most of the findings of the earlier GATT panels and further called into question the allocation of individual country quotas to the ACP. Under the new WTO rule of "negative consensus," a ruling can only be blocked if the benefiting party votes to reject the favorable panel decision. The European Union was thus obliged to abide by the ruling and bring the CMOB into conformity with the WTO. The deadline for implementing the reformed CMOB was January 1, 1999 (European Union 1999).

The main target of the WTO ruling was the licensing system, which acted as a cross-subsidy in favor of the traders of ACP and EU bananas and was viewed as a discriminatory mechanism at the expense of third-country importers, namely the dollar zone importers and the TNCs. As was expected, the WTO ruling received a negative greeting in the ACP countries, which expressed concerns that the removal of the licensing system would result in a redistribution of market shares, profits, and income in favor of the dollar traders and the TNCs. Another major concern for the ACP was the abolition of specific country quotas even though the global ACP export quota of 857,000 tons at nil duty was retained.

The EU response made it clear that the reformed regime would be WTO-compatible and not go beyond the requirements stipulated in the rules. This was because most of the provisions of the CMOB were not placed into question in the WTO verdict, notably the amount of the tariff quota, aid for EU OCT producers, the preferential system for the import of traditional bananas from the ACP, and preferential treatment for EU production.

The EU reforms did not satisfy the original complainants: the United States along with five Latin American countries (Ecuador, Guatemala, Honduras, Mexico, and Panama). These countries argued that the European Union's adoption of Council Regulation 1637/98 of 20 July 1998 and Commission Regulation 2362/98 of 28 October 1998 continued to restrict access for bananas from Latin America and thus were inconsistent with the WTO recommendations. Ecuador expressed dissatisfaction with the EU reform regime and called for the reconvening of the WTO panel.

The reconvened panel went beyond the original panel and appellate body and outlined three specific options for making the EU measures WTO-consistent. The first option was a tariff-only system; the second, a tariff-only system with a tariff quota for ACP bananas covered by a suitable waiver; and the third, a MFN tariff quota. The European Union expressed a divergent view and failed to implement the recommendations of the reconvened panel.

The failure of the European Union to implement, in a reasonable period, WTO-consistent reforms to the banana regime led the United States to pursue retaliatory measures. The United States claimed injury to the tune of $520 million. The European Union argued that the U.S. claim was too high. The case then went to arbitration to assess the level of nullification or impairment of benefits. The Dispute Settlement Body ruled in favor of the United States on 19 April 1999 and authorized parallel retaliation in the amount of $191.4 million per year. Ecuador sought and was granted similar retaliation measures against the European Union under the GATT, GATS, and TRIPS in the amount of $450 million per year, which was subsequently reduced to $201.6 million per year (Komuro 2000, 29–43).

The European Union, under intense pressure at home and from within the WTO, relented and came to an understanding with the United States in April 2001. The United States and Ecuador subsequently dropped retaliatory measures. The European Union agreed to the adoption of a WTO-compatible tariff-only regime with preferential access for the ACP to be implemented no later than January 1, 2006. In the interim, the transitional regime consists of a two-stage process: (1) a tariff quota system with an ACP duty exemption that runs from July 1, 2001, to December 31, 2001, and (2) a tariff-quota system that involves a transfer of 100,000 tons per year from the ACP toward third-country imports to run from January 1, 2002, to December 31, 2005 (*EC Council Regulations,* No. 2587/2001 & 896/2001). The transition regime called for a temporary tariff preference waiver at the WTO for ACP exporters. As agreed, the waiver was supported by the United States and Ecuador and was approved at the fourth WTO Ministerial Conference in Doha in November 2001.

The WTO banana agreement is far from a free trade regime and there are lingering concerns that another round of conflict may ensue. A tariff level still has to be set by the European Union. It is possible that the European Union may opt for a differentiated tariff regime to secure a share of the market for ACP suppliers. Even so, expectations are that this objective will prove increasingly difficult to maintain given the economic prowess of the banana TNCs to flood the market and drive prices down. It is assessed, for example, that the main beneficiary of the impending regime will be Chiquita, whereas Dole and independent banana producers from Ecuador will lose market share. The ACP members, especially the Windward Islands, may be forced out of the market. Consequently, there is much doubt whether the tariff-only arrangement can meet the obligations of the new Banana Protocol attached to the ACP-EU Economic Partnership Agreement, which commits the European Union to maintain the viability of ACP bananas in the EU market.

## Making Sense of the Trans-Atlantic Banana Wars

The trans-Atlantic banana wars demonstrate the increased rivalry and competition between the United States and the European Union. They also illustrate in poignant terms the contest between promarket and *dirigiste* perspectives. The contestation is evident in terms of interjudicial conflict between the integrationist perspective of the ECJ and the free trade opinions of the panel reports of the GATT/WTO. The various rulings of the GATT and the WTO favored the free trade perspective, which gained support from three World Bank studies (Borrell 1994; Borrell and Yang 1990, 1992). The essence of the argument is that free markets are more efficient and favorable to consumer welfare than distortive trade measures, hence the critique of the tariff-quota system and the licensing mechanism in the CMOB (Fitzpatrick and Associates 1990; McMahon 1998; Read 1994). An associated view was that visible compensatory mechanisms were a superior means for economic development and a better catalyst for diversification of those producers that were likely to be adversely affected by the liberalization of the EU banana import regime. The banana case reinforces the argument for the further institutionalization of free market solutions under the aegis of the WTO. The WTO rules and mechanisms are far more complex and intrusive than its predecessor, the GATT.[7] The results of the banana wars point to a shift toward open regionalism, tariffication, and the erosion of trade preferences. The main contention of the complainants (i.e., the United States and the dollar-zone banana exporters) was that the CMOB favored the banana suppliers, producers, and traders of the ACP and EU fruit at the expense of EU consumers and Latin American producers and traders.

The opposing side argued for a more interventionist approach, recognizing that the banana industry has an oligopolistic market structure and that medium- to long-term consumer and stakeholder welfare was only achievable through a managed import regime (Hallam 1997; Nurse and Sandiford 1995; Preville 2001). It was also argued that the free market approach did not take full account of transnational structures and business practices such as intrafirm transfers and collusive behavior that work against consumer welfare and fair competition. This position is supported by the fact that the U.S. banana TNCs, especially Chiquita (formerly known as the United Fruit Company), have been found guilty in the past of abusing their market power in both the U.S. and European markets (Litvak and Maule 1977). An additional argument leveled against the free trade option was that it does not take into account the social fallout and the problem of distributive justice for ACP producers who are unable to make the adjustment to a liberalized market.

The banana case also reeks of a double standard: free trade for peripheral agricultural exports but protection for agricultural production in the core. The OECD member countries spend $1 billion a day providing support measures and export subsidies for agriculture. By "distorting" world markets and prices, these policies render exports from the periphery uncompetitive and exacerbate their food import dependency. Core states continue to expand subsidies despite their commitments under the WTO Agreement on Agriculture to liberalize this sector. An example of this is the 2002 U.S. Farm Security and Rural Investment Act, which increases agricultural subsidies by 80 percent and provides $180 billion over ten years (UNDP 2003, 123–135). In the face of such evidence the free trade argument falls apart and becomes an apologia for the inequity of the capitalist world-system, underlining the fact that the core states do not preach what they practice (Chang 2002). It thus illustrates that the power of the free trade argument comes not from its explanatory or predictive capabilities but from its alignment with the interests of global power brokers.

How did the CMOB perform and who are the winners and losers? The evidence on welfare benefits and losses as well as changes in the market structure shows a fairly complicated picture. As Table 9-1 illustrates, the net effect of the CMOB for the period 1993–1998 was a total loss of 67.59 million ecus. When broken down, it is evident that there was a consumer welfare loss of 1,407.71 million ecus, which, in the main, was transferred to traders and producers (557.77 million) and to the national budgets (782.34 million) of the various EU member countries. When this data is disaggregated it is evident that the main losers were the consumers from the former free trade and tariff-imposing countries such as Germany, the Netherlands, Belgium-Luxembourg, and Sweden because of higher retail prices. Among the traders and producers, the beneficiaries

Table 9-1. Welfare Effects of CMOB, 1993–1998 (million ecus)

|  | Consumers (1) | Traders and Producers (2) | National Budgets (3) | Total (1+2+3) |
|---|---|---|---|---|
| Free trade countries | -1,249.78 | 220.57 | 757.54 | 271.67 |
| Tariff imposing countries | -466.22 | 454.45 | -96.97 | -108.75 |
| ACP supplied countries | 280.28 | -163.70 | -93.17 | 23.41 |
| Countries with EU production | 28.00 | 46.46 | 214.93 | 289.40 |
| Total | -1,407.71 | 557.77 | 782.34 | -67.59 |

*Source*: Badinger, Breuss, and Mahlberg 2002: 523.

were those supplying Latin American fruit to the same countries identified above. In contrast, the main losers were the ones that supplied ACP fruit (a loss of 163.70 million ecus). Other major beneficiaries of the CMOB were the various national budgets of the free trade importing countries (757.54 million ecus) because of tariff income, and the European Union–supplied territories (214.93 million) largely because of compensatory aid to EU banana producers.[8]

Table 9-2 illustrates that there has been little change in the market shares of the various suppliers over the period 1992 to 2002. If anything, the Latin American exporters have been marginal beneficiaries with a 3 percent rise in market share. On surface, this result conforms to the goals of the CMOB, which were, according to Franz Fischler, "to maintain the presence of ACP and Community bananas . . . and not to damage the interests of exporters of Latin American bananas" (European Commission 1995, 1).

The data in Table 9-2 does not capture differential performance within the ACP grouping. Falling prices, financial problems, bad weather, and weak competitiveness have plagued Caribbean producers, and their share of the market has declined over the period from 47 percent down to 40 percent of ACP imports. The decline in production has come largely from Jamaica and the Windward Islands, but this shortfall has been compensated for by increased exports from the Dominican Republic (FAO 2002).

Table 9-2. EU Banana Supply Market Share (percent), 1992 and 2002

|  | EU Producers | ACP Exporters | Latin American Exporters |
|---|---|---|---|
| 1992 | 21 | 19 | 60 |
| 2002 | 19 | 17.9 | 63.1 |

*Source*: Nurse and Sandiford 1995; FAO 2003.

# Corporate Globalization and the Concentration of Capital

TNCs are an important feature of the banana wars in terms of the alignment of their interests along with those of member states at the GATT/WTO. Thus the banana wars can be viewed as a case of interimperialist rivalry at the level of the firm.

How did the CMOB impact traders and retailers? A specific goal of the CMOB, especially the licensing system, was to encourage cross investments by the banana traders. Much of this did happen. For instance, Del Monte invested in operations in Cameroon and the Cote d'Ivoire. Dole acquired 35 percent of Jamaica Producers' UK operations at a cost of £18 million. Dole also expanded its presence in the French market and invested in production in Martinique and Guadeloupe. Fyffes, in particular, was very active in terms of acquisitions and joint ventures in consumer markets like Denmark, Sweden, France, the Netherlands, and Germany. Fyffes also entered into joint ventures for banana production in Jamaica and the Canary Islands. As a result of these initiatives, Fyffes was able to double its sales and market share by 1994. Geest invested in banana plantations in Costa Rica and expanded its trading network into Spain and Italy, and was able to expand its market share from 5 to 12 percent before the sale of its banana business to a joint venture between Fyffes and WIBDECO in January 1996. Fyffes continued its strategy of acquisitions throughout the 1990s. Its latest acquisition was the German subsidiary of Del Monte in late 2002 (*Banana Trade News Bulletin,* No. 27, Jan. 2003).

The only major firm that did not engage in these kinds of investments was Chiquita. Chiquita, along with the Colombian traders (e.g., UNIBAN), employed an alternative strategy. It anticipated that a free market regime would have been established and consequently boosted exports to the European Union prior to the SEM. This proved to be a miscalculation and Chiquita lost $284 million in 1992. The Colombian producers also lost $70 million in 1992 (Nurse and Sandiford 1995, 112). Chiquita's problems did not end there, however. The firm continued to lose more than $1 billion over the decade and got into bankruptcy problems that were solved in 2002 when its creditors struck an agreement to receive 95.5 percent of the company in exchange for the cancellation of $700 million of publicly held debt (*Banana Trade News Bulletin,* No. 26, Nov. 2002).

The results of these transformations in the EU banana industry are outlined in Table 9-3. The table shows that Chiquita has been the major loser, with its market share falling by half from 43 to 21 percent over the decade. In contrast, Fyffes has been the major beneficiary, increasing its share of the EU

Table 9-3. Banana Transnationals' Market Share in the EU, 1992 and 2002

| Firms | Chiquita | Dole | Del Monte | Fyffes | Geest | Noboa | Others |
|-------|----------|------|-----------|--------|-------|-------|--------|
| 1992  | 43       | 13   | 10        | 7      | 5     | n.a.  | 22     |
| 2002  | 21       | 13   | 11        | 20     | 0     | 6     | 29     |

*Source: Banana Trade News Bulletin,* No. 27 (Jan. 2003): 11.

**Table 9-4. Share of Multiples in Various EU Banana Markets, 2002**

|  | Italy | Spain | Ireland | Germany | France | UK | EU Avg. |
|---|---|---|---|---|---|---|---|
| Share (percent) | 66 | 40 | 66 | 70 | 74 | 82 | 66 |

*Source: Banana Trade News Bulletin*, No. 27 (Jan. 2003): 13.

market from 7 to 20 percent. This does not fully capture Fyffes' gains as it has a joint venture with WIBDECO that is not illustrated in the table. In summary, the changes in the corporate landscape in the EU banana market underscore one of the key goals of the SEM, to improve the competitiveness of European firms in the global economy.

Another feature of the EU banana market has been the increasing importance of bananas in retail business. In several of the large grocery chains, bananas have moved in status from exotic produce to a main sale item. In the United Kingdom, consumers spend more on bananas than any other supermarket food item. In tandem, supermarkets have expanded their share of the retail market for bananas in the major consumer markets. Across Europe the average market share of the multiples is 66 percent (see Table 9-4). The growth has been rapid over the last decade. In the United Kingdom, where the banana market showed the greatest growth, the multiples expanded their market share from 46.8 percent in 1992 to more than 82 percent in 2002 at the expense of independent retailers.

The increased market power of the retailers has resulted in lower margins for the other stakeholders in the industry. The retailers have been using bananas as a loss leader and for price wars to woo customers from the competition. In 1996, Asda, the third biggest UK retailer, initiated a price war with the likes of Tesco and Sainbury. In the most recent bout, consumer prices fell by 25 percent when Asda, which was acquired by Wal-Mart in August 2002, initiated a price war. The bulk of the burden of lower prices was passed on to the traders, exporters, and farmers. The transnational banana traders' margins have been squeezed through exclusive supply agreements. For example, Asda is supplied exclusively by Del Monte, and Tesco has reduced its suppliers from five to two and is paying these suppliers 30 percent less since early 2002 (*Banana Trade News Bulletin*, No. 28, 2003, 1–2). The large retailers also exercise their immense market power by redistributing the cost of new packaging and boxing technologies on producers and farmers (Grossman 1998).

## Peripheral Fragmentation and Marginalization

The trans-Atlantic banana wars demonstrate the disharmony of interests between Latin American and ACP banana producers (Sutton 1997). They were on opposing sides of the legal conflicts. The Latin Americans were in support of the U.S. complaint to the WTO, but the ACP supported the EU stance. At-

Table 9-5. Comparison Between Ecuador and the Windward Islands, Banana
Exports and Revenue Contribution, 1992–2001

|  | Banana exports to EU (volume – thousand tons) | | Bananas as percent of total exports | |
|---|---|---|---|---|
|  | 1992 | 2001 | 1992 | 2001 |
| Ecuador | 677.1 | 705.2 | 13.6 | 19.0 |
| Windward Islands | 274.5 | 83.0 | 46.8 | 28.6 |

*Source:* Nurse and Sandiford 1995; FAO 2002.

tempts by the European Union to split the Latin American group through the
BFA proved eventually to be unsuccessful. The basis of the divide between the
banana exporters stems from the fact that their principal export is thrown into
competitive markets, a function of mono-crop production, export concentration, and export dependence. It is also that there is a wide gap in production
costs between the Latin American producers ($180/ton) and the ACP ($463/
ton). In contrast, there was some harmony of interest between EU producers
and ACP exporters in terms of their support for the EU response to the WTO
complaints. The EU producers have a similar production cost profile to the
ACP and are highly dependent on protection from market forces to maintain a
share of the EU banana market. However, unlike the ACP, the EU producers
enjoy access to compensatory aid that has maintained their share of the
market. Whereas the banana trade is of negligible importance to importing countries, for the exporters bananas are a matter of life or death. They make a
sizeable contribution to foreign exchange earnings in both Latin American and
ACP exporters. Table 9-5 compares the export volume and revenue for Ecuador, the largest producer, with the Windward Islands, the most vulnerable of the
ACP exporters. The table shows that over the period 1992 to 2001, Ecuador
has become more dependent on banana exports, although its exports to the
European Union did not grow appreciably, largely because of the quantitative
restrictions that were in place. Ecuador's export growth occurred in other markets, for example the United States. The Windward Islands, on the other hand,
only export to the European Union. Their production and export earnings have
fallen dramatically due to the erosion of preference, increased competition,
falling prices, abandoned farms, and bad weather (e.g., hurricanes and drought)
(Addy 1998; Sandiford 2000).

The intensification of competition between banana exporters has been
accompanied by lower average prices for bananas in the European Union. It is
estimated that between 1990 and 2000 retail prices have dropped by 64 percent
in real terms against rising production costs (CBEA 2003). The price squeeze is
a function of both increased competition between major producers as well as
the expansion of the value added by traders and retailers such as the supermarkets. Farmers and growers have borne the largest share of the price squeeze.
The Windward Islands is the region that has been the most severely affected as
reflected in the decline of bananas' contribution to GDP (from 12 to 7 percent)

and employment (from 24,111 growers to 11,665) (Sandiford 2000). The socioeconomic conditions for banana workers and peasants in Latin America have deteriorated as well. For example, Costa Rica, the second largest exporter, has had huge job losses and wages have fallen by 40 percent in the last three years (*Banana Trade News Bulletin*, No. 28, July 2003, 4). These trends are indicative of the further marginalization of peripheral economies as explained by the conjunctural downturn in the world-economy since the early 1970s. For example, ACP countries have dropped from 8.4 percent of world commodity exports to 2.4 over the last three decades (UNDP 2003, 148).

The TNCs control the banana trade in Latin America and the ACP. Firms from producing countries also control some of the world trade. For example, Noboa of Ecuador, Jamaica Producers of Jamaica, WIBDECO of the Windward Islands, and Uniban and Banacol of Colombia control a large share of their country's exports and account for between 15 to 20 percent of world trade. Irrespective of ownership, especially in Latin America, the industry is associated with oligopolistic practices, the super-exploitation of labor, violence against unions, the political manipulation of governments, preemptory management tactics, and intrafirm transfers (Ellis 1981). Attempts by the producer countries to redress the imbalance in bargaining power through the establishment of a cartel in the mid-1970s, the Union de Paises Exportadores de Banana (UPEB) failed because of the political influence of the TNCs and the nonparticipation of large exporters like Ecuador and the Philippines. Efforts are currently underway to revive UPEB, but the organization still faces structural problems such as:

- longstanding competition for market shares, exemplified by the banana wars;
- the largest exporters (Ecuador and the Philippines) have a disproportionate world market share;
- the perishability of the product means it is unsuitable for buffer stocks;
- an oligopolistic market dominated by a few TNCs as producers and as traders and now retailers (supermarkets);
- variable cost of production (Dickson 2003, 5).

Given the failure of cooperation within the South in this context, there seems to be greater hope of change from the demand side. Consumer awareness is the key to the recent growth of fair trade and organic bananas. An alliance of trade unions, farmers' associations, consumer groups, and NGOs (from both sides of the Atlantic) has been promoting "ethical" bananas for the last decade or so. The demand for these bananas has crossed over into the mainstream supermarket trade. An increasing number of producers are moving toward fair trade and organic bananas because they enjoy better margins; for example, a 50 percent premium on the producer price. However, this trade is still highly concentrated. The Dominican Republic accounts for 80 percent of the EU market for organic bananas (FAO 2003). Fair trade and organic bananas account for only 3 percent of the import market in the European Union but are the fastest rising segments in the banana trade with around 30 percent annual growth in the main import markets (FAO 2003).

These trends point to the creation of new norms and practices such as fair trade, organic farming, and ecolabeling, which have the potential to address problems like social dumping, ecological despoliation, and the loss of genetic biodiversity. A coalition of plantation workers' unions from Latin America, small banana farmers from the Caribbean and Ecuador, and European NGOs and unions have been calling for an international agreement to address the negative social, economic, and environmental impact of the liberalization of the EU banana regime.[9] How far these initiatives will extend is still to be seen. Already there is some concern that the large retailers and companies, some of whom are party to the Ethical Trading Initiative, are compromising these standards through price wars and co-optive marketing strategies.[10] The banana case illustrates both the promise and challenge faced by many of the new social movements and the antiglobalization protesters in terms of countering the dehumanizing features of global capitalism.

## Hegemonic Competition, Bananas, and the World-System

What does world-system analysis tell us about the role of the periphery in an era of triadic competition? And how do the trans-Atlantic banana wars exemplify the case?

This chapter examined the origins and the global political economy of the trans-Atlantic banana wars. This war, which involved eight years of international legal challenges, is one of a number of contemporary trade disputes between the United States and the European Union that exemplify the increased intensity and instability of relations within the core, what Wallerstein (2003) refers to as triadic competition. This is evident in a process of realignment of geoeconomic and geopolitical roles; the most obvious example of this being the contest for market shares (states and firms) through the formation of regional trading blocs.

The banana wars also provide some insight into the other geopolitical cleavages articulated by Wallerstein (2003): the North-South cleavage that is manifested in the polarization of income between core and other zones and the Davos–Porto Alegre cleavage epitomized in the competing visions of world development between corporate globalization and civil society groups. As the banana case illustrates, the geopolitical cleavages are interconnected in terms of the contestation between free trade and fair trade ideologies as well as the conflict between and among stakeholders such as banana importers, banana exporters, the WTO, the European Commission, TNCs, retailers, farmers, and consumer groups. From this perspective, the banana wars tell a story about the changing global political economy and the trajectory of the world-system.

In summary, the banana case highlights three specific trends. The first is free trade hegemony and its institutionalization within the WTO and other multilateral institutions such as the World Bank and IMF. The case illustrates that the institutionalization of free trade ideology operates to maintain the status quo and has limited explanatory power because it does not come to grips with the transnational structure of the industry. In effect, the hegemony of free trade ideology operates as a mode of cultural violence (Galtung 1996) that validates global inequality and social injustice. The second is the increasing concentration of capital and polarization of income evident in the growth of corporate globalization. This was illustrated in the growth of power of both the banana TNCs and the supermarket retailers and the weakened position of peripheral states as well as independent firms and workers in both the periphery and the core. The last trend is the growing fragmentation of the periphery as displayed in the competition between the Latin American producers and the ACP. The lack of a cohesive position coming from peripheral states further exacerbates the marginalization process as exemplified in declining terms of trade and asymmetrical trade patterns. The rise of new social movements and new trade norms such as ethical and fair trade are part of an antiglobalization ethos that may offer a counterhegemonic alternative once they avoid the trap of co-optive marketing strategies and state apologists. In conclusion the banana case attests to the fact that the trajectory of the world-system is moving toward a scenario where the geopolitical cleavages will become increasingly bifurcated. The banana case is not an anomaly. Instead, it represents an intensification of long-standing secular processes that propel unequal capitalist development. The contradictions inherent in this process are mounting and will lead to a broader questioning of the viability and desirability of the existing civilizational order.

## Notes

1. A recent study by the Institute of Grocery Distribution forecasts that the top 25 supermarket groups will control 40 percent of the world retail distribution sector by 2009 (*Banana Trade News Bulletin* 24, November 2001).

2. The Lomé Convention provides the framework for trade and cooperation between the European Union and the ACP states. The Lomé Convention, with its special import regimes or protocols on bananas, sugar, rum, and beef, began in 1975 and was renewed three times (1980, 1985, and 1990) before expiring in 2000. The Lomé Convention was replaced by the Cotonou Agreement, which is valid for a period of 20 years, with periodic reviews every five years.

3. It should be noted that a waiver could have been sought and would almost certainly have been granted many years ago. The United States, for instance, was given a waiver for the preferences offered to the countries that benefit from its Caribbean Basin Initiative.

4. ACP banana exporters enjoyed protection under Article 1 of Protocol 5, which states that "in respect of its banana exports to the Community markets, no ACP state shall be placed, as regards access to its traditional markets and its advantages on those markets, in a less favourable situation than in the past or present" (Courier 1990, 150).

5. The licensing system can be summarized as follows: rights to import under the tariff quota (an annual quota) are allocated on the basis of past trade in third country and nontraditional bananas (66.5 percent of the tariff quota—Category A), on the basis of past trade in the EC and traditional ACP bananas (30 percent of the tariff quota—Category B), and to newcomers to trade in third country and nontraditional ACP bananas (3.5 percent of the tariff quota—Category C). Allocation of licenses to operators as part of Categories A and B are determined on the basis of the quantities of bananas marketed, weighted according to the three marketing activities of primary import (57 percent), secondary import (15 percent), and ripening (28 percent).

6. It is reported that Mr. Lindner of the American Financial Corporation gave $275,000 to the Democratic Party and $250,000 to the Republican Party in November and December 1994; in 1993, he gave $250,000 to the Democratic Party. AFC and its affiliates were the second largest contributors to both political parties during the 1993–1994 election cycle, with a total of $995,000 (*Caribbean Insight*, April 1995). For further details see Greenwald (1996) and McWhirter and Gallagher (1998).

7. The WTO incorporates new features like the single undertaking, binding implications for domestic policies and sanctions, or compliance mechanisms (UNDP 2003, 52–53).

8. Compensatory aid to the EU banana producers averaged 202 million euros per year between 1994 and 2001 (*Banana Trade News Bulletin* 27, January 2003).

9. The coalition includes: Coordination of Latin American Banana Trade Unions (COLSIBA); Windward Island Farmers' Association (WINFA); Small Farmers' Organization, Ecuador (UROCAL); and European Banana Action Network (EUROBAN) (*Banana Trade News Bulletin* 27, January 2003).

10. The Ethical Trading Initiative is an alliance of companies, nongovernmental organizations, and trade unions working to identify and promote good practices in the implementation of codes of labor practice (www.ethicaltrade.org).

# References

Addy, David. 1998. *Restructuring and the Loss of Preferences—Labour Challenges for the Caribbean Banana Industry.* Port of Spain, Trinidad and Tobago: International Labor Organization (Briefing Report).

Badinger, H., F. Breuss, and B. Mahlberg. 2002. "Welfare Effects of the EU's Common Organization of the Market in Bananas for EU Member States." *Journal of Common Market Studies* 40(3): 515–526.

*Banana Trade News Bulletin* (various issues).

Bergesen, A., and R. Schoenberg. 1980. "Long Waves of Colonial Expansion and Contraction, 1415–1969." In A. Bergesen, ed., *Studies of the Modern World-System.* New York: Academic Press, pp. 231–277.

Borrell, B. 1994. *EU Bananarama III.* Washington, DC: World Bank, International Economics Department.

Borrell, B., and Mow-Cheng Yang. 1990. *EC Bananarama 1992.* Washington, DC: World Bank, International Economics Department, WPS 523.

———. 1992. *EC Bananarama 1992: The Sequel—The EC Commission Proposal.* Washington, DC: World Bank, International Economics Department, WPS 950.

Bousquet, Nicole. 1980. "From Hegemony to Competition: Cycles of the Core?" In

T. Hopkins and I. Wallerstein, eds., *Processes of the World-System*. Beverly Hills: Sage, pp. 46–83.

Caribbean Banana Exporters Association. 2003. *Caribbean Bananas: A Case for Equitable Trading*. Available at: www.cbea.org.

Chang, Ha-Joon. 2002. *Kicking Away the Ladder: Development Strategy in Historical Perspective*. London: Anthem Press.

Chase-Dunn, C. 1978. "Core-Periphery Relations: The Effects of Core Competition." In B. Kaplan, ed., *Social Change in the Capitalist World Economy*. London: Sage, pp. 159–176.

Council Regulations (EEC) No. 1442/93 of 10 June 1993. "Laying Down Detailed Rules for the Application of the Arrangements for Importing Bananas into the Community." *Official Journal of the European Communities* L42/6.

Council Regulations (EEC) No. 404/93 of 13 February 1993. "The Common Organisation of the Market in Bananas." *Official Journal of the European Communities* L47/1.

*Courier.* 1990. *Lomé IV Convention* 120 (March–April).

Dickson, A. 2003. "Toward an International Agreement on Bananas: A Discussion Paper." Dublin: EUROBAN.

Ellis, F. 1981. "Export Valuation and Intra-Firm Transfers in the Banana Export Industry in Central America." In R. Murray, ed., *Multinational beyond the Market*. New York: John Wiley.

European Commission. 1994. *Report on the EU Banana Regime*. Brussels: Commission of the European Commission.

———. 1995. *Report on the Operation of the Banana Regime*. Brussels: Commission of the European Commission, IP/95/1105.

European Court of Justice. 1994. *Judgement of the Court—Case C-280/93*. Luxembourg: European Court of Justice.

European Union. 1999. "EU Proposal for New Banana Regime." Available at: http://www.cbea.org.

Everling, U. 1996. "Will Europe Slip on Bananas? The Banana Judgement of the Court of Justice and National Courts." *Common Market Law Review* 33: 401–437.

Fitzpatrick and Associates. 1990. *Trade Policy and the EC Banana Market: An Economic Analysis*. London: Sponsored by Dole Europe Ltd.

Food and Agriculture Organization. 2001. *Commodity Market Review, 1999–2000*. Rome: FAO, Commodities and Trade Division.

———. 2003. *Banana Information Note*. Rome: FAO, Commodities and Trade Division.

Francis, Anselm. 2000. "The Rule-Based System of the World Trade Organization: An Analysis." *Social and Economic Studies* 49(1): 113–142.

Galtung, J. 1996. *Peace by Peaceful Means: Peace and Conflict, Development, and Civilization*. London: Sage/PRIO.

GATT. 1993. *EEC—Import Regime for Bananas*. (GATT document DS32/7).

———. 1994. *EEC—Import Regime for Bananas*. (GATT document DS38/R).

Greenwald, John. 1996. "Banana Republican: Carl Lindner Is an Empire Builder Who Invests in U.S. Lawmakers and Harvests Favors from Them." *Time*, January 22, pp. 36–37.

Grossman, Lawrence S. 1998. *The Political Ecology of Bananas*. Chapel Hill: University of North Carolina Press.

Hallam, David. 1997. *The Political Economy of Europe's Banana Trade*. Reading, UK: University of Reading, Occasional Paper No. 5.

Jenkins, V. S. 2000. *Bananas: An American History.* Washington, DC: Smithsonian Institution Press.

Komuro, Norio. 2000. "The EC Banana Regime and Judicial Control." *Journal of World Trade* 34(5): 1–87.

Litvak, L., and C. Maule. 1988. "Transnational Corporations and Vertical Integration: The Banana Case." *Journal of World Trade Law* 11(6): 537–549.

McMahon, Joseph. 1998. "The EC Banana Regime, the WTO Rulings and the ACP: Fighting for Economic Survival?" *Journal of World Trade* 32(4): 101–114.

McWhirter, Cameron, and Mike Gallagher. 1998. "Chiquita Secrets Revealed: U.S. Helps Chiquita Fight Tariffs in Europe." *Cincinnati Enquirer,* May 3, available at http://www.nlsearch.com.

Nurse, Keith. 1998. "Third World Industrialization and the Reproduction of Underdevelopment." *Marronnage* 1(1): 69–97.

Nurse, Keith, and Wayne Sandiford. 1995. *Windward Island Bananas: Challenges and Options under the Single European Market.* Kingston, Jamaica: Friedrich Ebert Stiftung.

Petersmann, Ernst-Ulrich. 1994. "The Dispute Settlement System of the World Trade Organization and the Evolution of the GATT Dispute Settlement System since 1948." *Common Market Law Review* 31: 1157–1244.

Read, R. 1994. "The EC Internal Banana Market: The Issues and the Dilemma." *World Economy* 17(2): 219–235.

Sandiford, Wayne. 2000. *On the Brink of Decline: Bananas in the Windward Islands.* St. Georges, Grenada: Fedon Books.

Stewart, Taimoon. 1993. "The Third World Debt Crisis: A Long Waves Perspective." *Review: A Journal of the Fernand Braudel Center* 16(2): 117–171.

Sutton, Paul. 1997. "The Banana Regime of the European Union, the Caribbean and Latin America." *Journal of Interamerican Studies and World Affairs* 39(2): 5–36.

United Nations Development Project. 2003. *Making Global Trade Work for People.* London: Earthscan.

Wallerstein, I. 2003. "Geopolitical Cleavages of the 21st Century: What Future for the World?" In *South Centre High Level Policy Forum.* Geneva: South Centre, pp. 75–94.

# 10

# THE GREAT POWERS AND THE GLOBAL ENVIRONMENT IN THE TWENTIETH CENTURY

### John R. McNeill

When elephants fight, the grass gets trampled. So runs an East African proverb. When nations fight, the biosphere gets trampled. One of the major determinants of modern environmental history has been, and remains, the struggle for survival and power in the international system. In this chapter I will argue that historically international struggle has generally selected against ecological prudence in states and societies, and that the rigorous struggle of the twentieth century selected rigorously against ecological prudence. Further, I will argue that preparation for war and economic mobilization for war had stronger environmental consequences than did combat itself.

## I. Environmental Change and Its Causes in the Twentieth Century

Environmental change has always been part of the human experience. Since the first harnessing of fire several hundred thousand years ago, hominids and humans have changed the world's ecology. But in modern and contemporary times they have done so on a scale unprecedented in human history and with very few analogues in earth history. Humankind undertook a gigantic, uncontrolled experiment on the earth, altering land cover, atmospheric chemistry, biodiversity, biogeochemical flows, and much else. Just how large and how rapid was this experiment? The figures in Table 10-1 are intended to give some measurement to the twentieth century's environmental flux.

These are global figures, and they disguise great variations among places and societies. The 13- or 15-fold expansion of energy use around the world owes much more to the experience of the United States than to India. The table ignores some indices for which the coefficients of change would be infinite, such as releases of chlorofluorocarbons (which were not produced before the twentieth century but since the 1930s have thinned the stratospheric ozone layer that protects life on earth from ultraviolet-B radiation). Some of these figures are of course more reliable than others, and some more important than others. But the table gives the right impression nonetheless. For understanding environmental change in the twentieth century, I think the coefficients for en-

### Table 10-1. Coefficients of Change, c. 1890s to 1990s

| | |
|---|---|
| World population | 4 |
| Urban proportion of world population | 3 |
| Total world urban population | 13 |
| World economy | 14 |
| Industrial output | 40 |
| Energy use | 13–15 |
| Coal production | 7 |
| Oil production | 240 |
| Carbon dioxide emissions to atmosphere | 17 |
| Carbon dioxide concentration in atmosphere | 1.3 |
| Sulfur dioxide emissions to atmosphere | 13 |
| Lead emissions to atmosphere | 8 |
| Freshwater use | 9 |
| Marine fish catch | 35 |
| Cattle population | 4 |
| Pig population | 9 |
| Goat population | 5 |
| Sheep population | 1.8 |
| Horse population | 1.1 |
| Cropland | 2 |
| Pasture area | 1.8 |
| Irrigated area | 5 |
| Bird and mammal species | 0.99 (1% decrease) |
| Fine whale population | 0.03 (97% decrease) |
| Blue whale population (southern ocean only) | 0.0025 (99.75% decrease) |

Source: McNeill 2000: 361–62; webpage maintained by Dutch Ministry for the Environment (RIVM) at: http://arch.rivm.nl/env/int/hyde/index.html.

ergy use and population growth are the most significant. For what they imply about the future, I imagine that the 9-fold expansion in freshwater use and the 17-fold growth in carbon dioxide emissions will prove the most important.

Why did this tremendous flux occur when it did and how it did? The reasons are many, complex, and overlapping. Population growth, often cited as the principle driving force behind all manner of environmental change, did indeed matter. It is worth noting that about a quarter of all human-years ever lived were lived after 1900. But the energy system mattered even more. First, because it was based on fossil fuels: after 1890 they provided more than half of the energy used around the world. Fossil fuels are dirty. The carbon dioxide they emitted into the atmosphere promoted climate change. The sulfur dioxide they emitted fell as acid rain, damaging the biota of rivers and lakes and possibly damaging forests as well. But the pollution consequences of burning fossil fuels were only part of the larger picture. Digging coal, drilling for oil, and transporting oil were dirty affairs too. Fossil fuels allowed new technologies that exponentially increased the volume and pace of mining, to the point where it became practical to shear off mountaintops in search of coal, or to crush millions of tons of rock in search of a few grams of gold. Fossil fuels allowed the chainsaw, without which tropical deforestation, so characteristic of our times, could not have taken place nearly so quickly. Of course fossil fuels are not the only component of the twentieth century's energy system: hydroelectricity required dam building, often done on the gigantic scale; and nuclear energy, with its accidents and waste storage problems, had significant ecological effects too, although so far rather less calamitous than often feared.

The ideological fixations of modern times have also contributed to the pattern of twentieth-century environmental history. Under the tutelage of the economists, and inspired by self-interest, public servants and private individuals consistently sought to foment economic growth and secure monetary gain. They regarded the natural world as a storehouse of raw materials, without intrinsic worth. They saw little value in such abstractions as balance, stability, or resilience in ecosystems. The reigning ideas about appropriate individual and state behavior promoted rapid environmental change and justified it in the name of various higher goals: economic growth, political stability, social mobility. This was true of the capitalist world and truer still of the socialist world. The environment changed so much because prevailing ideas changed so little.

These were the most important reasons why the twentieth century had the environmental history that it did.[1] But there were other reasons. Among them was politics. It was conventional politics not environmental politics that mattered most. Even after 1966, when countries began to create environmental agencies, departments, and even ministries, real environmental policy was made elsewhere, in the powerful branches of government: the finance ministry, the trade ministry, the ministry of industry, and the defense ministry. In every country at all times these were more powerful than the environment ministry (or agency), and they made *de facto* environmental policy as accidental byproducts of their own affairs. One concern they all shared, to greater or lesser degrees, was security. It is this that I shall focus on here. Remember that it is, of course, a small part of the overall picture.

## II. The International System and Its Imperatives

The dominant characteristic of the twentieth-century international system was its highly agitated state. By the standards of prior centuries, the big economies and populous countries conducted their business with war very much on their minds, especially after about 1910. This contrasts sharply with the nineteenth century (here meaning 1815–1910), in which the great powers managed their competition almost peacefully, thanks to diplomatic skill and British hegemony. In effect they almost banished war to Asia and Africa, where it prevailed with heightened regularity in part because of colonial pressures from the great powers. But these conflicts required minimal mobilization on the part of the great powers: colonial wars were easy wars, mainly because of technological and organizational edges European states had developed, but also because they often were fought by colonial troops. But the situation changed with the rise of a united Germany after 1870, and acutely when German industrialization allowed greater German assertiveness after 1890. So the twentieth century would be different, an era of high anxiety, beginning with the run-up to World War I.

War efforts in the two world wars were all-consuming. Security anxiety between the world wars (1919–1939) and during the long Cold War (1945–1991) was high, given the perceived costs of unpreparedness. In the immediate aftermath of the Cold War, it seemed that this elevated security anxiety might, just might, be consigned to the dustbin of history. That hope now seems quaint, in light of nuclear proliferation, abundant regional crises, heightened terrorism, and vigorous reactions thereto. Once more, after 2001, security considerations easily trump all others for the United States, although not necessarily for other powers. Ever since 1914, states and societies have had strong incentives to maximize their military strength, to industrialize (and militarize) their economies, and, after 1945, to develop nuclear weapons. The international system, in Darwinian language, selected rigorously against ecological prudence in favor of policies dictated by short-term security considerations. There were moments of greater or lesser security anxiety, but the baselines levels, for the great powers, were always high.

The quest for state security has been in force, and affecting ecology, since states were first organized.[2] Ancient Sumer created a network of irrigation canals in Mesopotamia in order to maximize its grain crop and maintain an army powerful enough to resist and at times subdue its neighbors. In the long run that irrigation network led to salinization of farmlands, lower yields, less food, and crises that allowed neighbors to assert dominion over Sumer. Throughout most of the history of states, however, the rigor of state security concerns has been blunted by the success of large empires. Most people lived in circumstances either of imposed peace managed and maintained by the technocrats of bureaucratic empire, or else in an anarchic world in which states can scarcely be said to exist. Stable and enduring systems of competing states have been rare. Typically, they quickly collapsed into imperial unification or reunification. Notable and durable exceptions include the era of warring states in China (c. 770 B.C. to 221 B.C.) and in Greece from the first *poleis* (c. 800 B.C.) to Alexander the Great's unification (336 B.C.). In these times and places interstate struggle doubtless took its toll on landscapes, although details are obscure.[3] But in these times and places the scales of military and bureaucratic operations were comparatively small; the technologies involved were rudimentary. Consider the technology of destruction. Before 1800, the only powerful means of ecological damage were deliberate fire and the capacity to tear apart irrigation works, causing deliberate floods. So the ancient eras of anarchic competition in international systems were limited in their ecological impact. Modern times have seen the resurgence of international anarchy combined with ever-growing scales of operations and technological sophistication.

The current competitive international system has not yet collapsed or unified, but instead has evolved and grown so as to be effectively global. It originally emanated from the stalemate in sixteenth-century Europe among Hapsburg, Valois, and Ottoman rivals. None succeeded in reestablishing pan-European empire, which marked Europe off from the rest of the world. Elsewhere, at least in the major centers of population, large empires succeeded in unifying, usually by force, broad territories. In Europe the development of this pattern was checked by this improbable three-way stalemate. This extraordinary failure was codified by the Treaty of Westphalia in 1648, and a self-consciously self-regulating system of competing states was born, ratcheting up the rigor of intersocietal and interstate struggle. The constant competition of this system obliged (surviving) European states to evolve into ever more formidable political, fiscal, and military entities, which by the nineteenth century created states more powerful than those anywhere else in the world. In the long run the emergence and maintenance of this international system proved very favorable to Europe (although it entailed great strife and suffering for several generations of Europeans), and unfavorable to polities and people in the rest of the world. It was also deeply consequential for the biological, physical, and chemical condition of the planet.

Through imperialism and imitation the system of competing nation-states spread around the world in the last 200 years. In the twentieth century the rigor of struggle ratcheted up yet further, on account of the mounting requirements of competitiveness and the heavy costs of failure in an age of total war. By 1914, only an all-out effort gave any chance of survival in the European international system; by 1939–1945, losers in the competition risked annihilation. Higher stakes brought forth more strenuous effort and greater disregard for any goals other than immediate political and physical survival. By 1945–1991 even peacetime required, or seemed to require, the utmost preparedness for war and the conscientious cultivation of international formidability to the exclusion of many other considerations. The international system selected for those characteristics that promised power in the present moment: technological sophistication, mass industrial and agricultural production, and ideological conformity (on fundamental questions at least, and in some societies on more than that). The health of soils, waters, and air took a distant back seat.

## III. International Struggle and Environmental Change

Intersocietal competition affected the environment directly through warfare (the final arbitration of competition) and less directly through the preoccupation with military power: that is, through war and through preparedness for war.

### The Deeper Past

Until the twentieth century the technology of destruction did not produce vast environmental consequences of combat except in extraordinary circumstances. When men fought with clubs, spears, arrows, swords, lances, pikes, or muskets, they could do little damage to landscapes. Indeed, the more destructive wars so disrupted agriculture that they produced a fallowing effect, as in Brittany in the Hundred Years' War, or in Germany during the Thirty Years' War (Cintre 1992, 119–127).[4] Forests and wildlife recovered when and where farmers and herders could not conduct their daily business. So did fisheries when naval war, pirates, or privateers confined fishermen to port. The built environment, of course, has always been vulnerable to destruction in war, usually through fire. Victors have torched countless cities; retreating armies have scorched earth aplenty. The Mongols, in their thirteenth-century conquest of Iraq, devastated a flourishing irrigation network, flooding arable lands, creating (or re-creating) swamps. While the Mongols' efforts edged Iraq more nearly to a state of nature, from the cultivators' point of view—not initially shared by the Mongols—this was environmental damage on a large scale.[5] From any point of view it amounted to vast and enduring environmental change. But such cases were quite rare, essentially confined to landscapes of irrigation.

Preparation for war, rather than combat, typically provoked more serious environmental changes. In Europe for instance, the navy-building programs of Venice and Genoa in the eleventh through sixteenth centuries, and then of Britain, France, and Spain in the seventeenth and eighteenth centuries, severely depleted the supply of tall fir and spruce and stout oak in Mediterranean and Atlantic Europe. All states developed forest conservation programs so as to save more specialized timber for navies, but this proved inadequate in every case. By the eighteenth century, Europe's wooden navies sought ship timber in Indonesia, India, Brazil, Canada, and elsewhere around the world (Albion 1926; Appuhn 2000; Bamford 1956; Lane 1965; Merino Navarro 1981, 181–267; Miller 2000).

## Combat's Environmental Consequences in the Twentieth Century

In the twentieth century, as the technology of destruction grew vastly more powerful, preparation for war, as in remoter times, wrought greater and more lasting environmental change than did war itself. The direct environmental effects of warfare in the twentieth century have been vast, destructive, but usually fleeting. The battle zones at the western front of World War I created small deserts, where little but rats, lice, and men could live—and few lived for long. But these zones are hard to detect today, except where carefully preserved: elsewhere their recovery and assimilation to the French and Belgian countryside is nearly complete. The more mobile campaigns of World War II produced less concentrated damage to landscapes (except for cities),[6] although certain episodes were destructive enough. In 1938 Chinese troops, in an effort to forestall Japanese advance, deliberately breached the dikes that held the Hwang Ho in place, flooding broad areas of North China and killing people (almost all Chinese), drowning crops, sweeping away bridges, roads, over 4,000 villages, and millions of tons of soil: a disaster to be sure, but one soon made invisible by the careful labor of millions of Chinese peasants.[7] By 1947 the Hwang Ho dikes were repaired. The "war erosion" of the Russian and Ukrainian plains (1941–1945) is perhaps the next greatest example of combat-derived environmental change (cities excepted) from World War II, and in the grand sweep of Soviet soil history it ought probably to be considered trivial (Alayev, Badenkov, and Karavaeva 1990; Sobolev 1945, 1947). In general, the theaters of operations in World Wars I and II involved ecologically, economically, and socially resilient places, so the environmental impacts of combat lasted comparatively briefly. Some unexploded ordnance lingers on, especially in eastern Europe, bomb craters remain here and there, forests are still recovering, and the destabilizing effects of tank tracks on dunes in the North African desert still linger, but very little of significance in the way of combat-derived environmental change will prove lasting.

The environmental impact of the 1991 Gulf War, a subject viewed with great alarm at the time because of its conspicuous oil fires and spills now seems not as great as many first feared. It is too soon to comment on its durability, which for marine ecosystems at least may be considerable. About 10 million barrels of oil flowed into the Gulf, the equivalent of 40 Exxon Valdez spills. The fires, despite initial alarms, appear to have had a negligible impact on the atmosphere and climate (Hawley 1992; Hobbs and Lawrence 1992). In Kuwait the war had the effect of enriching desert environments. So much lethal ordnance (unexploded mines, cluster bombs) remained amid the shifting sands of the Kuwaiti desert that all prudent Kuwaitis refrain from hunting and joyriding, favorite prewar pastimes of prosperous Kuwaitis. Bird populations grew 100–fold after the war. Grasses flourished to the point where they reminded some observers of prairies. Similar, if temporary, consequences arose from the desert campaigns in Libya and Egypt in 1942–1943.[8] Thus in exceptional cases the heavy use of explosive ordnance in conventional war has permitted more rapid recovery from environmental damage.

One perhaps durable effect of the 1991 Gulf War is the near-elimination of the marshes that for several millennia had spread over the lower reaches of the Tigris-Euphrates. These were home to populations disloyal to Saddam Hussein in his war with Iran in the 1980s, and who rose in revolt against him in 1991. They were crushed. As a *coup-de-grâce,* the Iraqi dictator ordered the draining of the marshes beginning in 1993 (based on a plan drawn up in 1989), a form of ecological warfare that destroyed birds, fish, reed beds, and a way of life for a few hundred thousand people. Attempting to destroy the ecological and economic basis of life of one's enemies is a practice with a long pedigree. In the twentieth century, energy-intensive machinery made such projects far easier than in times past, when fire was the only efficient tool for such operations. In this case, with the fall of Saddam, it is possible that engineers will attempt to create the marshes anew. If so, the episode of the Iraq marshes will be just another case of fleeting environmental damage from war (see Nicholson and Clark 2002).

## The Impact of Guerrilla War

As a rule, more enduring environmental change came from the guerrilla wars of the twentieth century. Great variability exists in the ecological impact of these wars, but on the whole they were disproportionately important in environmental change because they invariably involved systematic attempts at habitat destruction, similar to that which Saddam Hussein undertook from 1993. Guerrilla fighters inevitably sought to hide from the firepower of their enemies, and except in urban settings that meant hiding in forest and bush—using vegetation as cover. After the dawn of air reconnaissance and bombing (the 1920s, practically speaking), hiding in remote areas proved insufficient: vegetation cover was required. Those fighting against guerrillas found it advantageous to destroy that vegetation, and used the tools at hand to do so.

In some instances, this produced durable consequences for vegetation and soils, notably in drier mountainous regions with high erosion potential, such as those around the Mediterranean. The antiguerrilla campaigns in the Rif mountains of Morocco (1921–1926), in the mountains of northwestern Greece (1942–1949), and in the Algerian Tell (1954–1961) all entailed widespread forest burning, often through air power. All these wars left scars still visible today, and reduced both the biomass and the economic potential of these districts. The consequences may last for centuries. The numerous wars in Africa since 1970, often intersocietal but not international, have led to heightened rates of desertification and ecological damage of many sorts. These too are likely to be durable in their effects, as for climatic, geological, economic, and social reasons the resilience of the affected ecosystems is weak. Ethiopia is perhaps the saddest example of this, but much the same situation prevails in Mozambique, Angola, Chad, and Somalia (Rubenson 1991; Timberlake 1987, 162–173). In Vietnam, where defoliation figured prominently in U.S. tactics, the durable results of war are less conspicuous but no less real: geology, climate, and human agency have combined to permit quick repair of most but not all of the damage. Bomb craters (about 20 million all told) and deforested zones remain throughout the country, testament to the U.S. antiguerrilla effort (De Koninck 1999; Westing 1976, 1984). Guerrilla wars in Central America in the 1970s and 1980s have also accelerated forest clearance and added to the chemical poisoning of waterways (Faber 1992; Rice 1989).

## Impacts of War Refugees

Additionally, both conventional and guerrilla warfare routinely disrupted local ecologies through the mass migration of refugees. As thousands or millions left war zones, their impact in disturbing or managing their home environments was lost. This at times proved ecologically helpful, but in some cases, such as terraced mountains, mass emigration led to accelerated erosion because terraces fall apart without constant upkeep. Whatever the consequence of war refugees' departure, their arrival somewhere else almost always proved stressful ecologically as well as in other respects. A careful study of the environmental effects of 3.5 million Afghan refugees in northwest Pakistan in the 1980s provides a grim picture. Suddenly heightened demand for arable land and fuel wood, and the Afghans' inevitable ignorance of local ecology, combined to devastate Pakistan's largest remaining forest zone (Allen 1987). Africa's decolonization and postcolonial conflicts since the 1950s created refugees in the millions, obliged to occupy landscapes they often understood poorly and in which they hoped to have no long-term stake.

Previous centuries of course featured war refugees. But the twentieth century was distinctive for the number of refugees, greater than in the past because human numbers grew so much greater, and because warfare became much more dangerous. Moreover, only rarely in the twentieth century could war refugees find unoccupied lands into which to move; much more often they had to crowd into landscapes already thickly settled. Thus their impacts were probably greater because ecological buffers had already been worn thin in the lands obliged to accept them.

## Impacts of Preparation for War

Combat in general, whether guerrilla or conventional, even including refugee impacts, had a lesser impact than the business of war production and preparing for war. This was because more societies sought to prepare for war than actually fought wars; because many societies saw fit to maintain their preparedness for decades on end, and wars themselves were (usually) comparatively brief; and because the big economies and populous societies were, most of them, deeply involved in the geopolitical wrangling of the twentieth century. It was also true because, with the transportation systems and integrated markets that had developed since 1870 or so, the demand for war material, and thus the impacts of economic mobilization for war, reached into nearly every nook and cranny of the globe.

Preparedness for war implied maximizing immediate wealth, putting much of it at the disposal of the state, and mobilizing as much labor as quickly as possible. It concentrated the efforts of tens of millions of people, and all the technology that states could muster. Countless states sacrificed the quality of their soils, waters, and urban air in concentrated efforts to maximize production and stockpiles of food, rubber, oil, steel, uranium, soldiers, and other strategic substances. In World War I the British government encouraged farmers to plow every imaginable acre. Labor shortage prevented farmers from caring for their lands as they would have wished. British grain production increased by 30 percent in the course of the war, but much marginal land was damaged in the process (Horn 1984). Britain's war efforts of course extended to the empire, to Australian wheat fields, Canadian forests, and South African mines. During World War II in colonial Southern Rhodesia (now Zimbabwe), for example, the British revived the practice of forced labor on settlers' farms, trying to maximize production of food and tobacco, and bled the African farms of their labor supply. African farms thus lacked the labor needed to manage soils and wildlife, and settlers' farms extended cultivation at the expense of surrounding bush (Johnson 2000).

Fascist states regarded preparation for war during peaceful interludes as a sacred duty. In the 1920s, Mussolini, well informed about food shortages in Germany and Austria in the latter stages of World War I, thought that Italy needed to be self-sufficient in grain. He launched a Battle for Wheat, and did not care that this policy promoted forest clearance of sloping and otherwise marginal lands at home, accelerating the erosion of soils over subsequent decades.[9] He also tried to make Italy energy-independent, which involved promoting dam-building in the Alps for hydropower.

Crash programs of economic mobilization proliferated in wartime and in times when war loomed on the horizon. Such programs often amounted to a form of environmental roulette, but societies, whether fascist and militarist in orientation or merely anxious about war, played willingly because the ecological bills fell due much later than the political and military ones did.

## Military Pronatalism

International competition encouraged maximization not merely of food and energy harvests, but of the human crop as well. Emperors and kings for many centuries typically encouraged reproduction, in part because they wanted to ensure a ready supply of army recruits. Modern states sometimes made it a staple of policy. Fascist Italy, Third Republic France, Ceausescu's Romania, Mao's China, and the Syria of Hafez al-Assad all sought to raise birth rates in order to provide more troops to fight possible enemies: military pronatalism.

Normally populations have responded desultorily to their leaders' efforts to get them to reproduce more exuberantly. Romanians under the dictator Nicolae Ceausescu were the great exception, a product of special circumstances. In 1965 Romania was very much a Soviet satellite, but Ceausescu had in mind a rather more independent foreign policy than Moscow wished. He concluded that Romania needed more people, preferably 30 million by the year 2000, so he banned all forms of birth control and abortion. He set his secret police the task of ensuring that Rumanian women were not shirking their reproductive duties. Romania's birth rate doubled in 1966. Maternity wards were deluged, and delivering mothers wedged in two to a bed. But after Ceaucescu's over-throw in 1989, women went on a reproduction strike, so Romanians fell well short of the population target he set. Pronatalism in most of Europe continues to suffer from its association with nationalistic dictators, including Mussolini, Hitler, and Stalin, and nowhere has matched the hopes of its sponsors.[10]

Mao, like Ceausescu, usually thought more people meant more security. From the time of the Korean War (1950–1953) he anticipated a nuclear attack by the United States, which was not a far-fetched fantasy since General MacArthur in 1951 recommended just that. After the Sino-Soviet split in 1958, Mao also feared nuclear attack from the Soviets. He concluded that China's best defense lay in raising its population so that it could better withstand nuclear war. For Mao, a large population was a form of military capital, China's way to combat technologically more advanced enemies—something he had learned in his struggles against the Japanese between 1937 and 1945. He surprised Nikita Khrushchev in 1957 with his views:

> We shouldn't be afraid of atomic missiles. No matter what kind of war breaks out— conventional or thermonuclear—we'll win. As for China, if the imperialists unleash war on us, we may lose more than 300 million people. So what? War is war. The years will pass and we'll get to work producing more babies than ever before.[11]

Mao's successors were horrified by the rapid population growth Mao encour-aged, and in 1976 turned to the most restrictive birth control program ever implemented.

The twentieth century witnessed many other cases of "military pronatalism," a policy that, when successful, could lead to imbalance between population and environment, overintensive resource exploitation, environmental degradation, and perhaps a higher probability of war. Occasional efforts persisted into the 1990s, despite the evolution of warfare that increasingly rewarded industrial strength and high technology more than mere manpower.

## Military Industrialization

Most states, however, recognized early in the twentieth century that military power rested on industrial might more than upon a massive population. Several shuffled their priorities accordingly, building military-industrial complexes so as not to be caught unprepared in the event of war. The British and Germans began this policy in the nineteenth century, and were soon imitated by the Japanese. The lessons of World War I, in which the Russian army lacked the necessary armament to fight the Germans effectively, drove home the importance of having one's own heavy industry. So from World War I onward, all great powers and some not-so-great encouraged the emergence of metallurgical and armaments industries within their national territories and their empires. These industries inevitably involved heightened levels of air and water pollution. Furthermore, they intensified resource use, especially for coal and iron, with attendant environmental effects from mining.

The most dramatic examples came where the state enjoyed maximal latitude to direct economic development, as in Stalin's Soviet Union and Mao's China. In both cases security anxiety helped to motivate heroic overnight industrialization campaigns (which in both cases had other motives as well). The dirty industrialization of the Soviet Union beginning in 1929 reflected Stalin's fear that his country would be crushed by its enemies if it did not become an industrial power within ten years. He was correct in this assessment, although it is certain that sufficient industrialization to resist Hitler could have been achieved at lower environmental (and human) cost than Stalin was prepared to exact.

After the defeat of the Germans in 1945, the Soviets embarked on grand plans for the harnessing of nature in the service of the state, formalized in the 1948 "Plan for the Transformation of Nature" (Josephson 2002, 28). The deepening Cold War made it seem necessary that no drop of water should flow to the sea unused, no forest should be left unharvested. Giant hydroelectric dams served as the centerpiece of this plan, but it also involved a comprehensive restructuring of the Soviet Union's ecology. Cost constraints prevented Stalin and his successors from realizing their most grandiose ambitions: The Soviets never managed to divert the Siberian rivers to Central Asia, or reroute the Pacific Ocean's Japan cold current. But they built a sprawling military-industrial complex with very few checks on pollution, and kept secret the environmental and health consequences of their efforts (Feshbach and Friendly 1992; Josephson 2002; Weiner 1999).

In 1958 the Chinese embarked on an industrialization that was even dirtier than the Soviet effort. Mao had become fixated on the idea of surpassing British steel production, and encouraged Chinese peasants to make steel in their backyards. They made plenty of steel, most of it useless, and in the process accelerated the deforestation of China in their quest for fuel for their tiny smelters (Shapiro 2001). After Mao's death in 1976, China continued its industrialization program, although in more conventional forms.

Meanwhile, South Korea and Taiwan proceeded apace with their own pollution-intensive industrializations, nurtured by the United States, whose interest in economic development in East Asia was mainly geopolitical. The U.S. security agenda required the rapid industrialization of its allies (as it had the post-1950 reindustrialization of Japan) to counter the emergence of China. All of these efforts, capitalist or communist, were notably successful except Mao's Great Leap Forward. In every case, pollution levels and other environmental concerns carried a very low priority until about 1990. And in every case, especially the Great Leap Forward, the environmental consequences proved unfortunate.

In the United States a military-industrial complex emerged in the twentieth century too, although there top-down state planning played a much smaller role. Domestic nonmilitary demand was so strong that the steel mills of Pittsburgh and Gary, the coal mines of West Virginia and Wyoming would have thrived even without security anxiety. Nonetheless, tentatively and temporarily in World War I, and exuberantly from 1942 onward, the United States subsidized and otherwise encouraged military industry, adding a fillip to the demand for steel, coal, bauxite, electricity, and other enterprises, all of which carried profound ecological consequences.

## Nuclear Weapons Industry

The starkest illustration of how security anxiety propelled the great powers to indulge in reckless environmental change comes from the nuclear weapons programs of the United States and Soviet Union. At least nine countries built nuclear weapons in the twentieth century, although only seven admitted doing so: the United States, United Kingdom, France, Soviet Union, China, India, and Pakistan. Israel and South Africa also developed nuclear weapons and pretended they had not (South Africa after 1994 dismantled its program). No component of the world's military-industrial complexes could rival nuclear weapons for state support, for freedom of action with respect to environmental consequences, and for protection from public and press scrutiny.

The U.S. nuclear weapons complex was born in 1942 and by 1990 involved some 3,000 sites in all. The United States built tens of thousands of nuclear warheads, and tested more than a thousand of them, mainly in Nevada and on small Pacific atolls. The jewel in the nuclear weapons crown was the Hanford Engineering Works, a sprawling bomb factory on the Columbia River in the bone-dry steppe of south-central Washington state. It opened during World War II and built the bomb that flattened Nagasaki in 1945. Over the next 50 years, Hanford engineers intentionally released billions of gallons of low-level radioactive wastes into the Columbia River, and accidentally leaked some more into groundwater. In 1949, shortly after the Soviets had exploded their first atomic bomb, the Americans conducted a secret experiment at Hanford. The fallout detected from the Soviet test prompted questions about how quickly the Soviets were able to process plutonium. In response, U.S. officials decided to use "green" uranium, less than 20 days out of the reactor, to test their hypotheses about Soviet activities. The Green Run, as it was known to those in on the secret, released nearly 8,000 curies of iodine-131, dousing the downwind region with radiation at levels varying between 80 and 1,000 times the limit then thought tolerable. (The officially tolerable limit has been lowered since then). The local populace learned of these events in 1986, when Hanford became the first of the U.S. nuclear weapons complexes to release documents concerning the environmental effects of weapons production. The Green Run shows the environmental liberties the Americans took under the influence of Cold War security anxiety.[12] That was the tip of the iceberg. More environmentally serious were the wastes, which in the heat of the Cold War were left for the future to worry about. A half century of weapons production around the United States left an archipelago of contamination, including tens of millions of cubic meters of long-lived nuclear waste. More than half a ton of plutonium is buried around Hanford alone. No one has yet devised a technically feasible and politically acceptable solution to the problems posed by the U.S. nuclear weapons industry (Fioravanti and Makhijani 1997; U.S. Department of Energy 1995).

The Soviet nuclear program began with Stalin, who wanted atomic weapons as fast as possible, whatever the human and environmental cost. The Soviet command economy was good at such things: a large nuclear weapons complex arose from nothing in only a few years. Soviet engineers built about 45,000 warheads and exploded about 715 between 1949 and 1991, mostly at Semipalatinsk (in what is now Kazakhstan) and on the Arctic island of Novaya Zemlya. They also used nuclear explosions to create reservoirs and canals and to open mine shafts. In 1972 and 1984 they detonated nuclear bombs to try to loosen ores from which phosphate (for fertilizer) was derived. They experimented with nuclear explosions as a means of salt mining. They dumped much of their nuclear waste at sea, mostly in the Arctic Ocean, some of it in shallow water. They scuttled defunct nuclear submarines at sea. Most of the world's known reactor accidents befell the Soviet Union's Northern Fleet, based at Archangel.

The Soviets had only one center for reprocessing used nuclear fuel, at Mayak in the upper Ob basin of southwestern Siberia, now easily the most radioactive place on earth. It accumulated 26 metric tons of plutonium, 50 times Hanford's total. From 1948 to 1956 the Mayak complex dumped liquid radioactive waste into the Techa River, an Ob tributary, and the sole source of drinking water for 10,000–20,000 people. Some 124,000 people in all were exposed to heightened radiation in this way. After 1952, storage tanks held some of Mayak's most dangerous wastes, but in 1957 one exploded, raining 20 million curies down onto the neighborhood—equivalent to about 40 percent of the radiation released at Chernobyl. About 270,000 people lived in the contaminated territory. After 1958 liquid wastes were stored in Lake Karachay, a shallow pond some 45 hectares in area. In spring 1967 a drought exposed the lake bed's radioactive sediments to the steppe winds, sprinkling dangerous dust, with 3,000 times the radioactivity released in the 1945 bombing of Hiroshima, over an area the size of Belgium and onto a half million unsuspecting people. By the 1980s, anyone standing at the lakeshore for an hour received a lethal dose of radiation (600 rentgens/hour). A former chairman of the Soviet Union's Supreme Soviet Subcommittee on Nuclear Safety, Alexander Penyagin, likened the situation at Mayak to 100 Chernobyls. No one knows the extent of contamination in the former Soviet Union because the nuclear complex was so large and so secret. Much of the complex was shut down in the last years of the Soviet Union, but the mess remained and post-Soviet Russia and Kazakhstan could not afford to clean it up even if the technical and political obstacles to doing so were overcome.[13] The lethal residues of the British, French, Chinese, Indian, Pakistani, Israeli, South African (and perhaps a few other) nuclear weapons programs were, mercifully, not on the superpower scale.[14]

Taken as a whole, the nuclear programs of the great powers left a remarkable legacy. They burdened posterity with an apparently intractable long-term waste-management obligation. They exploded about 400 atomic devices above ground after 1945, sprinkling some 200 million tons of radioactive material around the earth. Underground testing irradiated underground chambers in the earth's crust. Moreover, undersea testing, practiced by the French in Polynesia, leaked plutonium into the Pacific (Danielsson and Danielsson 1986). The magnitude of these leaks remains secret, but their durability is well known: plutonium's half-life is 24,000 years. Nuclear weapons programs also gobbled up nearly a tenth of the commercial energy deployed worldwide after 1940 (Smil 1994, 185). The environmental changes resulting from nuclear weapons production and testing, which will persist long after the wars and tensions of the twentieth century are forgotten, were driven exclusively by international security concerns.

## Transportation Infrastructure

Beyond the more or less direct environmental impacts of industrialization and weapons programs, there are indirect environmental consequences of state actions driven, at least in part, by security anxiety. Consider transportation infrastructure. German railroads, the trans-Siberian railroad, Brazilian Amazonian highways, the Karakoram Highway connecting Pakistan and China, and even the U.S. interstate system were built partly or entirely for military reasons.[15] Each investment in rails or roads led to rapid economic change (generally regarded as beneficial), rapid social change (often controversial), and unanticipated environmental change (normally ignored). People and businesses flocked to the new roads and railroads, almost like iron filings to a magnet. The U.S. interstate system strongly affected land use, population distribution and densities, and, through promoting trucking and automobile travel at the expense of rail transport, air quality and energy use. It is true, of course, that highways and railroads also exist in places where military motives played no role in their construction. In light of this it is fair to say that, in contrast to nuclear weapons, the world's networks of roads and railroads would exist approximately as they are even absent security anxiety. The point here is a limited one: the extent, location, and timing (of construction) of much of the twentieth century's transportation infrastructure had military motives, and in myriad ways that infrastructure affects the environment.

## Military Reserves

Twentieth-century security anxiety has led also to the proliferation of military reserves—bases, firing ranges, security zones, and the like. These military islands have unusual environmental histories. Border security zones, such as those between Greece and Bulgaria, between Iran and the Soviet Union, or the DMZ in Korea carried (and in Korea still carry) much richer vegetation cover and wildlife than the lands around them, because of restricted human access. Some firing ranges are oases of ecological stability because people are kept out. Regular artillery barrages form less of a threat to wildlife and vegetation than quotidian human activity in most cases. The Culebra National Wildlife Refuge in Puerto Rico was until 1975 a U.S. Navy gunnery and bombing practice site; navy gunners unwittingly protected the seabirds and turtles that make Culebra a place of unusual biodiversity (Hein 1990). The U.S. military today maintains about 10 million hectares of military reserves, equivalent to the size of Kentucky. Much of the land has been used only lightly and retains plant and animal species that are rare elsewhere. Fort Stewart in Georgia, for example, is home to 5 percent of the world's population of red-cockaded woodpeckers as well as to the U.S. Army's Third Infantry Division. Since 1988 the Nature Conservancy and the U.S. military have been working together to inventory and preserve the unusual biodiversity of these lands (Nickens 1993; Pope 2003).

More commonly, however, military bases are islands of extreme environmental damage. The sorry tale of Soviet bases in eastern Europe is only the most famous example. Czechs and Poles say decades will be needed to clean up the mess left behind by the Soviet Army, which dumped diesel fuel into groundwater, disposed of chemical wastes with no regard for the local environment, and treated radioactive material cavalierly. Wherever states operated bases on foreign territory, something in which the British, French, Americans, and Soviets specialized for much of the twentieth century, commanders and troops rarely resisted the temptation to regard ecological damage as acceptable—or, in cases where forces felt hostility from the local population, even desirable.

## Conclusion

In most societies, politics, institutions, and mentalities have evolved so as to provide security as their foremost goal. This has been more true since about 1910 than at most times in the deeper past. Hence, our politics and institutions—our social choice mechanisms—are ill-adapted to the complex demands of ecological prudence, in which everything is connected to everything, and everything is always in flux. In Darwinian terms, the international security anxiety of the twentieth century selected for states and societies that emphasized military power and industrial strength over all else: survival of the dirtiest. When the ecology movement gathered force in the 1970s, it did so in a moment of detente, which provided an opening for other items on political agendas. Since then it has flourished best in societies with minimal risks of war. Ecological concern on the part of states remained hostage to fortune.[16] In 1990 when the war clouds were gathering over the Persian Gulf, President Bush asked the U.S. Congress to exempt the military from all environmental laws, and Congress complied. After 2001, his son asked that oil companies be allowed to drill for oil in the Arctic National Wildlife Refuge in Alaska, on the grounds that in time of war Americans cannot let caribou get in the way of strategic requirements. In March 2003, as the United States prepared to attack Iraq, the president and secretary of defense pressed Congress for a permanent, blanket exemption from environmental regulations for the U.S. military. The twentieth century's pattern, in which great power security anxiety put a ceiling on environmental preservation and actively fomented ecological change, bids fair to hold in the twenty-first century as well.

## Notes

1. Fuller treatment can be found in McNeill (2000, 267–356).

2. Westing (1980) provides a list of 26 wars with a capsule description of their ecological cost.

3. In the Second Punic War the Roman efforts to defeat Hannibal led to ecological damage in southern Italy that, according to one observer, was visible more than 2,000 years later (Toynbee 1965, 11–35). Caesar's legions energetically burned the forests of Gaul (Corvol and Amat 1994; Demorlaine 1919).

4. Between 1420 and 1440 the Breton marches lost 20 to 80 percent of their population, and almost all land was abandoned for decades and returned to second-growth forest. See also Duby (1968, 296–302) where he says the Hundred Years' War led to a resurgence of forest in wide areas throughout France. On the Thirty Years' War, see Makowski and Buderath (1983) (thanks to David Blackbourn for this reference).

5. The Mongols did rebuild the water system in Baghdad and eventually saw the attractions of higher revenues from irrigated farming. Details can be found in Christensen (1993).

6. Hewitt (1983) reports that about 750 square kilometers of German and Japanese cities were flattened by aerial bombing in World War II.

7. The Dutch used a similar tactic to forestall a French invasion in the 1670s, inflicting great flood damage on their own country, and many marauding or occupying armies have purposely flooded other people's lands.

8. Reported anonymously in *Environment* (1993), 35(4): 22; on Egypt and Libya, see Westing (1980, 111). Westing also reports parallel events in the North Atlantic fisheries, where World War II temporarily halted harvesting, so stocks flourished until peace permitted renewed fishing.

9. Mussolini may have had an equally unintended impact, this time beneficial, upon Italian landscapes, by his campaign to reduce the populations of Italian goats. He regarded the goat as an unfascist animal.

10. Details on Rumania are in Kligman (1998), and Chesnais (1995, 171–178).

11. Shapiro (2001, 32) quotes *Khrushchev Remembers: The Last Testament* (Boston: Little, Brown, 1974, 255). Or so Khrushchev wrote; he had reasons to disparage Mao.

12. Details of this episode are in Caufield (1990) and Gerber (1992). In arguing that the United States ought not to adhere to radiation guidelines approved by the International Commission on Radiological Protection, one U.S. nuclear mandarin in 1958 said, "the nation's security may demand the exposure of people to higher levels of radiation than those just established by the International Commission" (Caufield 1990, 130).

13. See Cochran, et al. (1994); Herndon (1995); Josephson (2000); Nilsen and Bohmer (1994); Nilsen and Hauge (1992); Yablokov (1995). A useful general study of the Soviet nuclear weapons program to 1956 is Holloway (1994). The latest assessment, highly technical, is Egorov, et al. (2000).

14. See Danielsson (1990) on the French in Polynesia; Makhijani, Hu, and Yih (1995) for a global survey.

15. *Economist* (10 October 1992) recounts the story of Eisenhower's 1919 cross-country convoy drive and his role in establishing the federal interstate highway program in 1956. He also admired the military potential of Germany's autobahns in the campaigns of 1945.

16. Britain relaxed its air and water pollution regulations during World War II in hopes of spurring industry to greater production levels; indeed coal smoke over cities served military purposes because it made it harder for German bombers to see their targets.

# References

Alayev, E. B., Y. P. Badenkov, and N. A. Karavaeva. 1990. "The Russian Plain." In B. L. Turner et al., eds., *The Earth as Transformed by Human Action*. New York: Cambridge University Press, 543–560.

Albion, Robert G. 1926. *Forests and Sea Power: The Timber Problem of the Royal Navy, 1652–1862*. Cambridge, MA: Harvard University Press.

Allan, N. J. R. 1987. "Impact of Afghan Refugees on the Vegetation Resources of Pakistan's Hindu Kush—Himalaya." *Mountain Research and Development* 7: 200–204.

Appuhn, Karl. 2000. "Inventing Nature: Forests, Forestry, and State Power in Renaissance Venice." *Journal of Modern History* 72(4): 861–889.

Bamford, Paul. 1956. *Forests and French Sea Power, 1660–1789*. Toronto: University of Toronto Press.

Caufield, Catherine. 1990. *Multiple Exposure*. Harmondsworth, UK: Penguin.

Chesnais, Jean-Clause. 1995. *Le crépuscule de l'Occident*. Paris: Laffont.

Christensen, Peter. 1993. *The Decline of Iranshahr: Irrigation and Environments in the History of the Middle East, 500 B.C. to A.D. 1500*. Copenhagen: University of Copenhagen Museum Tusculanum Press.

Cintré, René. 1992. *Les marches de Bretagne au moyen age: Économie, guerre et société en pays de frontière, XIV–XVe siècles*. Pornichet: Editions Pierre.

Corvol, Andrée, and Jean-Paul Amat. 1994. *Forêt et guerre*. Paris: L'Harmattan.

Danielsson, Bengt, and Marie-Thérèse Danielsson. 1986. *Poisoned Reign: French Nuclear Colonialism in the Pacific*. Harmondsworth: Penguin.

De Koninck, Rodolphe. 1999. *Deforestation in Vietnam*. Ottawa: International Development Research Centre.

Demorlaine, J. 1919. "Importance stratégique des forêts dans la guerre." *Revue des eaux et forêts* 57: 25–30.

Duby, Georges. 1968. *Rural Economy and Country Life in the Medieval West*. Columbia: University of South Carolina Press.

Egorov, Nikolai, Vladimir Novikov, Frank Parker, and Victor Popov, eds. 2000. *The Radiation Legacy of the Soviet Nuclear Complex.* London: Earthscan and IIASA.

Faber, Daniel. 1992. *Environment under Fire.* Boston: Monthly Review Press.

Feshbach, Murray, and Alfred Friendly. 1992. *Ecocide in the USSR.* New York: Basic Books.

Gerber, Michelle. 1992. *On the Home Front: The Cold War Legacy of the Hanford Nuclear Site.* Lincoln: University of Nebraska Press.

Hawley, T. M. 1992. *Against the Fires of Hell: The Environmental Disaster of the Gulf War.* New York: Harcourt, Brace, and Jovanovich.

Hein, P. 1990. "Between Aldabra and Nauru." In W. Beller, P. d'Alaya, and P. Hein, eds., *Sustainable Development and Environmental Management of Small Islands.* Paris: UNESCO.

Hewitt, K. 1983. "Place Annihilation: Area Bombing and the Fate of Urban Places." *Annals of the Association of American Geographers* 73(2): 257–284.

Hobbs, Peter V., and Lawrence F. Radke. 1992. "Airborne Studies of the Smoke from the Kuwait Oil Fires." *Science* 256: 987–991.

Horn, Pamela. 1984. *Rural Life in England in the First World War.* Dublin: Gill and Macmillan.

Johnson, David. 2000. *World War II and the Scramble for Labour in Colonial Zimbabwe, 1939–1948.* Harare: University of Zimbabwe Press.

Josephson, Paul. 2002. *Industrialized Nature.* Washington, DC: Island Press.

Kligman, Gail. 1998. *The Politics of Duplicity: Controlling Reproduction in Ceausescu's Romania.* Berkeley: University of California Press.

Lane, Frederic C. 1965. *Navires et constructeurs à Venise pendant la Renaissance.* Paris: S.E.V.P.E.N.

Makowski, Henry, and Bernhard Buderath. 1983. *Die natur dem menschen untertan: Ökologie im spiegel der landschaftsmalerei.* Munich: Kindler.

McNeill, J. R. 2000. *Something New under the Sun: An Environmental History of the Twentieth-Century World.* New York: W. W. Norton.

Merino Navarro, José P. 1981. *La armada española en el siglo XVIII.* Madrid: Fundación Universitaria Española.

Miller, Shawn. 2000. *Fruitless Trees: Portuguese Conservation and Brazil's Timber.* Palo Alto, CA: Stanford University Press.

Nicholson, Emma, and Peter Clark. 2002. *The Iraqi Marshlands.* London: Politico's Publishing.

Nickens, Eddie. 1993. "Operation Conservation: A Conservancy-Aided Project to Defend a Top-Secret Military Resource." *Nature Conservancy* 43(2): 24–29.

Pope, Carl. 2003. "Is This All We Can Be?" *Sierra* 88(4): 8–9.

Precoda, Norman. 1991. "Requiem for the Aral Sea." *Ambio* 20(3–4): 109–114.

Rice, Robert A. 1989. "A Casualty of War: The Nicaraguan Environment." *Technology Review* 92 (May–June): 63–71.

Rubenson, Sven. 1991. "Environmental Stress and Conflict in Ethiopian History: Looking for Correlations." *Ambio* 20(5): 179–182.

Shapiro, Judith. 2001. *Mao's War against Nature: Politics and the Environment in Revolutionary China.* New York: Cambridge University Press.

Sobolev, S. S. 1945. "Soil Erosion in the Territory of the Ukrainian SSR and the Struggle against It after the Reconstruction of Agriculture Following the German Occupation." [In Russian.] *Pochvovedenia*: 216–221.

———. 1947. "Protecting Soils in the USSR." *Journal of Soil and Water Conservation* 2: 123–132.

206    *John R. McNeill*

Timberlake, Lloyd. 1987. *Africa in Crisis.* London: Earthscan.

Toynbee, A. J. 1965. *Hannibal's Legacy.* 2 vols. London: Oxford University Press.

Westing, A. H. 1976. *Ecological Consequences of the Second Indochina War.* Stockholm: SIPRI.

————. 1980. *Warfare in a Fragile World.* London: Taylor and Francis.

————. 1984. *Herbicides in War: The Long-Term Ecological and Human Consequences.* London: Taylor and Francis.

————, ed. 1990. *Environmental Hazards of War: Releasing Dangerous Forces in an Industrialized World.* Newbury Park, CA: Sage Publications.

Worster, Donald. 1985. *Rivers of Empire.* New York: Pantheon.

# CONTRIBUTORS

**Giovanni Arrighi** is director of the Institute for Global Studies in Culture, Power, and History at Johns Hopkins University and author of *The Long Twentieth Century*.

**Christopher Chase-Dunn** is director of the Institute for Research on World-Systems, University of California at Riverside, professor of sociology at the University of California at Riverside, and author of *Rise and Demise: Comparing World-Systems*.

**Peter Gowan** teaches internal relations at London Metropolitan University and is the author of *The Global Gamble: Washington's Faustian Bid for World Dominance*.

**John Gulick** teaches sociology at the University of Tennessee.

**Andrew Jorgenson** teaches sociology at Washington State University at Pullman.

**Çağlar Keyder** teaches sociology at the State University of New York at Binghamton and Bogaziçi University, Istanbul, and is the author of *State and Class in Turkey: A Study in Capitalist Development*.

**John R. McNeill** teaches history at Georgetown University and is the author, most recently, of *The Human Web: A Bird's Eye View of World History*.

**Keith Nurse** teaches international relations at the University of the West Indies and is the coauthor of *Windward Island Bananas: Challenges and Options under the Single European Market*.

**Ravi Arvind Palat** teaches sociology at the State University of New York and is the author of *Capitalist Restructuring and the Pacific Rim*.

**Thomas Reifer** teaches sociology at the University of San Diego and is the editor of *Hegemony, Globalization, and Anti-Systemic Movements*.

**Faruk Tabak** teaches at the Walsh School of Foreign Service at Georgetown University and is the coeditor of *Informalization: Process and Structure*.

**Immanuel Wallerstein** is the director of the Fernand Braudel Center for the Study of Economies, Historical Systems, and Civilizations at the State University of New York at Binghamton, and is the author, most recently, of *Decline of American Power*.

# INDEX

# POLITICAL ECONOMY OF THE WORLD-SYSTEM ANNUALS SERIES

## *Immanuel Wallerstein, Series Editor*

I.  Kaplan, Barbara Hockey, ed., *Social Change in the Capitalist World Economy.* Political Economy of the World-System Annuals, 01. Beverly Hills/London: Sage Publications, 1978.

II.  Goldfrank, Walter L., ed., *The World-System of Capitalism: Past and Present.* Political Economy of the World-System Annuals, 02. Beverly Hills/London: Sage Publications, 1979.

III.  Hopkins, Terence K. & Immanuel Wallerstein, eds., *Processes of the World-System.* Political Economy of the World-System Annuals, 03. Beverly Hills/London: Sage Publications, 1980.

IV.  Rubinson, Richard, ed., *Dynamics of World Development.* Political Economy of the World-System Annuals, 04. Beverly Hills/London: Sage Publications, 1981.

V.  Friedman, Edward, ed., *Ascent and Decline in the World-System.* Political Economy of the World-System Annuals, 05. Beverly Hills/London/New Delhi: Sage Publications, 1982.

VI.  Bergesen, Albert, ed., *Crises in the World-System.* Political Economy of the World-System Annuals, 06. Beverly Hills/London/New Delhi: Sage Publications, 1983.

VII.  Bergquist, Charles, ed., *Labor in the Capitalist World-Economy.* Political Economy of the World-System Annuals, 07. Beverly Hills/London/New Delhi: Sage Publications, 1984.

VIII.  Evans, Peter, Dietrich Rueschemeyer & Evelyne Huber Stephens, eds., *States versus Markets in the World-System.* Political Economy of the World-System Annuals, 08. Beverly Hills/London/New Delhi: Sage Publications, 1985.

IX.  Tardanico, Richard, ed., *Crises in the Caribbean Basin.* Political Economy of the World-System Annuals, 09. Newbury Park/Beverly Hills/London/New Delhi: Sage Publications, 1987.

X.  Ramirez, Francisco O., ed., *Rethinking the Nineteenth Century: Contradictions and Movements.* Studies in the Political Economy of the World-System, 10. New York/Westport, CT/London: Greenwood Press, 1988.

XI.  Smith, Joan, Jane Collins, Terence K. Hopkins & Akbar Muhammad, eds., *Racism, Sexism, and the World-System.* Studies in the Political Economy of the World-System, 11. New York/Westport, CT/London: Greenwood Press, 1988.

XII.  (a) Boswell, Terry, ed., *Revolution in the World-System.* Studies in the Political Economy of the World-System, 12a. New York/Westport, CT/London: Greenwood Press, 1989.

XII.  (b) Schaeffer, Robert K., ed., *War in the World-System.* Studies in the Political Economy of the World-System, 12b. New York/Westport, CT/London: Greenwood Press, 1989.

213

XIII.   Martin, William G., ed., *Semiperipheral States in the World-Economy.* Studies in the Political Economy of the World-System, 13. New York/Westport, CT/London: Greenwood Press, 1990.

XIV.    Kasaba, Resat, ed., *Cities in the World-System.* Studies in the Political Economy of the World-System, 14. New York/Westport, CT/London: Greenwood Press, 1991.

XV.     Palat, Ravi Arvind, ed., *Pacific-Asia and the Future of the World-System.* Studies in the Political Economy of the World-System, 15. Westport, CT/London: Greenwood Press, 1993.

XVI.    Gereffi, Gary & Miguel Korzeniewicz, eds., *Commodity Chains and Global Capitalism.* Studies in the Political Economy of the World-System, 16. Westport, CT: Greenwood Press, 1994.

XVII.   McMichael, Philip, eds., *Food and Agrarian Orders in the World-Economy.* Studies in the Political Economy of the World-System, 17. Westport, CT: Greenwood Press, 1995.

XVIII.  Smith, David A. & József Böröcz, eds., *A New World Order? Global Transformations in the Late Twentieth Century.* Studies in the Political Economy of the World-System, 18. Westport, CT: Greenwood Press, 1995.

XIX.    Korzeniewicz, Roberto Patricio & William C. Smith, eds., *Latin America in the World-Economy.* Studies in the Political Economy of the World-System, 19. Westport, CT: Greenwood Press, 1996.

XX.     Ciccantell, Paul S. & Stephen G. Bunker, eds., *Space and Transport in the World-System.* Studies in the Political Economy of the World-System, 20. Westport, CT: Greenwood Press, 1998.

XXI.    Goldfrank, Walter L., David Goodman & Andrew Szasz, eds., *Ecology and the World-System.* Studies in the Political Economy of the World-System, 21. Westport, CT: Greenwood Press, 1999.

XXII.   Derluguian, Georgi & Scott L. Greer, eds., *Questioning Geopolitics.* Studies in the Political Economy of the World-System, 22. Westport, CT: Greenwood Press, 2000.

XXIV.   Grosfoguel, Ramón & Ana Margarita Cervantes-Rodriguez, eds., *The Modern/Colonial/Capitalist World-System in the Twentieth Century: Global Processes, Antisystemic Movements, and the Geopolitics of Knowledge.* Studies in the Political Economy of the World-System, 24. Westport, CT: Greenwood Press, 2002.

XXV.    (a) Dunaway, Wilma A., ed., *Emerging Issues in the 21st Century World-System, Volume I: Crises and Resistance in the 21st Century World-System.* Studies in the Political Economy of the World-System, 25a. Westport, CT: Greenwood Press, 2003.

XXV.    (b) Dunaway, Wilma A., ed., *Emerging Issues in the 21st Century World-System, Volume II: New Theoretical Directions for the 21st Century World-System.* Studies in the Political Economy of the World-System, 25b. Westport, CT: Greenwood Press, 2003.

XXVI.   (a) Reifer, Thomas Ehrlich, ed. *Globalization, Hegemony & Power.* Political Economy of the World-System Annuals, 26a. Boulder, CO: Paradigm Publishers, 2004.

XXVI.   (b) Friedman, Jonathan & Christopher Chase-Dunn, eds. *Hegemonic Decline: Present and Past.* Political Economy of the World-System Annuals. Boulder, CO: Paradigm Pubishers, 2005.

XXVII.  Tabak, Faruk. *Allies as Rivals: The U.S., Europe and Japan in a Changing World-System.* Political Economy of the World-System Annuals, 27. Boulder, CO: Paradigm Publishers, 2005.